CAMBRIDGE

Progress Plus

ENGLISH LANGUAGE
GCSE for AQA
Student Book

Lindsay McNab, Imelda Pilgrim, Marian Slee

CAMBRIDGE
UNIVERSITY PRESS

University Printing House, Cambridge CB2 8BS, United Kingdom

Cambridge University Press is part of the University of Cambridge.

It furthers the University's mission by disseminating knowledge in the pursuit of education, learning and research at the highest international levels of excellence.

www.cambridge.org
Information on this title: www.cambridge.org/9781107452978 (Paperback)
www.cambridge.org/9781107453005 (Cambridge Elevate-enhanced Edition)
www.cambridge.org/9781107453036 (Paperback + Cambridge Elevate-enhanced Edition)

First published 2015

Printed in Dubai by Oriental Press

A catalogue record for this publication is available from the British Library

ISBN 978-1-107-45297-8 Paperback
ISBN 978-1-107-45300-5 Cambridge Elevate-enhanced Edition
ISBN 978-1-107-45303-6 Paperback + Cambridge Elevate-enhanced Edition

Additional resources for this publication at www.cambridge.org/ukschools

Cambridge University Press has no responsibility for the persistence or accuracy of URLs for external or third-party internet websites referred to in this publication, and does not guarantee that any content on such websites is, or will remain, accurate or appropriate. Information regarding prices, travel timetables, and other factual information given in this work is correct at the time of first printing but Cambridge University Press does not guarantee the accuracy of such information thereafter.

....

Approval message from AQA

This textbook has been approved by AQA for use with our qualification. This means that we have checked that it broadly covers the specification and we are satisfied with the overall quality. Full details of our approval process can be found on our website.

We approve textbooks because we know how important it is for teachers and students to have the right resources to support their teaching and learning. However, the publisher is ultimately responsible for the editorial control and quality of this book.

Please note that when teaching the GCSE English Language (8700) course, you must refer to AQA's specification as your definitive source of information. While this book has been written to match the specification, it does not provide complete coverage of every aspect of the course.

A wide range of other useful resources can be found on the relevant subject pages of our website: www.aqa.org.uk

Contents

Introduction

Dear Student,

You are about to start on your GCSE course in English Language. It is likely that, as you read this, you have already studied English for many years, steadily developing your skills in reading, writing and spoken English. This text book will help you to:

- build on the skills you already have
- achieve the best result you can in your GCSE exams
- equip you with the English Language skills you need for further study across a range of subjects.

Your final GCSE exams are based on assessment objectives provided by the government. This text book develops the skills outlined in these assessment objectives, with each unit targeting a clearly defined area. Each unit provides staged instruction and tasks, enabling you to build your expertise, and ends with an 'Assess your progress' section which allows you to check how well you have done.

In addition to this, there are tests designed to reinforce your learning across a number of units, a 'Spoken language' unit to help you make a formal presentation, and an exam section that provides sample papers, expert advice, annotated sample answers and suggestions for purposeful revision. Throughout the book, you will find links with Cambridge Elevate, CUP's digital platform, where you can find further activities and support.

The source materials in this text book have been carefully selected to interest, engage and challenge you. They include a range of genres and text types drawn from the 19th, 20th and 21st centuries. You will also find two 'Wider reading' units, which are designed to extend your interest and independence in reading, as well further the development of specific reading skills.

The tasks set for reading, writing and spoken language are varied. You will be asked to work on your own, or in pairs or small groups. You will examine detail, meaning and authorial methods and styles, and will learn how to answer questions about these in focused and purposeful ways. You will also develop your own writing skills to ensure you target your purpose and audience, and organise and express your ideas clearly and effectively.

Here, at the start of your GCSE course, there is much to be learnt and much to be achieved. We hope you find it an interesting, enjoyable and rewarding experience.

We wish you all the best with your studies.

The author team

How to use this book

Your final GCSE exams are based on a number of assessment objectives. This textbook develops the skills outlined in these assessment objectives, with each unit targeting a clearly defined area. You will see which assessment objective is covered at the beginning of the unit you are studying when you see (AO1).

There are 27 units and an additional exam preparation section in this book. As you work through the book you will explore different aspects of reading, writing and speech. Also included are two 'Wider reading' units, which are designed to extend your interest and independence in reading, as well as further the development of specific reading skills, and a 'Spoken language' unit to help you make a formal presentation. Each unit provides staged instructions and tasks, enabling you to build your expertise as you go. Most units end with an 'Assess your progress' section, which allows you to test your understanding and check how well you have progressed throughout that unit.

You will also find 'Test your progress' units that give you the opportunity to test yourself on what you have learnt over the previous units under timed conditions.

The exam preparation section provides sample papers, advice, annotated sample answers and suggestions for purposeful revision to help you get ready for your exams.

Working on Cambridge Elevate

As you work through the book you will find links to Cambridge Elevate, the Cambridge University Press digital platform. At these points, you are invited to complete a task, listen to an extract or watch a video to help you reinforce your learning.

 When you come across this icon, you will be led to a video.

 If you see this icon, listen to an audio extract.

 Complete an activity when you see this icon.

  These icons indicate sections dealing with grammar and links to spelling activities later in the book.

Take advantage of working on Cambridge Elevate to get the most out of your study of Progress Plus – and good luck!

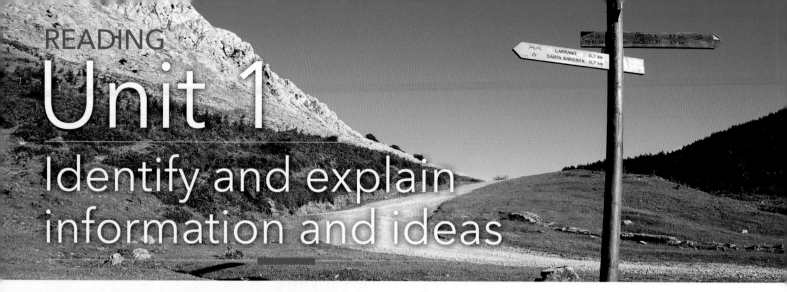

READING
Unit 1
Identify and explain information and ideas

YOUR READING

Every day you need to read a wide range of items. However, you don't read them all in the same way. When reading the ingredients list in a recipe, you need to read every word to make sure you don't miss anything. In contrast, when reading a text message, a quick glance is sometimes all that is needed.

ACTIVITY 1

1 Create a table to list the different types of things you might read in a normal week, your reasons for reading them and whether you read them closely or quickly glance at them.

What I read	Reason	Close/glance
sports news	interest	close
lesson timetable	to find next lesson	glance

> **Watch a video about reading skills on Cambridge Elevate.**

2 In small groups:

a compare your records of reading to find out if you read more or less than the others in your group

b talk about what you most and least enjoy reading

c list in order of importance why it is important to have good reading skills.

3 Your group has been selected to give a televised presentation as part of a government campaign targeting teenagers to promote the benefits of reading. Work together on your presentation. Discuss:

a the points you want to make

b the order in which you should make these points

c how to make your presentation interesting, lively and effective.

Practise delivering your presentation in front of another group.

READ FOR DETAIL

You read for many reasons. Sometimes this may be to find a specific detail. You do not need to read every word closely. Think about how you scan the pages of a bus timetable – your eyes move over the text quickly until they focus on the key words that locate the detail you are looking for. Sometimes you need to find several details and link them together. This requires closer reading.

ACTIVITY 2

Find out how well you read for detail by reading Source A from *Guinness World Records*.

1 Find specific details in Source A to answer these questions:

a What name is given to videos that quickly spread across the internet?

b Which type of video dominates the YouTube chart?

c What is the nationality of the star who has had over a billion views?

2 Select and link details from the text to answer this question:

What, according to the passage, are the consequences of video uploading?

3 Check your answers with another student. Amend them if necessary.

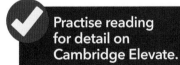

Practise reading for detail on Cambridge Elevate.

Source A

FACT FILE: VIRAL VIDEOS

TAKING OVER THE WORLD, ONE VIEW AT A TIME

'Viral' videos are well named. They spread across the internet faster that you can type 'You've got to see these kittens, they're sooo cute!' Such popularity has seen the business of uploading videos become professionalised, and only the home-made 'Charlie bit my finger — again!' makes it into YouTube's all-time Top 10. The chart is otherwise dominated by music videos, but for the first time pop is a truly global phenomenon. 15

It's no longer true that everything comes from the West and the USA in particular. As a result of online videos, stars such as 20 a certain stylish South Korean can rack up over a billion views in less than six months. Video uploading remains a powerful hybrid of 21st- 25 century technology and personal recommendation that has the potential to bring down a government … or simply embarrass grandma. 30

From *Guinness World Records 2014*

GET THE DETAIL RIGHT

Being able to find, understand and use appropriate detail is an important skill, particularly when filling in forms.

Many of you will apply for a driving licence sometime in the future. This can be done online or on paper. Source B is taken from the official application form and guidance notes from the Driver and Vehicle Licensing Agency (DVLA). The DVLA does its best to help people complete the form correctly, but it has to provide instructions for a wide range of applicants. It is up to you to work out what to do. If you get it wrong, you will have to reapply.

Read Source B, then answer the questions that follow.

Source B

Section 5 – Your proof of identity

Part B – Documents enclosed to prove your identity.

We will accept the following current documents.

- A passport or travel document or
- a Biometric Residence Permit (BRP), or
- an EC/EEA National Identity Card (with the exception of ID cards issued by the Swedish Post Office).

We will not accept photocopies.

If you are sending one of these, you must provide a recent photo of yourself but you do not need to have your photo signed and you do not need to fill in the section 'Signing a photo to verify identity (if necessary)'.

If the documents you provide are not in English, you will need to provide a translation that has been issued in the UK and signed by an official translator.

Do not send your passport in if you need it within 4 weeks.

If this is the case you should consider delaying your licence application until you can send us your passport.

If you **do not** have a digital UK passport, or you have one but you do not want us to check your identity with the Identity and Passport Service, you can use the Premium Checking Service (see section 'Premium Checking Service at the Post Office®') as long as your UK passport is in your current name. Your passport will be sent securely with your application to DVLA.

- **A UK birth or adoption certificate and one other supporting identity document (see the note below).**
If you were born in the UK and do not have your UK birth or adoption certificate, or the one you have does not show your full name or country of birth, contact your local register office.

Note – a birth or adoption certificate is not absolute proof of your identity; you must also send one of the following documents:

- Your **National Insurance (NI) card** or a **letter** from the Department for Work and Pensions showing your NI number.
- A **photocopy** of the **front page** of a **benefits book** or an **original letter** about a claim for state benefit.
- A **P45**, **P60** or **payslip**.
- A **marriage certificate** or **divorce papers** (decree nisi or decree absolute).
- A **student union card** or **school record**.

Note – the National Insurance Number cannot be a temporary number (usually starting with TN).

- **If you have reached State Pension age**, you can provide originals of one of the following:
  - A bank or building society statement, issued in the last three months, showing your pension payment.
  - A letter from the Department for Work and Pensions confirming your eligibility for the state pension and showing your NI number.

- **UK Certificate of Naturalisation.**
If your name is different from that shown on your digital UK passport, current photocard licence or the documents you are enclosing, you must provide proof of your name.

We will accept:
- a marriage or civil partnership certificate;
- a decree nisi or decree absolute; or
- any deed-poll declarations.

The evidence you provide must show a clear link between the name on your identity document or digital UK passport and your current name.

ACTIVITY 3

1 Which of the following statements are correct?

a Original identity documents must be provided.

b If you do not have the original documents, you can use a photocopy.

c Translations of documents not in English will not be accepted.

d A passport must be accompanied by a recent photo of yourself.

e A UK birth or adoption certificate must be sent with your National Insurance card.

f State pensioners only need to provide a statement from their bank or building society.

2 Now decide what documents you need to complete Section 5B of the application form.

USE DETAIL TO EXPLAIN

Being able to identify and use detail correctly is the first step to being a good reader. The next step is being able to use detail to explain.

In Source C, the writer describes what happened to him one morning in India. As you read it, think about how you would use the detail to explain why the writer ended up in 'the dust'.

You will realise that there are several points which explain this:

- He and his pony were attacked by a swarm of tree bees.
- The pony was bucking and rearing to try and get rid of the bees.
- The writer was trying to protect his face and limbs, making it difficult to stay on the pony.
- The pony bucked angrily and it was this that finally threw the writer into the dust.

To give a full explanation, you would need to include all these points and link them together.

Practise using detail to explain on Cambridge Elevate.

Source C

Of the many vicious pests in Northeastern India, the tree bee, half cousin of the Indian hornet, tops the list. These bees go about in immense swarms, making their hives in the highest trees. Unlike the hornet, which will sting only when thoroughly 5 annoyed, the tree bee has the habit of swooping down in attacking thousands, for no apparent reason, and chasing a person for his life.

One sunny morning, riding along a dusty cart track, I found myself, without the least warning, 10 the centre of such an assault. The sky above me suddenly became thick with bees. With an icy shiver down my spine, I put my pony to a gallop, but the bees were after us in earnest. My pony jumped, bucked, reared and lashed out in all 15 directions to rid himself of the bees, while I, attempting to protect my face and limbs, had the greatest difficulty in staying on. In a few moments, an angry buck threw me into the dust.

From *Tea Pests* by J. Beagle-Atkinson

ACTIVITY 4

1 Read Source D. Explain why the girl missed the bus. Aim to link all the reasons in your answer.

2 Compare your explanation with that of another student. Have you missed any essential details?

USE PUNCTUATION

Dashes

Used singly, a dash can indicate a comment or an afterthought at the end of a sentence:

Rushing down the street she finally rounded the corner, only to see the Number 41 disappearing from view – just her luck!

In pairs, dashes have the same function as brackets:

Of course, she hadn't heard the alarm – had probably turned it off in her sleep – and only woke when a police car, siren blaring, passed the house.

ACTIVITY 5

1 Copy the following sentences, adding dashes where appropriate:

Aunt Kath had been in her life for as long as she could remember the best aunt in the world. Even when she had started to get ill and that was many months ago she had still always had time for her youngest niece.

2 Using dashes, write two sentences of your own about a favourite relative.

SUMMARISE DETAIL

A summary is a short statement that brings together a series of main points. Summarising is a skill that you use in conversation every day. Think about the following questions:

What did you do at the weekend?
How was the holiday?
What's he like?
How did the match go?

Source D

It had been a late night. Her Mum had been upset and she had stayed up to talk with her, leaving her school bag firmly shut and her Maths homework untouched. She would be in trouble, she knew; no doubt Mr Jenkins would pass some sarcastic remark and hand out detention as well.   5

Of course, she hadn't heard the alarm – had probably turned it off in her sleep – and only woke when a police car, siren blaring, passed the house. She'd rushed to get dressed, grabbed a quick bowl of Cheerios and then, just as she was leaving the house, the phone rang. She thought it   10
might be news from the hospital about her Aunty Kath and so she went to answer it. She hung up and ran out the door. Rushing down the street, her hair blowing over her eyes, she finally rounded the corner, only to see the Number 41 disappearing from view – just her luck!   15

When you answer questions like these, you do not give every single detail. It would take too long and your listener would get bored. Instead, you pick out the main details and link them together.

When writing about texts, you may need to summarise what you have read. To do this, you must identify:

- the key details you need to include
- the details you can leave out.

Read the following paragraph. Key words are underlined.

For many nations within the <u>Caribbean Sea</u>, <u>coral reefs</u> provide vital <u>protection</u> from the rages of frequent summer <u>hurricanes</u> and from <u>coastal erosion</u>, as well as helping to build the region's beautiful white sand <u>beaches</u>. Many island and coastal <u>residents</u> are also <u>highly dependent</u> on coral reef <u>fisheries</u> for both their <u>food</u> supplies and <u>livelihoods</u>. Coral reef-<u>related tourism</u>, particularly scuba diving, also represents a <u>major source of revenue</u> across the Caribbean.

Adapted from www.coral-reef-info.com

Using the key details to help, you could summarise the paragraph in the following way:

Caribbean coral reefs provide protection from hurricanes and coastal erosion and help build the sandy beaches. Many residents depend on the reef fisheries for their food and livelihoods, with reef-related tourism being a major source of revenue.

ACTIVITY 6

1. Identify the key details in Source E, then use them to write a summary of the paragraph. Aim to use no more than 50 words.

2. Compare your summary with that of another student. Have you included the same key details? Are there details you need to add or leave out? Improve your summary if you need to.

Source E

The Greater Caribbean region is heavily dominated by fringing reefs, which are reef systems which grow fairly close to or directly from shore, with an entirely shallow lagoon or no lagoon at all. In many cases these are quite extensive and well developed, such as those that parallel much of the coast of Cuba, and the east coasts of Andros Island and Eleuthera in The Bahamas. Fringing reefs also encircle most of the smaller islands of the Caribbean region such as Aruba, Bonaire, Antigua, and the Cayman Islands, providing some of the best Caribbean snorkelling opportunities to be had.

Adapted from www.coral-reef-info.com

WORK OUT MEANING

When you are reading, you will come across words you do not know. You can usually make a reasonable guess at their meaning by looking for clues in the context – the words that come before and after.

Read the following sentences:

Coral reefs are one of the greatest natural wonders of the world's oceans. They come in a seemingly endless <u>array</u> of shapes and colours and teem with life.

The word 'array' may be new to you. However, there are clues to its meaning. The first sentence tells you it is something to do with why coral reefs are one of the 'greatest natural wonders of the world's oceans'.

'Seemingly endless' and 'shapes and colours' also help. They suggest a range or group or collection. The dictionary definition of 'array' is 'an impressive display or collection'.

It is not just unfamiliar words that can cause problems for the reader. Writers often use **figurative language** to express an idea, so the reader has to work out what is being suggested. Read Source F and the following explanation.

The Langdale Pikes, hills in the Lake District, are called the 'peacocks of Lakeland'. Clearly the hills are not peacocks, but the writer uses this metaphor to suggest that they are very beautiful and stand out from the surrounding hills. The writer reinforces the metaphor in the second sentence with the word 'boastfully', suggesting the pride and flamboyance of a peacock.

Source F

The Langdale Pikes are the peacocks of Lakeland, receiving admiring gazes from the tourists in the car parks of Dungeon Ghyll and on the shores of Windermere. From here their near-vertical flanks of rock can be seen rising boastfully into the clouds.

From *Collins Rambler's Guide: Lake District*
by John Gillham and Ronald Turnbull

ACTIVITY 7

1 Work with a partner to figure out the meaning of the underlined words in the following extract. Read the whole passage first to get the overall meaning, then look for clues in the context. If you are still not sure, check in a dictionary.

I knew that in a moment the bullies would decide to search the store room and, <u>inevitably</u>, I would be discovered. Sadly, I was right. Kenners was first. He opened the door slowly, scenting his victim. Smiling <u>sadistically</u>, he glanced at my huddled form in the corner. <u>Summoning</u> my last ounce of courage, I turned to face my <u>nemesis</u>. When the first blow fell, <u>excruciating</u> pain quickly followed.

 Practise working out meaning on Cambridge Elevate.

2 The next extract is more challenging. Read it through and then, with your partner, work out the meanings of the underlined words. For each underlined word, choose a **synonym** that could replace it in the passage.

The <u>irksome</u> <u>monotony</u> of my daily life had produced a most unpleasant feeling in my mind. Not only had I lost much of my <u>wonted</u> energy, but a kind of <u>lethargy</u> seemed to have crept over me; a most <u>indefinable</u> reluctance to move about had <u>imperceptibly</u> gained <u>ascendancy</u> over my actions; – to walk, to speak (and here I must not forget to mention that my voice had become extremely <u>feeble</u>) – to apply myself to drawing, reading, or in fact, to make the slightest <u>exertion</u> of any kind whatever, had become absolutely <u>irksome</u> to me.

From *The English Governess in Egypt* by Emmeline Lott

3 The following extracts are from a novel. With your partner, identify the effects of the underlined uses of figurative language.

The sun was up, the room already too warm. Light filtered in through the net curtains, hanging suspended in the air, <u>sediment in a pond</u>. My head felt <u>like a sack of pulp</u>.

The lights around the dressing-room mirror were small round bulbs, as in theatres; they cast a flattering light, but I was not flattered: I looked sick, my skin leached of blood, <u>like meat soaked in water</u>.

The orange tulips are coming out, crumpled and raggedy <u>like the stragglers from some returning army</u>. I greet them with relief, <u>as if waving from a bombed-out building</u>.

From *The Blind Assassin* by Margaret Atwood

4 Copy the following sentences and underline the uses of figurative language. Annotate the images to explain the effects of the images that the writer has used.

The trees I walk beneath are wilting umbrellas, the paper is damp under my fingers, the words I write feather at the edges like lipstick on an aging mouth. Just climbing the stairs I sprout a thin moustache of sweat.

From *The Blind Assassin* by Margaret Atwood

INFER MEANING

Writers do not always tell us everything. Often they leave it to the reader to work things out – to **infer** meaning.

Watch a video on inferring meaning on Cambridge Elevate.

ACTIVITY 8

1 Read Source G and work out:

a how Mr Barber's son died
b why the writer's parents felt they could trust Mr Barber
c how the parents feel about the writer, their daughter.

When writing an answer to a question about your reading, aim to:

- explain why you think as you do
- refer to the text to support your ideas.

Take the question: **How do you think Mr Barber's son died?**
One possible answer is:

I think he died in an awful accident. It seems as though he was playing with another boy with 'a rifle with no safety', probably meaning no safety catch, and it was fired accidentally and killed him.

Note how inverted commas are placed before and after words taken directly from the text.

Now think about the question: **Why do the narrator's parents feel they could trust Mr Barber?**
A possible answer is:

It seems as though they trust him because he lost his son in a tragic accident. This is 'significant' for them. They think that because he knows how easily a death can occur that he will take extra care with their daughter: 'They could put me in his hands because he knew how careful he had to be.'

Note how a colon is used to introduce a long, direct quotation.

2 Answer this question:

How do you think the parents in Source G feel about their daughter?

Quote directly from the passage to support your ideas. Punctuate your quotation(s) accurately.

Source G

My parents enrolled me in a driver's education class. Mr. Barber conducted driving lessons after school in the back parking lot at Mercy. He had lost a son. It happened in 1980. There was a rifle with no safety and two boys. His boy died.   5

Mr. Barber was a good driving instructor – calm, measured, with a wry sense of humour. I looked at him at every stoplight, at every corner, every pause in traffic, my hands on the wheel at ten o'clock and two o'clock, and heard my father's   10
voice saying, "He lost his son too, baby". For my parents this death was significant. They could trust him. They could put me in his hands because he knew how careful he had to be.

From *Name All the Animals* by Alison Smith

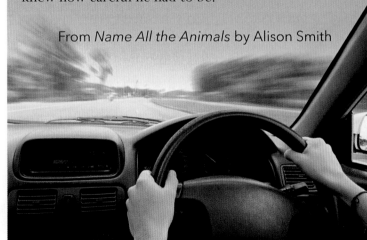

Source H

A gun is fired. Startled antelopes look up from their grazing as
the noise echoes across the savanna. As the reverberation fades,
one of Africa's most incredible animals struggles to take his last
breath through his punctured lungs. All is quiet apart from the
sound of the hunter's footsteps on the brittle grass. He squats by   5
the bloodstained carcass, still holding his gun, and smiles as his
picture is taken. Victory shots are fired into the air as the proud
hunter gets into the car, driven by his guide, and goes back to
the hunting camp where he is served a meal and a stiff drink.
The skinners then get to work carefully removing the tawny   10
coat from the carcass. Vultures circle above the mass of meat
and, as the last car leaves, they descend and finish off what the
hunter has left behind.

One of the most magnificent male lions in our study area has
been killed. Armagnac will soon be flown halfway across the   15
world, where on arrival his head will be stuffed and mounted
on the hunter's wall, along with the photograph. His skin will
be used as a carpet, and the hunter will tell his friends about his
trip to Africa, with a few embellishments. Above him Armagnac
will stare into oblivion with his new glass eyes.   20

From *The Lion Children* by Angus, Maisie and Travers McNeice

Assess your progress

Read Source H and answer the questions. They will help you assess how
well you:

- identify, explain and infer meaning based on detail
- use evidence to support your ideas
- summarise detail.

1 A gun is fired twice in the passage. Explain why.

2 What will happen to Armagnac's head and skin?

3 What is the meaning of the following words in the passage:

     reverberation   embellishments   oblivion

4 How do you think the writer feels about the hunter and what he has
done? Use evidence from the passage to support your ideas.

5 List the points you would include in a summary of the passage.

Compare your answers with those of
another student. Correct or add to your
answers if you feel they can be improved.

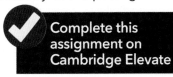
**Complete this
assignment on
Cambridge Elevate**

FURTHER PROGRESS

One of the best ways to
develop reading skills is to
read widely. In this unit, you
have read a range of non-
fiction and fiction texts. Aim
to spend an extra two hours a
week reading. Keep a record
of what you read and make
sure that over the next few
months you read both fiction
and non-fiction texts.

Unit 2

Examine how writers use language to affect readers

Make progress

- explore how writers' purposes affect their language choices
- explore the effects of grammatical features
- explore how writers use imagery
- explore how writers use language to create tone.

UNDERSTAND PURPOSE

When you explore a writer's use of language, it is helpful to think about the **purposes** of the writing – what the writer's intentions were. Some forms of writing may have more than one purpose. Health and safety leaflets, for example, have the purpose of informing readers about aspects of health and safety, but the writer may also intend to describe and persuade.

The purpose of writing may be to:

- entertain
- inform
- express a point of view
- explain how to do something
- argue
- persuade.

 Find out if the purpose of reading will change in the future on Cambridge Elevate.

ACTIVITY 1

1 Work with another student. Look at the list of purposes for writing. Discuss any main purposes for writing that you think could be added to the list, then copy the list and add up to four of your own ideas.

2 When you have completed your list, look at each purpose in turn and, next to each one, make a note of any kind of writing that is mainly for that purpose – for example next to 'entertain' you might note down 'song lyrics'.

3 Choose three of the kinds of writing you have identified. Which ones have more than one purpose? For example song lyrics may be intended to entertain, but many songs also express a point of view about the world or describe an event in the writer's life.

 Watch a video about the purpose of reading on Cambridge Elevate.

EXAMINE THE EFFECTS OF LANGUAGE CHOICES

Writers use language to achieve their purpose. In the following text, the writer's purpose is to provide clear instructions about how to reach a destination.

By changing the language slightly, the writer can make the journey seem simple and worth doing.

Whatever the purpose of the writing, writers choose words that will engage the reader.

10:45 AM

< Back   New Message   Cancel

To Cassandra Duncan

Drive south on the M40 until you reach the A34 exit for Oxford. Exit the motorway and take the first left at the roundabout. The hotel is on the left-hand side, a kilometre down the road.

Write message ...   Send

Simple, factual place names give clear information about the route.

Direct, simple verbs (including imperatives) are used to give clear instructions.

Take the _easy_ drive south on the M40 until you reach the A34 exit for Oxford. _Simply_ exit the motorway and take the first left at the _big_ roundabout. The _beautiful_ hotel is on the left-hand side, _just_ a kilometre down the road.

Adjectives emphasise how simple the journey is.

Adverbs emphasise how straightforward the journey is.

An adjective persuades readers to use the hotel.

ACTIVITY 2

1 Read Source A, which contains information about King Henry VIII.

Source A

After the ending of his marriage to Anne of Cleves, Henry married Catherine Howard. He was 49, overweight and suffering from an ulcer on his leg, and she was around 18 years old. After a few months, rumours began to emerge that she was being unfaithful to the King.

Now read Source B, in which a writer provides the same information but in a different way. Pay particular attention to the underlined words and phrases.

Source B

Having been put off by the looks of his last wife, Henry went for a younger, more attractive model in the shape of Catherine Howard, aged only about eighteen when they were married. Unfortunately the attraction was not mutual; for some reason Catherine did not seem to fancy the bloated, ill-tempered King, over thirty years her senior, who was now barely able to walk due to a running ulcer on his leg.

From *An Utterly Impartial History of Britain* by John O'Farrell

2 Read Source B again, then look at the following comments about the way the writer uses language to achieve certain effects and engage the reader. Which ones do you agree with?

a The writer provides information in a formal, serious way, showing great respect for the importance of the topic.

b The writer keeps his own feelings about the topic to himself and presents it factually.

c The writer tries to engage the modern reader by presenting the facts in everyday, informal language.

d The writer's language choices show he is approaching his subject in a light-hearted, comic way to entertain the reader.

3 Work with another student. Explain your choices with reference to particular words and phrases in the extract. In your pairs, decide which of the four statements is most appropriate and why.

EXPLAIN LANGUAGE CHOICES

The following extract provides factual information about an industrial landmark in the north of England.

Ferrybridge power station is situated on the River Aire, in West Yorkshire. It is the third coal-fired power station to be built on the site since 1924. The power station, often referred to as 'Ferrybridge C', first fed electricity into the national grid in February of 1966. Ferrybridge C has two 198m (650ft) high chimneys and eight 115m (380ft) high cooling towers, which are the largest of their kind in Europe.

From sse.com

A response to the writer's use of language might be:

The writer provides factual information and keeps their opinions about the feature hidden. The writing is full of facts about place, time and size. One fact, that the cooling towers are 'the largest of their kind in Europe', might show the writer trying to persuade the reader of their importance.

identifies a main purpose in a general statement	identifies a specific detail and suggests a possible effect on the reader

ACTIVITY 3

Source C is also about the Ferrybridge cooling towers. Read the extract and answer the following questions.

1 Work with another student.

a Identify words and phrases in the passage that show the writer is doing more than simply providing information.

b Find words that show the writer is trying to influence the reader's opinion about the cooling towers.

2 In your pairs, talk about each word or phrase you have identified. Together, write an explanation of the effect of each word or phrase. You could begin each explanation with the words 'This has the effect of …'.

3 Share your list of words and explanations with another pair. Discuss your findings.

4 In your group of four, copy out Source C in the centre of a clean sheet of paper. Annotate the extract to draw attention to the words and phrases that have been chosen for effect. You could arrange these sheets into a wall display to share your findings with the class.

 Look at a copy of the extract to help you with your ideas for Question 4 on Cambridge Elevate.

EXPLORE THE EFFECTS OF ADJECTIVES AND NOUN PHRASES

Writers can influence readers through their choice of particular words and phrases.

Adjectives are words used to enhance the meaning of **nouns**:

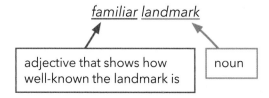

familiar _landmark_

adjective that shows how well-known the landmark is | noun

A **noun phrase** is a group of words that acts like a noun. The phrase contains a noun and words that modify its meaning. In the phrase 'familiar landmark', the noun 'landmark' is modified by the adjective 'familiar'. Look at this annotated example:

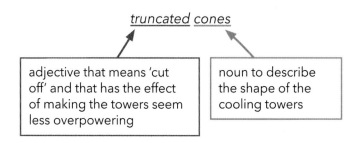

truncated _cones_

adjective that means 'cut off' and that has the effect of making the towers seem less overpowering | noun to describe the shape of the cooling towers

Noun phrases are not always modified by adjectives. In the phrase 'clouds of water vapour', for example, the noun is 'clouds' and it is modified by 'of water vapour' – and 'water vapour' is a noun phrase too.

Source C

Ferrybridge power station cooling towers, West Yorkshire

(At junction of M62 and A1)

The eight cooling towers at Ferrybridge power station dribble clouds of water vapour like a group of amiably smoking giants as they stand beside the junction of the M62 and A1, a familiar landmark to drivers, their truncated cones flaring gently out towards the top. You could drop a Big Ben inside each one, and still have room for a Tyrannosaurus Rex on top.

From *Never Eat Shredded Wheat*
by Christopher Sommerville

ACTIVITY 4

Read Source D, then answer these questions:

1 What are your first impressions of the writer's purposes?

2 Select three noun phrases. For each one, explain the effects of the adjectives attached to the nouns.

3 Now think about the effect the writer is hoping their use of noun phrases will have on the reader. Use your ideas from Question 2 to help you write an answer to this question:

How does the writer use noun phrases to influence the reader's view of Edinburgh?

You could use the following as your starting point:

The writer begins by using noun phrases in which several adjectives are used to persuade the reader that Edinburgh is a wonderful place. In the first two sentences, two compound adjectives – 'must-see' and 'world-class'– are packed together to emphasise just how great the city is.

EXPLORE THE EFFECTS OF VERBS AND ADVERBS

A writer's choice of verbs can influence readers. For example there are several verbs of movement from which a writer can choose, all of which have slightly different effects on the reader.

The old man <u>walked</u> past the bus stop.

In this sentence, the verb 'walked' is neutral and has little effect on the reader other than providing some basic information.

The old man walked <u>slowly</u> past the bus stop.

The addition of an **adverb** can modify the meaning of the verb and might change the effect. The use of 'slowly' provides more information and might have the effect of emphasising the man's age.

The old man <u>limped</u> past the bus stop.

Changing the verb can have a similar effect. Here, the use of 'limped' suggests infirmity and pain, and might have the effect of making the reader feel sorry for the old man.

Source D

Edinburgh is a must-see, world-class tourist destination, boasting everything from iconic landmarks to beautiful coastlines, renowned festivals to the fun of Hogmanay – meaning there's certainly something of interest for   5
everyone, of any age.

A UNESCO World Heritage Site, the Scottish capital is a mix of the medieval grandeur of the Old Town and the Georgian elegance of the New Town, while the vibrant and contemporary bars,   10
restaurants and boutiques ensure that Edinburgh never feels old-fashioned.

Spend time exploring Edinburgh's leading tourist attractions, from the dramatic Arthur's Seat with its spectacular views over the city, to Edinburgh   15
Castle, settled on an extinct volcano. After taking in the splendour of the sights, a night out at one of the many bars, pubs or clubs will put you in the party spirit – a perfect way to round off a stay in this uniquely charming city.   20

ACTIVITY 5

Work with another student. Look at the following extract from a travel book, which describes something that most people would find rather unappealing!

Shutting my door, <u>I was undisturbed</u> by a cockroach, as big as a mouse and markedly faster on its feet, which <u>shot out from</u> under the bed, <u>brown-blurred</u> its way across the linoleum and <u>swung a right</u> through the door of the bathroom partition.

From *Into the Heart of Borneo*
by Redmond O'Hanlon

1 Discuss each of the underlined phrases, focusing on the **verbs**. What do they suggest about:

a the movement of the cockroach?
b the attitude of the writer?

2 Decide which of the following statements best describes the effect of the writer's verbs:

a They emphasise his disgust.
b They show his admiration for the insect.
c They show he isn't really bothered by the insect.
d They add drama to the description.

3 What impression of himself do you think the writer is hoping to give the reader?

WRITE ABOUT THE EFFECTS OF WORDS

So far you have explored some of the effects that a writer's choice of words can have. Now read Source E, which contains two extracts from a 19th-century novel. When you have read the passages, answer the following questions.

ACTIVITY 6

1 Work on your own. Focus on the writer's use of adjectives, noun phrases, adverbs and verbs. Write about the ways in which he uses language to give an impression of the narrator's state of mind.

2 Read through what you have written. Highlight where you have:

a identified adjectives, noun phrases, verbs and adverbs
b commented on the effects of the identified words
c commented on a possible range of effects.

Source E

The evening, I remember, was still and cloudy; the London air was at its 5
heaviest; the distant hum of the street-traffic was at its faintest; the small
pulse of the life within me, and the great heart of the city around me,
seemed to be sinking in unison, languidly and more languidly, with the
sinking sun […]

The quiet twilight was still trembling on the topmost ridges of the heath; 10
and the view of London below me had sunk into a black gulf in the shadow
of the cloudy night, when I stood before the gate of my mother's cottage.

When I rose the next morning and drew up my blind, the sea opened
before me joyously under the broad August sunlight, and the distant
coast of Scotland fringed the horizon with its lines of melting blue. 15

From *The Woman in White* by Wilkie Collins

INVESTIGATE THE EFFECTS OF IMAGERY

Writers use **imagery** to describe features and achieve different effects. Imagery is usually associated with particular figures of speech, such as **metaphor**, **simile** and **personification**.

Metaphor is when one thing is described as though it is another. In the phrase 'he was drowning in homework', for example, the stress of homework overload is being described as though it were the same as drowning.

Simile is when a thing is compared to something else using the words 'like' or 'as'. For example the phrase 'talking to him was like wading through treacle' suggests that the conversation was difficult.

Personification is when something that is not alive is described as though it were human or living. In the phrase 'The news was like a punch to his heart', for example, 'news' – which is not a living thing – is described as though it were a person hitting someone.

Being able to identify these language features is only the first step. You also need to be able to explore the effects of figurative language on the reader.

In Source C, the writer described the cooling towers at Ferrybridge using the simile 'like a group of amiably smoking giants'. This simile could be identified and its possible effects discussed in the following way:

The simile makes the huge towers seem appealing rather than eyesores. The writer compares the towers to 'giants' to suggest their enormous size. The idea of 'giants' might make some readers feel uncomfortable, but 'amiably smoking' gives the reader an image of a bunch of friendly giants chatting and enjoying a cigarette. Although 'smoking' might suggest unhealthiness, 'amiably' makes them seem harmless and friendly to the reader.

identifies the feature	
focuses on effect	
shows the possible effect rather than insisting on an effect	

 Watch a video about figurative language on Cambridge Elevate.

ACTIVITY 7

In the following extract, the writer describes his experience of leaving a mosquito-ridden swamp in a boat.

For the next ten minutes, I conducted a thorough search-and-destroy mission on any remaining mosquitoes that had hitched a lift with us. They were lined up on the inside of the canoe's hull like aeroplanes on an aircraft carrier, and perched in large numbers on every object below the level of the vessel's sides.

From *Surviving Extremes* by Nick Middleton

1 Copy the extract onto a clean sheet of paper and annotate it, drawing attention to the effects of the writer's use of figurative language.

2 Consider the extract as a whole. Which of the following words best describes the tone of the writing?

jokey	serious	angry	something else

3 Work with another student. Read Source F – a Victorian woman's account of a close encounter with a pair of rhinos.

a As you read, identify the writer's use of figurative language. The first two examples are underlined for you.

b Comment on the effects of the figurative language and explain how it helps the reader understand the experience being described. Before you start, look again at the example that describes the effects of a simile.

Source F

The rhino was only momentarily taken aback. Before I had time to skip out of his sight he had made up his mind to charge me. The <u>angry thunder of his snort</u>, mingled with <u>a screech like an engine blowing off steam</u>, lent me wings. When I dared throw a glance over my shoulder I saw that both rhino were bearing   5
down on me with frightening speed. The boys had a start of me, and as I raced after them across the vistas of stone bare as asphalt without a blade of cover anywhere, conviction swept over me that this time the game was up.

Though I ran and ran as I had never run in my life before, and   10
my heart pounded in my ears and my lungs stiffened with the pain of drawing breath, time went suddenly into slow motion. Each step was weighted with lead; I wanted to fly over the ground and, as in some horrid nightmare, I felt as though I were scarcely moving.   15

From 'Speak to the Earth' by Vivienne de Watteville, in *The Virago Book of Women Travellers*

EXPLORE HOW WRITERS CREATE TONE

The word **tone** is used to describe the attitude of the writer. There are many possible tones – for example sarcastic, angry, disgusted, sad, excited, amused, and so on.

Compare the tone of the following extracts:

The proposed railway line will carve its way through some of our most beautiful countryside, butchering ancient woodland and massacring wildlife. Its supporters should be ashamed of themselves.

The words 'carve' and 'butchering' show how strongly the writer feels. You can sense the anger in the powerful image of living creatures being 'massacred'.

The proposed railway line will bring us the delights of shiny trains flying through the countryside, as fast as a bullet and just as destructive.

The words here are more sarcastic than angry. The writer clearly does not really mean the train will bring 'delights'. The image of the 'bullet' suggests that instead of being a 'delight', the railway line will destroy things.

ACTIVITY 8

1 Work in pairs. Read Source G. What words would you use to describe the writer's tone?

2 Identify the words and images that the writer uses to create this tone.

3 In your pairs, produce a short commentary on the tone of the writing, using some of the features you have identified.

Source G

Italians will park anywhere. All over the city you see them bullying their cars into spaces about the size of a sofa cushion, holding up traffic and prompting every driver within three miles to lean on his horn and give a passable imitation of a man in an electric chair. If the opening is too small for a car, the Romans will decorate it with litter – an empty cigarette packet, a wedge of half-eaten pizza, twenty-seven cigarette butts, half an ice-cream cone with an ooze of old ice-cream emerging from the bottom, danced on by a delirium of flies, an oily tin of sardines, a tattered newspaper and something truly unexpected, like a tailor's dummy or a dead goat.

From Neither Here Nor There by Bill Bryson

Assess your progress

Sources H and I focus on the severe storm that devastated large parts of southern England in 1987. Answer the following questions before reading Source J and completing Question 5.

1 Source H is a newspaper report written soon after the event. Comment on the effects of the verbs and noun phrases in the report. What are the writer's purposes?

2 Source I is an extract from a natural history book in which the writer remembers the storm. Which words have similar effects to those in the newspaper report?

3 Think about Sources H and I together. Write about the different effects achieved by each writer through the use of:

   a adjectives and noun phrases

   b verbs and adverbs

   c imagery.

Organise your ideas using a template on Cambridge Elevate.

4 When you have finished, compare your responses with another student's.

   a How well were you able to identify and comment on features of language?

   b What do you need to revisit and improve in your writing?

Complete this assignment on Cambridge Elevate.

Source H

At least seventeen people were killed yesterday as Britain's worst-ever storm ravaged the country at 100 mph leaving chaos and devastation in its wake.   5

Last night a Sealink ferry was aground at Folkestone, thousands of homes and buildings were wrecked, cars were crushed and trees   10 uprooted.

London was blacked out for six hours in the storm and road and rail networks were paralysed.   15

The hurricane, which in Guernsey gusted to 110 mph, struck with astonishing ferocity in the early hours.

From an article in the *Daily Mirror*
by Ann Gripper

Source I

It was lucky that the storm hit England in the middle of the night. The ferocity of the wind – which was sucking matter into its path as well as simply blowing it flat – would have caused carnage if more humans had been about. Despite the   5 widespread failure of power-lines and telephone cables, stories began to trickle through. There had been fatalities, mainly people crushed in their cars by falling trees. The caravan settlement at Canvey Island, one of the victims of the storm-surge flood   10 in 1953, had been wrecked again. In Brighton, the streets were full of splintered glass as the gale flounced through, sucking out shop windows and bringing down many of the city's lovingly protected elms – then whipping one of the   15 Pavilion's stone finials from its plinth and dropping it through the ceiling. In its last hours, the storm seemed to take a fancy to churches. Stained-glass windows were blown out. All that was left of Cransford Baptist Chapel in Suffolk was a single   20 wall, and rows of pews standing under the sky.

From *Beechcombings: The Narratives of Trees* by Richard Mabey

Source J

Source J is an extract from a novel. In it, Samad takes a final look around his home before leaving it to find safety from the storm. Read the text closely.

5 The following comments all help describe this extract. Support each comment with reference to details from the text.

a The storm is shown to be both terrifying and destructive.

b The writer creates a vivid image of how dangerous the storm can be for ordinary people.

c There is some humour in this description of the storm.

d The writer's main aim is to create comedy out of a dangerous event.

Once in the kitchen Samad flashed his torch around: kettle, oven hob, teacup, curtain and then a surreal glimpse of the shed sitting happy like a treehouse in next door's horsechestnut. He picked up the Swiss army knife he remembered leaving 5 under the sink, collected his gold-plated, velvet-fringed Qu'rãn from the living room and was about to leave when the temptation to feel the gale, to see a little of the formidable destruction, came over him. He waited for a lull in the wind 10 and opened the kitchen door, moving tentatively into the garden, where a sheet of lightning lit up a scene of suburban apocalypse: oaks, cedars, sycamores, elms felled in garden after garden, fences down, garden furniture demolished. 15

It was only his own garden, often ridiculed for its corrugated-iron surround, treeless interior and bed after bed of sickly smelling herbs, that had remained relatively intact.

He was just in the process of happily formulating 20 some allegory regarding the bending Eastern reed versus the stubborn Western oak, when the wind reasserted itself, knocking him sideways and continuing along its path to the double glazing, which it cracked and exploded effortlessly, 25 blowing glass inside, regurgitating everything from the kitchen out into the open air. Samad, a recently airborne colander resting on his ear, held his book tight to his chest and hurried to the car.

From *White Teeth* by Zadie Smith

FURTHER PROGRESS

Choose a substantial paragraph from a text you have enjoyed – fiction or non-fiction. Design a poster, on which the paragraph is written out in the centre with particular features of language highlighted. Draw lines out from the highlighted sections, then place comments about the language feature and its effects around the text. Focus on things such as the use of adjectives, adverbs, noun phrases and imagery.

Unit 3

Understand how writers structure texts to affect readers

Make progress (AO2)
- examine how writers use sentences of different lengths for effect
- consider the sequence of details in sentences and paragraphs
- explore the effects of contrasting sentence and paragraph lengths
- develop comments on writers' use of sentences and paragraphs.

UNDERSTAND THE EFFECT OF SHORT SENTENCES

Writers choose particular sentence structures depending on why they are writing (their purpose) and who they are writing for (their audience). If they are writing for young children, for example, and their purpose is to offer clear advice, a writer will probably use short sentences:

Secondary school is different from primary school.

There are five or more lessons a day. Each lesson has its own set of books and its own homework. You need to be well organised.

The school may give you a planner. This will really help. Otherwise you will need to get a diary.

Each sentence is a straightforward statement. This makes the advice seem simple and clear. Short sentences can be used to achieve a range of effects.

Read the following short text:

He glanced behind him. They were still there. He ran. His lungs were burning. He could hear them. A car sped by. Red tail-lights flared. It stopped. A door opened. 'Get in!'

The reader needs to pause at the end of each short sentence. The effect of this is to capture the gasps of breath of the person being chased in the story.

ACTIVITY 1

Read Source A, which is an extract from a ghost story. In it, the writer combines the use of short sentences with repetition. Two short sentences have been underlined as example and there is brief commentary about their effects.

1 Identify and copy three other examples of the writer's use of short sentences in Source A. For each one, write a brief commentary about its effect on the reader.

INVESTIGATE THE EFFECT OF LONGER SENTENCES

Writers usually vary the length of their sentences. Longer sentences, with more than one **clause**, introduce variety and make texts more interesting and engaging for the reader.

Writers decide where to place clauses in sentences to influence the reader. Look at this sentence from *Mansfield Park* by Jane Austen:

To the education of her daughters Lady Bertram paid not the smallest attention.

The most obvious way to write the sentence would be:

Lady Bertram paid not the smallest attention to the education of her daughters.

By beginning the sentence with 'To the education of her daughters', the writer draws the reader's attention to the education of young women first and saves Lady Bertram's attitude to that education until the end. This has the effect of making the topic seem more important, and saves Lady Bertram's ignorance as a surprise.

 Complete a 'clause crossword' on Cambridge Elevate.

Source A

'I know it's you!' Edward shouted, and he heard the fear in his own voice. 'You're playing ghosts again, aren't you? <u>Aren't you?</u>'

> Repeating 'Aren't you?' in a short sentence emphasises Edward's doubts.

And then there was silence. <u>No sound at all</u>. Edward sat up in bed and listened. The awful 5 slithering noise had stopped. It had gone. The ghost had gone.

> This short sentence – without a verb – repeats the idea of 'silence' and has the effect of making the reader feel there is something sinister about the lack of noise.

He hugged himself with relief. It had been a dream, that's all. He'd imagined it. Just as Julie imagined things. Imagined ghosts. 10

Then he heard the breathing again. The shuddering, choking breaths. and he knew that the thing hadn't gone. That it was still there. Outside his door. Waiting. Waiting.

From 'Such a Sweet Little Girl' by Lance Salway, in *A Nasty Piece of Work and Other Ghost Stories*

ACTIVITY 2

1 Work with another student. Read the following sentences then discuss why you think the writers have structured the sentences in the ways they have. The main clause has been underlined in each one.

   a Contrary to what you may have heard about tourism overdevelopment on the island, <u>Mallorca is one of the great natural destinations of the Mediterranean.</u>

   b Unaware of the incoming tide, <u>the family walked across the bay.</u>

   c <u>The murderer</u>, staggering backward to the wall and shutting out his sight with his hand, seized a heavy club and <u>struck her down</u>.

2 Choose two of the sentences. Write an explanation of why you think the writer has shaped the sentence in the way they have.

EXPLORE THE EFFECT OF LONG SENTENCES

Writers can increase the impact of details by concentrating large amounts of information into long, single sentences.

ACTIVITY 3

Read the following extract and think about how the writer uses sentence length for effect:

A fearful man, all in coarse grey, with a great iron on his leg. A man with no hat, and with broken shoes, and with an old rag tied round his head. A man who had been soaked in water, and smothered in mud, and lamed by stones, and cut by flints, and stung by nettles, and torn by briars; who limped, and shivered, and glared and growled; and whose teeth chattered in his head as he seized me by the chin.

From *Great Expectations* by Charles Dickens

Now read the following comments by different students exploring the structure of the extract.

Student A *The first sentence is quite short and tells you about the colour of his clothes and the chain round his leg. The second sentence tells you something about what the convict is wearing, such as his broken shoes and the rag round his head instead of a hat. The long third sentence gives you a very clear picture of the convict. It shows how frightening he seems to the child: 'growled', for example, makes him sound like a mad dog.*

Student B *The first two sentences give the reader some details of the convict's appearance. They show what the child can see – the colour of his clothes, the chain on his leg, the rags of clothes he is wearing. The third sentence is different. A list of verbs is presented. They focus on pain and suffering: 'soaked … smothered … lamed … cut … stung … torn'. By building the list of these kinds of verbs, the writer influences the reader to see the convict as a character deserving of some sympathy.*

1 Student B gives the better response. Can you explain why?

2 Compare your explanation with that of another student. If you missed some good points, add them.

ACTIVITY 4

Great Expectations is a novel – a work of fiction. Writers of non-fiction use the same technique of packing a lot of information into long sentences to influence readers. Read Source B, then discuss the following questions with another student:

1 There are only two sentences in this long extract. In what ways does the first sentence add impact to the second?

2 Choose details from the second sentence that are in direct contrast to the following examples of vocabulary from the first:

   a 'din and bustle'
   b 'teem with every luxury'
   c 'most beautiful'.

3 What is the purpose of the dashes in the first sentence?

4 What word does the writer use to describe the change between the two scenes he describes? What does this word suggest?

5 Think about the writer's use of the colon (:) and semi-colon (;) in the second sentence. Now read the following comment on these. Do you agree? Is there anything you would add?

The colon after 'The change is marvellous' shows that the writer is introducing examples of the 'change'. The semi-colons are used between different aspects of the change because each change is described in some detail already, using commas. The semi-colons make it easier for the reader to identify the different changes.

6 Use the results of your discussions to write an answer to this question:

How does the writer draw attention to the extreme differences between different parts of London?

Use quotations from the extract to illustrate your points.

Source B

You seem for a time to leave the day, and life, and habits of your fellow-creatures behind you – just to step out of the din and bustle of a crowded thoroughfare – to turn aside from streets whose shops teem with every   5 luxury – where Art has brought together its most beautiful varieties, – and you have scarce gone a hundred yards when you are in *The Rookery*. The change is marvellous: squalid children, haggard men, with long uncombed   10 hair, in rags, most of them smoking, many speaking Irish; women without shoes or stockings – a babe perhaps at the breast, with a single garment, confined to the waist by a bit of string; wolfish looking dogs;   15 decayed vegetables strewing the pavement; low public houses; linen hanging across the street to dry; the population stagnant in the midst of activity; lounging about in remnants of shooting jackets, leaning on the window   20 frames, blocking up the courts and alleys; with young boys gathered round them, looking exhausted as though they had not been to bed.

From *The Rookeries of London*
by Thomas Beames

CONSIDER CONTRASTING SENTENCES

Writers often use short sentences to deliberately contrast with longer sentences in order to create particular effects. For example:

The casualties alone were almost double the entire strength of the British Expeditionary Force which had set off in August 1914 to meet the Germans at Mons. And forty thousand of them were dead.

From *Somme* by Lyn Macdonald

The opening sentence mentions 'casualties' and 'double', but the reader is not aware of the true extent of the casualties until the following sentence. The large number stands out because it has been placed in such a short sentence.

ACTIVITY 5

In Source C, the writer describes a character's thoughts about a Caribbean island. Read the extract, then answer these questions:

1 What effect is created by the phrase 'a black dash of crows'?

2 The writer could have written 'overhead'. What is gained by the phrase 'against the sky'?

3 What is the most noticeable aspect of the lizard and which words give that impression?

4 How does the writer add interest to the description of cicadas?

5 What impression of insects is given in the fourth sentence?

6 What is the purpose of the final short sentence?

7 Comment on how the writer has structured her ideas and sentences to create a picture of the island for the reader.

Source C

A black dash of crows flew home against the sky. A tree lizard scuttled up the bark licking grubs with its lightning tongue. Cicadas hissed rhythmic as cymbals. The sparks of fireflies buzzed   5
my head like thoughts escaping, while dots of bees returned to the hives, oblivious they were now working for me. This was a beautiful island.

From *Small Island*
by Andrea Levy

ORGANISE SENTENCES IN PARAGRAPHS

Writers organise words into sentences to create particular effects. They also organise sentences into paragraphs to shape meaning.

Read Source D. The commentary shows how the ideas are structured.

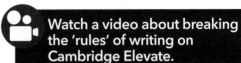

Watch a video about breaking the 'rules' of writing on Cambridge Elevate.

Source D

Their gradual exodus to messaging apps such as WhatsApp, WeChat and KakaoTalk boils down to Facebook becoming a victim of its own success. The road to gaining nearly 1.2 billion monthly active users has seen the mums, dads, aunts and uncles of the generation who pioneered Facebook join it too, spamming their walls with inspirational quotes and images of cute animals, and (shock, horror) commenting on their kids' photos. No surprise, then, that Facebook is no longer a place for uninhibited status updates about pub antics, but an obligatory communication tool that younger people maintain because everyone else does.

5

10

All the fun stuff is happening elsewhere. On their mobiles.

From an article in *The Observer* by Parmy Olson

The opening sentence introduces the idea of Facebook as a 'victim' of its own success.

This leads into a second sentence in which the writer explains what was meant by 'victim' – that a medium intended for young people has become popular with older generations.

In the third sentence the writer explains the impact of this increasing popularity.

This new paragraph could have been attached to the end of the previous one, but the writer separates it to add impact to the main point being made about young people.

ACTIVITY 6

Read Source D again, then answer these questions:

1. Which phrase in the second sentence connects with 'its own success' in the first?

2. Which phrase in the third sentence connects it to the second sentence?

3. Why do you think the writer split the short second paragraph into two sentences?

Now read the film review in Source E and answer the questions that follow.

Source E

The prospect of another superhero movie, another superhero-saves-the-planet yawn, didn't exactly fill me with enthusiasm. I've had my fill of incomprehensible or non-existent plots, all just an excuse for some explosion of mega-expensive 5
special effects in which, of course, no one important dies. Certainly not our superhero.

But something remarkable has been achieved with this latest instalment of the Marvel franchise; something almost shocking. This is a political film. 10
Forget all those fantastical, evil sub-human creatures chasing after some mythical gift of everlasting life, these superheroes are actually tackling real political issues like civil liberties, government surveillance and national security. It's brilliant to see. 15

4 Explain how the writer uses short sentences for effect.

5 How does the writer structure his sentences to emphasise the points he wishes to make?

6 Compare your answers to Questions 1–5 with those of another student. How well have you understood how writers structure sentences and paragraphs for effect?

EXPLORE PARAGRAPH COHESION

To expand upon an idea, writers build up a sequence of connected sentences in a paragraph. Source F is from an essay by George Orwell, written early in the 20th century. At the end of the previous paragraph the writer had noticed a condemned man step aside from a puddle as he was being led to the gallows. Read the paragraph and the annotations which explain the structure of the first three sentences, and then complete Activity 7.

Source F

It is curious, but till that moment I had never realised what it means to destroy a healthy, conscious man. When I saw the prisoner step aside to avoid the puddle, I saw the mystery, the unspeakable wrongness, of cutting a life short when it is in full tide. This man was not dying, he was alive just as we were alive. 5
All the organs of his body were working – bowels digesting food, skin renewing itself, nails growing, tissues forming – all toiling away in solemn foolery. His nails would still be growing when he stood on the drop, when he was falling through the air with a tenth-of-a-second to live. His eyes saw the yellow gravel and 10
the grey walls, and his brain still remembered, foresaw, reasoned – reasoned even about puddles. He and we were a party of men walking together, seeing, hearing, feeling, understanding the same world; and in two minutes, with a sudden snap, one of us would be gone – one mind less, one world less. 15

'Till that moment' picks up the detail of seeing the man avoid the puddle in the previous paragraph. The sentence introduces an idea.

The writer develops 'what it means' and asserts that it is wrong to kill someone.

'The prisoner' has become 'this man' and the writer focuses on how alive he was. The personal pronoun 'we' connects the man to other people.

From 'A Hanging' by George Orwell in *Essays*

ACTIVITY 7

1 Focus on the last four sentences in Source F. For each one, comment on how it:

a develops the idea of 'what it means to destroy a healthy, conscious man'
b builds directly on the sentence before it.

2 Write a short explanation of how Orwell **structures** and **develops** his ideas about the wrongness of capital punishment.

STRUCTURE TEXTS USING PARAGRAPHS

Both fiction and non-fiction texts are divided into paragraphs. Writers organise and link paragraphs to guide and influence readers.

ACTIVITY 8

Writers of reviews provide information and opinions about something. Source G is from a review of *12 Years a Slave* – a film based on the true story of Solomon Northup, a free man who was kidnapped and enslaved.

Source G

Northup's original account, written in just five months after his release, was highly influential in generating opposition to slavery, a movement that continued to gather momentum throughout the 1850s and helped provoke the American Civil War. 5

It might, in fact, be one of the most important books of which few of us had ever heard until McQueen resolved to adapt it.

Despite the celebrity that Northup enjoyed until his death sometime in the 1860s or 1870s (nobody knows 10 exactly when), it is moving to think of the millions, 150 years on, who will now become familiar with his name. It is high time his story was told again.

In doing so, McQueen pulls no punches. In the film's two most memorably intense scenes, his 15 camera lingers almost defiantly on unspeakable pain and degradation.

The first is after Northup has nearly been hanged by Tibeats. Instead he is left in the noose for hours on end, desperately keeping the toes of his tattered 20 shoes in contact with the mud beneath, to keep his neck from breaking. It would be interesting to know how many cinema-goers find themselves instinctively flexing their feet in empathy, reaching for the non-existent mud. I did. 25

From an article in the *Mail Online* by Brian Viner

1 Work with another student. Discuss the answers to the following questions:

a The first paragraph is not about the film. Why does the writer include this information?

b The second paragraph begins with the pronoun 'It'. What phrase in the first paragraph does this refer to?

c How does the third paragraph develop from the previous one?

d To what does 'In doing so', at the beginning of the fourth paragraph, refer?

e What would a reader expect to follow the fourth paragraph?

f What phrase instantly connects the final paragraph to the previous one?

g Comment on the effect of the very short final sentence.

h Explain the ways the writer sequences the four sentences in the final paragraph to have an effect on readers.

2 On your own, write an explanation of the ways in which the writer structures the review to influence the reader.

UNDERSTAND DIALOGUE

In fiction, dialogue is organised so that each character's words are placed in their own paragraph. This can lead to sequences of very short paragraphs that can be arranged to have a variety of effects on the reader.

 Listen to how writers use dialogue on **Cambridge Elevate.**

ACTIVITY 9

1 Work in groups of three to read Source H. Two of you should read the spoken words of Bingo and Bertie while the third reads Bertie's words as narrator.

Source H

'Jeeves tells me you want to talk to me about something,' I said.

'Eh?' said Bingo, with a start. 'Oh yes, yes. Yes.'

I waited for him to unleash the topic of the day, but he didn't seem to want to get going. Conversation languished. He stared straight ahead of him in a glassy sort of manner.   5

'I say, Bertie,' he said, after a pause of about an hour and a quarter.

'Hallo!'   10

'Do you like the name Mabel?'

'No.'

'No?'

'No.'

'You don't think there's a kind of music in the word,   15
like the wind rustling gently through the tree-tops?'

'No.'

He seemed disappointed for a moment; then cheered up. 'Of course you wouldn't. You always were a fat-headed worm without any soul, weren't you?'   20

From *The Inimitable Jeeves* by P.G. Wodehouse

2 Talk about your reading and how it might be improved. Then read it aloud again. Think in particular about:

a any clues about the tone of the **dialogue**

b the use of repetition

c any contrast between the two speakers.

3 Work on your own. Complete the following tasks:

a Comment on the way that Bingo's first line is structured and its effect on the reader.

b Comment on the three consecutive uses of 'No'. What is the intended effect?

c Write a short commentary in which you explain the tone of this text by drawing attention to the way it is structured.

I turned and descended the flight of shallow, worn stone steps, and, pushing open a heavy oak door which had been left ajar, entered the Cross Keys Inn.

For a few seconds, until my eyes grew 5 accustomed to the gloom, I could see nothing. The hallway was cold and had a dank, below-ground smell, mingled with the fumes of smoke and ale, which must have permeated those walls over 10 scores, perhaps hundreds, of years, for this was clearly an immensely old house.

I stood still, expecting to hear voices, or have someone appear. There was nothing. All was dark and silent, save 15 for, somewhere within, the heavy ticking of a grandfather clock.

And then, without warning, there came a sudden terrible cry – a screech or scream, like the cackle of a crone, 20 or the **caterwaul** of some creature in its death throes. It came once, ripping into the quiet building, and then twice more, a dreadful noise that made me start forward, and set 25 my heart racing, as I looked wildly about me. A great fear rose from somewhere deep inside me. The noise had awakened terrors, and dim formless memories, though I neither 30 recognised nor recalled the sound.

And then, there was silence again, and only the awful recollection of it was left hanging upon the air.

From *The Mist in the Mirror* by Susan Hill

Vocabulary

caterwaul: a shrill howling or wailing sound

FURTHER PROGRESS

Choose one kind of writing found in a newspaper, such as film review, editorial comment, article, report or letter. Find three short examples and print them on a large piece of paper. Add annotations that highlight features of structure such as how they begin and end, and how sentences are varied for effect.

Unit 4
Consider writers' ideas and perspectives

Make progress (AO3)
- understand perspective
- consider how culture, time and events can affect perspective
- investigate how writers influence their readers

WHAT IS PERSPECTIVE?

The way you see something often depends on where you are standing. It is the same for writers. Their viewpoint – or perspective – can be influenced by many things, such as the culture in which they have grown up, the time in which they are writing or by particular events that they have experienced or seen.

UNDERSTAND THE INFLUENCE OF CULTURE ON PERSPECTIVE

Sometimes the culture in which writers have grown up is reflected in their work. Culture is the name for the ideas, knowledge, beliefs and customs that are shared by the people of an area, a country, a race or a social group. You can also think of culture as a way of life reflected in everyday activities.

ACTIVITY 1

Read Source A, in which the writer – who was brought up in one of China's most remote regions – remembers an event from her childhood. Then answer the questions that follow.

Source A

It was the eighth birthday of the Guan's eighth child. Guan Jie, or No. 8 as he was better known, was the fourth son and the youngest of the Guans. Since eight, and especially double eight, is a lucky number, a number to bring in fortune and wealth, and Madame   5
Guan was a great believer in such things, the day called for a big celebration. [...] Having carefully removed the lid, which had an elaborate handle on one side, Jing started to put into the soup some finely cut potato slices, bean curd and rice noodles before adding some   10
wafer-thin slices of beef, lamb and mutton. There were also dishes piled high with Chinese cabbage waiting to go in. Jing did all of this with considerable skill, her every move watched avidly by a group of children, all waiting to tuck into the scrumptious Mongolian Hot   15
Pot. Between tasks, she had to fend off the greedy children, eager to dip into the hot pot for meat slices before they were ready. [...] We children were soon fighting for pieces of meat, and in fact for everything in the pot. No. 8 was head of the pack at our table.   20
He, taking advantage of his birthday, managed to hog most of the delicacies in the pot. Slurping contentedly, he started a game of paper-scissors-stone. The winner would win the chance to dip in the pot before him. The competition started reasonably fairly, and ended   25
in tears when No. 8 cheated a girl out of her chance to secure the last bit of beef. The tears only ended when Jing offered her mutton to the girl.

From *Lion's Head, Four Happiness* by Xiaomei Martell

1 Work with another student. Discuss what you learn from this extract about the following aspects of the writer's culture:

a names
b beliefs
c food
d birthday celebrations.

 Listen to some descriptions of different birthday celebrations on Cambridge Elevate.

2 Answer the following questions and discuss the reasons for your answers with your partner:

a In what ways is this birthday celebration different from birthday celebrations in your culture?
b In what ways is it similar?

3 Look at the structure of the text. At which point do you realise that this is a first-person account?

4 With your partner, discuss the following questions:

a Why might the writer have included this account in her autobiography?
b What do you think is the writer's attitude towards her culture?

INVESTIGATE THE INFLUENCE OF TIME AND EVENTS ON PERSPECTIVE

The time when something is written and the events that a writer witnesses can affect their viewpoint. However, two people writing at the same time might have different experiences of the same event, and this could affect their ideas and their perspective. During the First World War, for example, a soldier writing home from the battlefields of France may have demonstrated a very different view of the war than a recruiting officer based in London.

Read the fact file about the First World War.

> **Facts**
> - The First World War lasted from 1914 to 1918.
> - It was a global military war with 70 million participants.
> - 15 million people were killed.
> - Thousands of women lost husbands and fiancés in the war.

ACTIVITY 2

Study Source B, which is a poster created during the First World War.

1 Answer the following questions:

a What is the purpose of this poster? Who is the intended **audience**?
b From what perspective or point of view has this text been written?
c What ideas about war can you see in the poster?
d Look at the punctuation in the poster:

- Why are there so many questions?
- What is the effect of the words in capital letters?
- A dash is used to indicate a longer pause than a comma; how is the dash used for impact in the poster?

2 Sometimes apparently simple words have an extra meaning that is implied rather than stated. For example the phrase 'If not, don't YOU THINK he should be?' implies that the reader should feel guilty that her 'best boy' is not wearing a soldier's uniform and that it is her duty to encourage her boyfriend to join the army.

Copy and complete the following table to show the implied meanings of the phrases in the left-hand column. The first one has been done as an example.

Phrase	Implied meaning
'you and your country are worth fighting for'	Stresses the importance of country. Makes reader feel a sense of pride and respect for her country and also for herself.
'do you think he is <u>WORTHY</u> of you?'	
'Don't pity the girl who is alone'	
'neglects his duty to his King and Country'	
'the time may come when he will <u>NEGLECT YOU</u>.'	

3 How would you sum up the attitude to war displayed in the poster?

4 This poster was produced while the war was going on. What impact do you think the time it was written has on the way its message is expressed?

Source B

TO THE
YOUNG WOMEN
OF LONDON

Is your "Best Boy" wearing Khaki? If not don't <u>YOU THINK</u> he should be?

If he does not think that you and your country are worth fighting for—do you think he is <u>WORTHY</u> of you?

Don't pity the girl who is alone—her young man is probably a soldier—fighting for her and her country—and for <u>YOU.</u>

If your young man neglects his duty to his King and Country, the time may come when he will <u>NEGLECT YOU.</u>

Think it over—then ask him to

JOIN THE ARMY TO-DAY

Printed by David Allen & Sons Ltd., Harrow, London, etc.

EXAMINE DIFFERENT PERSPECTIVES

You are going to look at another text based on events in the First World War. However, this one was published many years later, in 1967. The extract is from an autobiography in which someone is looking back and describing an event that took place during the war.

ACTIVITY 3

Read Source C, then answer the questions that follow.

Source C

Then the blow fell. On the afternoon of September 4th – too late to get married that day – a further telegram arrived ordering Jack to leave Victoria for service overseas early on the 7th. There was nothing to be done, but to cancel the honeymoon plans. [...] 5

Jack was twenty-six and I was twenty, and both of us were, I think, very young for our ages. In the tense emotional climate of the time, we had little conception of what we were doing and little idea 10 of what we might be committing ourselves to. [...]

Early the following morning, a day and a half after our marriage, I saw him off from Victoria along with a train-load of other cannon fodder.

Five weeks later the War Office 'regretted to 15 inform me' that Capt. J. W. Wooton of the 11th Battalion Suffolk Regiment had died of wounds.

He had been shot through the eye and died forty-eight hours later on an ambulance train; and in due course his blood-stained kit was **punctiliously** 20 returned to me.

Thus before I had reached my twenty-first birthday, I had experienced the deaths of my father, my brother, my favourite school friend and the husband to whom I had been married in theory 25 for five weeks and in practice for something less than forty-eight hours. In ten years I had learned little about life, much about death. [...]

My troubles were, of course, in no way unusual. What happened to me happened also, in one form 30 or another, to thousands of my contemporaries.

From Barbara Wootton's autobiography, in *The Virago Book of Women and the Great War*

 Vocabulary

punctiliously: correctly, with attention to detail

1 From which perspective is this text written?

2 What is the writer's experience of war?

3 What does the final paragraph tell you about the writer's attitude to war?

4 The writer is looking back on her wartime experiences after many years. What effect might this have on her account?

5 In pairs, come up with a brief explanation of the impact that the following details from the text have on the reader. For example you might describe the effect of the phrase 'very little idea of what we were committing ourselves to' as:

This suggests that they were naïve and innocent and makes the reader realise that they had no idea of what the future may bring. They seem unaware of the impact that war could have on their lives.

a 'train-load of other cannon fodder'
b 'his blood-stained kit was punctiliously returned to me'
c 'I had learned little about life, much about death'
d 'My troubles were, of course, in no way unusual'.

6 What differences are there between Sources B and C in the writer's ideas about war and their perspectives? In your answer you should comment on:

a the writers' audience and purpose
b the ideas they put across
c the organisation of the text
d the language they use.

When you have finished, swap with another student and indicate on each other's work where you have included each of the features listed. Add anything that you have missed.

🔊 **Listen to an audio clip of Source C on Cambridge Elevate.**

INVESTIGATE HOW WRITERS INFLUENCE READERS

Read the following statements about teenagers:

The biology of human sleep timing, like that of other mammals, changes as we age. This has been shown in many studies. As puberty begins, bedtimes and waking times get later. This trend continues until 19.5 years in women and 21 years in men.

From an article in New Scientist by Russell Foster

Recent research confirms what we've all known for a long time: teenagers are lazy. Give them half a chance and they'll stay in bed all day long.

The first statement is **objective**. It gives facts about teenagers and sleep without trying to influence the reader's view of them. There is no evidence of the writer's opinion.

The second statement influences the reader by giving a negative view of teenagers. It distorts the facts to suit the writer's viewpoint. The phrase 'what we've all known for a long time' suggests that both the writer and reader are already prejudiced against teenagers.

The phrase 'teenagers are lazy' is a biased statement. **Bias** can be shown in either a **negative** or **positive** way. Writers use bias to influence their readers. If there is no bias in a statement and no attempt to influence readers, it is said to be **neutral**.

ACTIVITY 4

1 With another student, talk about the following statements and decide whether they are positive, negative or neutral, biased in favour of teenagers or biased against them. Explain the reasons for your choice in each case.

a Teenage thugs wearing hoodies are clearly intimidating, and the Bluewater Shopping Centre was quite right in its decision to ban them.

b Some years ago Bluewater Shopping Centre banned boys wearing hoodies because they were considered intimidating.

c There has been undeserved victimisation of teenagers in shopping centres, where it is unfairly assumed that innocent teen shoppers are all shoplifters or troublemakers.

d Retailers report an increase in the number of hours teenagers spend in shopping centres at the weekend, as well as evidence of higher spending.

e Teenagers give shopping centres a welcome boost. 'We're delighted to have them here. Their lively presence and willingness to spend money are hugely important to us,' said one major retailer.

 Watch two people discuss their opinions of 'hoodies' on Cambridge Elevate.

2 Write three more statements about teenagers. One should be positive, one negative and one neutral.

USE LANGUAGE TO INFLUENCE READERS

Bias can be detected in a writer's use of language, where particular words are intended to influence readers in a positive or a negative way. Look at the following paragraphs, in which two writers have used the same facts about a beach to produce very different descriptions.

Facts
- long beach
- palm trees
- hot weather all year round
- fast-moving tides
- crowded at weekends
- two cafés.

The warm sun shines down on the palm-fringed beach with its miles of soft golden sand. After a relaxing swim in the turquoise sea you can enjoy a delicious lunch in one of the lively beachside cafés.

The blazing sun beats down relentlessly on the beach, where tall palm trees provide little shelter. Strong currents make swimming dangerous, however inviting the sea may look. At weekends it is advisable to avoid the uncomfortably crowded cafés serving unappetising food.

Here is an extract from one student's commentary on the use of language in these paragraphs:

The first decsription uses the facts to present a <u>favourable</u> image of the beach, with the use of adjectives such as 'warm', 'relaxing' and 'delicious'. <u>The noun phrases</u> 'palm-fringed beach' and 'lively beachside cafés' add to this image. The sun 'shines' – a verb with a <u>positive association</u>, unlike the more negative 'beats down', used in the second description.

Adjectives used in the second description – 'blazing', 'dangerous' and '<u>unappetising</u>' – present a negative image of the beach, as does the noun phrase 'uncomfortably crowded cafés'.

> identifies positive bias

> detailed focus on language use

> considers effect on reader

> identifies negative bias

ACTIVITY 5

1 Look at the following facts about a house. Then write two short descriptions of the house, one making the house seem attractive and the other making it seem unattractive.

Remember that the words you choose for each description should influence readers either positively or negatively. Think carefully about the reaction your choice of words may provoke in the reader. For example the word 'home' has associations of comfort, love and security, whereas the word 'house' simply suggests a dwelling-place.

Facts
- three-bedroomed house
- large garden
- on the outskirts of a city
- buses every two hours
- views of hills
- station two kilometres away
- close to motorway
- one primary school nearby
- other schools in city.

2 When you have finished, swap your work with that of another student. Write a commentary on the way your partner has used language to influence the reader. You should refer to:

a their choice of vocabulary and its positive or negative associations
b the effect of adjectives, verbs and noun phrases on the reader.

INVESTIGATE IDEAS AND VIEWPOINTS

So far you have looked at bias and objectivity and writers' use of facts. You have examined the ways writers select language to put across their ideas and to influence their readers. Now you are going to investigate the way that ideas and viewpoints are conveyed in a longer text.

Source D

ARROGANT, ABUSIVE AND OH-SO SMUG — WHY DO SO MANY CYCLISTS THINK THEY'RE ABOVE THE LAW?

Getting more people on to bikes in London seemed to me to be a good idea — encouraging health-giving exercise, reducing traffic congestion and generally turning the city into a calmer, gentler and more civilised place. 5

How wrong can you be! For far from being calm, gentle or civilised, many cyclists have proved to be the exact opposite. While this of course by no means applies to them all, large numbers of cyclists have brought a new level of aggression and indeed menace 10 to our city streets.

As a pedestrian, I have encountered this on innumerable occasions. A few weeks ago, at a major intersection in Central London, I started to cross the road when the green man flashed up at the lights. 15

Out of the corner of my eye, I saw something hurtling towards me and sprang backwards just in time. A cyclist had jumped the red light and almost knocked me down as he sped across the junction.

Furious, I shouted after him that he had jumped the 20 lights. To my astonishment, he stopped and looking back over his shoulder, shouted abuse at me for having dared to try to interrupt his progress by crossing the road. [...]

What possible justification could there be for 25 abusing a pedestrian — and when the cyclist himself had just put her in danger by breaking the law? Surely an apology to me was in order rather than a tirade?

But it seems that, while obeying the law or rules of the road may be obligatory for lesser mortals such 30 as car drivers, cyclists believe they are above such irritating trifles.

In short, they behave as if they are the lords of the universe.

From an article in the *Daily Mail* by Melanie Phillips

ACTIVITY 6

Read Source D, a newspaper article about cyclists.

1 Answer the following questions to trace the development of the writer's ideas:

   a What is the first point that the writer makes about cycling?

   b How does her opinion change in paragraph 2?

   c What event changed her mind?

   d What point does the writer raise in paragraph 5?

   e What is the writer's conclusion?

 Vocabulary

tirade: an outburst of anger or criticism

trifle: something unimportant

2 With another student, discuss the following:

   a From which point of view or perspective is the article written?

   b How does the writer's perspective explain the opinions she expresses in the article?

   c Sum up the ideas about cyclists in London.

   d Why do you think the writer has used an **anecdote** (a personal story) to put across her opinions on cyclists?

3 In the article, the writer uses punctuation to draw attention to her ideas and to shape the reader's response. With your partner, discuss the effect on the reader of the following:

a   question marks
b   exclamation marks
c   dashes.

ACTIVITY 7

If you look again at the anecdote in Source D, you may be able to detect bias in the use of language. Here is an extract from a student's commentary on bias in the article:

The writer says that she saw something 'hurtling' towards her. The use of this word suggests that that the cyclist was moving fast in an uncontrolled manner. This impression is confirmed with the use of the word 'sped.' The cyclist shouts 'abuse' at her, giving the impression that he was rude and angry. The word 'dared' implies that the writer of the article was wrong in the eyes of the cyclist, even though she was crossing the road correctly. Together, the use of these words conveys a negative bias towards cyclists.

selects vocabulary for comment
explores implication of 'hurtling'
makes links between words
explores impact on reader
draws conclusion about effects of vocabulary

1 Using the student response as a model, write a further paragraph exploring the ways in which the writer of Source D influences her readers. You should:

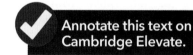
Annotate this text on Cambridge Elevate.

a   select examples from the text
b   explain the effect of particular words and phrases
c   draw your conclusion about the use of bias, whether negative or positive.

Assess your progress

Read Source E, an article about a campaign started by *The Times* newspaper. Then answer the following questions. They will help you assess how well you:

- work out the writer's perspective
- trace the development of the writer's ideas
- examine ways in which the article influences readers.

1 Work out the sequence of the writer's ideas by writing a short phrase or sentence to sum up the content of each paragraph.

2 Think about why the campaign was started. From what perspective is the article written?

3 What ideas about cycling are expressed in the article?

4 Select examples from the first paragraph to explain how the writer has used language to influence the reader.

5 How does the writer's use of language in the second paragraph draw attention to the facts and influence the reader?

6 What are the similarities and differences in the attitude towards cycling and cyclists in Sources D and E?

Compare your answers with those of another student to check that you have included all the necessary information. Add anything that you missed.

Complete this assignment on Cambridge Elevate.

Source E

The response to our Cities Fit For Cycling campaign has been heartening but it has not yet gone far enough

Mary Bowers is a news reporter at *The Times* and, among her colleagues, a popular one. For the past year, however, while many of them have spoken 5 to her, she has not spoken to them. For a year ago yesterday, Mary was knocked from her bike at a junction in front of the offices where she worked. Crushed and 10 horrifically injured, she has not yet regained full consciousness.

This newspaper makes no apology for having begun a campaign on such a personal basis, only an 15 apology for not having begun one earlier. Since Mary's accident, more than 100 cyclists have died on Britain's roads. The youngest was eight years old; the oldest 20 was 80. So far in 2012, eleven have died outside London, three in Edinburgh and two on the same stretch outside Nottingham. Those who survived injury in 25 2011 – Mary was one – number a startling 19,108, with more than 3000 seriously injured.

This time last year *The Times* began to advocate cities fit 30 for cycling. The response has been overwhelming. Thirty-six thousand members of the public have pledged their support, as have all three major 35 political parties. Winning Best Media Campaign award at the National Transport Awards, this newspaper's campaign was described as 'relentless, informed 40 and passionate'.

The campaign has prompted behavioural changes, encouraging drivers of heavy vehicles to fit suitable mirrors and turning 45 alarms. While cyclists too can always benefit from taking greater care, statistics show clearly that the vast majority of incidents between motor vehicles and bikes 50 are caused by driver, rather than cyclist error. But the stated aim of this campaign has never been to change drivers or cyclists. Rather, it has been to change the cities in 55 which they cycle and drive.

From www.thetimes.co.uk

FURTHER PROGRESS

Search online to find two articles in the national press about teenagers. For example:

- 'Hoodies from the past' in *The Guardian*.
- 'How Media Demonises Teenagers' in *The Independent*.

1 From what perspectives are the articles written?

2 What ideas are presented about teenagers in the text?

3 Compare and contrast the views of teenagers that are presented in the two articles.

Complete this test to assess your progress in the skills covered by Units 1–4.

You have **45 minutes**.

Route to success:

- Read the passage closely. Remember to think about what you are reading.
- Read all the questions carefully before starting to answer.
- The number of marks for each question will give you a clue as to how much time you should spend on each one.
- Remember to refer to the text to support points you make.

Source A is taken from the opening of the memoir *Cider with Rosie*. In it, the writer recalls his arrival at the remote Cotswold village of Slad.

Source A

I was set down from the carrier's cart at the age of three; and there with a sense of bewilderment and terror my life in the village began.

The June grass, amongst which I stood, was taller than I was, and I wept. I had never been so close to grass before. It towered above me and all around me, each blade tattooed with tiger-skins of sunlight. It was knife-edged, dark, and a wicked green,   5 thick as a forest and alive with grasshoppers that chirped and chattered and leapt through the air like monkeys.

I was lost and didn't know where to move. A tropic heat oozed up from the ground, rank with sharp odours of roots and nettles. Snow-clouds of elder-blossom banked in the sky, showering upon me the fumes and flakes of their sweet and giddy suffocation. 10 High overhead ran frenzied larks, screaming, as though the sky were tearing apart.

For the first time in my life I was out of the sight of humans. For the first time in my life I was alone in a world whose behaviour I could neither predict nor fathom: a world of birds that squealed, of plants that stank, of insects that sprang about without warning. I was lost and I did not expect to be found again. I put back my head and   15 howled, and the sun hit me smartly on the face, like a bully.

From this daylight nightmare I was awakened, as from many another, by the appearance of my sisters. They came scrambling and calling up the steep rough bank, and parting the long grass found me. Faces of rose, familiar, living; huge shining faces hung up like shields between me and the sky; faces with grins and white teeth 20 (some broken) to be conjured up like genii with a howl, brushing off terror with their broad scoldings and affection. They leaned over me – one, two, three – their mouths smeared with red currants and their hands dripping with juice.

'There, there, it's all right, don't you wail any more. Come down 'ome and we'll stuff you with currants.'   25

And Marjorie, the eldest, lifted me into her long brown hair, and ran me jogging down the path and through the steep rose-filled garden, and set me down on the cottage doorstep, which was our home, though I couldn't believe it.

That was the day we came to the village, in the summer of the last year of the First World War. To a cottage that stood in a half-acre of garden on a steep bank above a 30 lake; a cottage with three floors and a cellar and a treasure in the walls, with a pump and apple trees, syringa and strawberries, rooks in the chimneys, frogs in the cellar, mushrooms on the ceiling, and all for three and sixpence a week.

From *Cider with Rosie* by Laurie Lee

Read all the questions carefully before starting to answer.

- The number of marks for each question will give you a clue as to how much time you should spend on each one.
- Remember to refer to the text to support points you make.

1 **Focus on lines 1 to 16 only. Explain why the narrator put back his head and howled (lines 15-16).** **6 marks**

> **AO1** This question tests your skill in selecting and using detail to explain.

2 **Focus on lines 17 to 33 only. What do you learn about the relationship between the narrator and his sisters?** **8 marks**

> **AO1** This question tests your skill in using detail to infer meaning.

3 **Now consider the whole text. Explain how the writer has structured this account of his first day in the village.** **8 marks**

> **AO2** This question tests your skill in explaining how writers structure their writing.

4 **Focus on lines 1 to 16 only. How does the writer use language to create a picture of a frightening world?** **8 marks**

> **AO2** This question tests your skill in explaining and commenting on how language is used for effect and to influence readers.

5 **Think about the whole text again. The writer is recalling an incident from his childhood. How does he capture the perspective of a three-year-old child?** **8 marks**

> **AO3** This question tests your skill in explaining how a writer conveys perspective or viewpoint.

✓ **Complete this assignment on Cambridge Elevate.**

READING
Unit 6
Compare writers' ideas and perspectives

Make progress (AO3)
- develop comparison skills
- compare the ideas and language of two texts
- study the features of a written comparison before writing your own.

WHAT IS COMPARISON?

When you compare, you consider the similarities and differences between two things, people or events.

ACTIVITY 1

1 With another student, look closely at the two photographs and talk about what they show. List the similarities and differences between them.

Now look at the transcript of two students discussing these photographs.

Student 1: Well, there are trains in <u>both</u> photos.

Student 2: Yeah, and they're both trains in mountainous country – look at those <u>rocks</u>. They've both got those.

Student 1: I know, but the rocks in the first picture are loads <u>closer</u> – they look quite dangerous. Looks like the train's driving into those scary mountains in the background.

Student 2: Yeah, well it could be <u>dangerous</u> on the second railway as well. See how the train's just come out of the rocks? Could be it's a tunnel, and look how high that viaduct is.

| point of similarity |
| identifies similar feature |
| point of difference |
| begins to explore image more closely |

The students begin by stating what is obvious in the content of the photographs: both show trains in mountainous country. They then look more closely, finding details that are similar and different. Finally, they comment on details that require interpretation, such as how dangerous the journey on each train could be.

2 Did the students in the transcript find the same similarities and differences as you?

3 Look again at the photographs to see if you can find more similarities and differences. Aim to go beyond the obvious and make your own interpretations.

COMPARE TEXTS

You are now going to compare two texts. To do this you will focus on the similarities and differences in:

- purpose and audience
- the writers' ideas and perspectives
- how language reveals the writers' attitudes and influences readers.

ACTIVITY 2

Read Sources A and B. Source A appeared in the scientific magazine *Nature* in 1880, when London was badly affected by fog. Source B is a letter written to a modern national newspaper.

Source A

Those who know it well have had enough of it. Like other evils of great magnitude, its ill effects have not been very startling and sudden. It was hard to believe that so harmless looking and quiet a thing could do so much mischief. The unseen and little   5
noticed causes of death and disease, however, are the most fatal. Smoke in London has continued probably for many years to shorten the lives of thousands, but only lately has the sudden and palpable rise of the death-rate in an unusually dense and prolonged fog   10
attracted much attention to the depredations of this quiet and despised destroyer.

It is certain that private houses, and not factories, are chiefly responsible; for some of the very worst fogs have occurred on Sundays and Christmas   15
Day, 1879, was nearly dark. In winter more than a million chimneys breathe forth simultaneously smoke, soot, sulphurous acid, vapour of water, and carbonic acid gas, and the whole town fumes like a vast crater, at the bottom of which its unhappy   20
citizens must creep and live as best they can.

From 'London Fogs' by R. Russell

> 💬 **Vocabulary**
>
> palpable: plainly seen
> depredations: damage

Source B

Sir,

No one can deny that the recent days of extremely
unpleasant air pollution in London have not been
stressful for all of us, particularly those poor souls
suffering from respiratory diseases. However it is   5
all too easy for us to blame Saharan dust, climate
change or even spring sunshine.

While unusual weather conditions may have picked
up Saharan dust and blown it over us, sadly the
blame lies closer to home. The real culprit is our   10
own air pollution. The murky skies over London
and southern England are filled with tiny particles
of pollution from our own traffic, power stations,
farming, construction sites, central-heating boilers
and industry. We are all far too complacent about   15
the pollution we cause. Indeed, many would say
we are happily ignorant.

Until our government acts more responsibly and
develops a sensible policy to combat this evil,
illnesses and deaths caused by air pollution will   20
continue to increase.

Yours faithfully,

Keith Cooper

1 Copy the table, leaving plenty of space for
answers. Think about the questions in the first
column before writing your answers in the
second and third columns. Where you can, use
details from the texts to support what you say.

2 Work with another student. Use your
completed tables to help you list:

a similarities between the texts
b differences between the texts.

3 Look at how the fog and the air pollution are
described in the two texts:

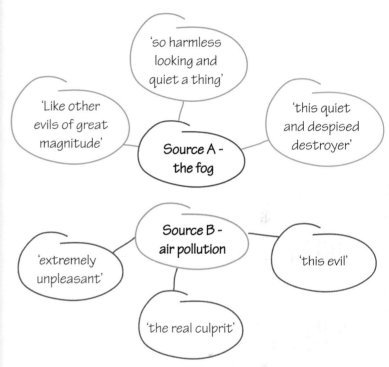

Write a paragraph commenting on:

a the similarities and differences in the
descriptions
b how the descriptions influence the reader.

	Source A	Source B
Where did the text first appear?		
Who is the intended audience?		
Why was the text written – what is its purpose?		
What is the text about?		
What/who does the writer blame?		

4 Now think about the following extracts from the texts:

Source A: It is certain that private houses, and not factories, are chiefly responsible; In winter more than a million chimneys breathe forth simultaneously smoke, soot, sulphurous acid, vapour of water, and carbonic acid gas, and the whole town fumes like a vast crater, at the bottom of which its unhappy citizens must creep and live as best they can.

Source B: We are all far too complacent about the pollution we cause. Indeed many would say we are happily ignorant.

What do they reveal about the writers' different attitudes to those responsible for the problem?

DEVELOP COMPARISONS: PURPOSE AND AUDIENCE, AND WRITERS' PERSPECTIVES

You are now going to build your skills in writing comparisons. To prepare for this you will gather evidence on a range of features, starting with purpose and audience, and writers' perspectives.

Read Source C, which is an extract from an autobiography written in 1959. The writer describes a family visit to his cousins.

Source C

'Step out, young men!' our Mother says crisply. She begins to teach us a hymn; the kind that cries for some lost land of paradise, and goes well with a tambourine. I've not heard it before (nor ever since), but it entirely enshrines our outing – the 5 remote valley in which we find ourselves, the smell of hot straw on the air, dog-roses and distances, dust and spring waters, and the long day's journey to the sheep-folds of our wild relations.

They are waiting for us with warm ginger- 10 beer, and a dinner of broad beans and bacon.

Aunty Fan says 'Annie, come in out of the sun. You must be ready to drop.' We go indoors and find our Uncle Charlie hacking at the bacon with a bill-hook. Young cousin Edie and her cautious brothers seem 15 to be pondering whether to punch our heads. Our Gramp comes in from his cottage next door, dressed in mould-green corduroy suiting. We sit down and eat, and the cousins kick us under the table, from excitement rather than spite. Then we play with 20 their ferrets, spit down their well, have a fight, and break down a wall. Later we are called for and given a beating, then we climb a tree by the earth-closet. Edie climbs the highest, till we bite her legs, then she hangs upside down and screams. It has been 25 a full, far-flung, and satisfactory day; dusk falls and we say good-bye.

From *Cider with Rosie* by Laurie Lee

 Vocabulary

ferret: weasel-like animal used to catch rabbits

earth-closet: outside toilet

Now read Source D, an extract from a novel written in 1847. The narrator, Jane Eyre, describes her cousin John Reed and recalls an event from her childhood.

Source D

John Reed was a schoolboy of fourteen years old; four years older than I, for I was but ten: large and stout for his age, with a dingy and unwholesome skin; thick lineaments in a spacious visage, heavy limbs and large extremities. He gorged himself 5 habitually at table, which made him bilious, and gave him a dim and bleared eye and flabby cheeks.

John had not much affection for his mother and sisters, and an antipathy to me. He bullied and punished me; not two or three times in the week, 10 nor once or twice in the day, but continually: every nerve I had feared him, and every morsel of flesh in my bones shrank when he came near.

He spent some three minutes in thrusting out his
tongue at me as far as he could without damaging   15
the roots: I knew he would soon strike, and while
dreading the blow, I mused on the disgusting and
ugly appearance of him who would presently deal
it. I wonder if he read that notion in my face; for,
all at once, without speaking, he struck suddenly   20
and strongly. I tottered, and on regaining my
equilibrium retired back a step or two from
his chair.

From *Jane Eyre* by Charlotte Brontë

Vocabulary

lineaments: features

visage: face

antipathy: a strong dislike

ACTIVITY 3

1 Work with another student. Look at the
statements and decide which are relevant to
Source C, which are relevant to Source D and
which are relevant to both. Record your answers
in a table with three columns, headed 'Source
C', 'Source D' and 'Both'.

a   The writer's purpose is to inform the reader.
b   The writer's purpose is to entertain the
reader.
c   The text is written for adult readers.
d   The writer describes a real event from
childhood.
e   The writer describes an imagined event
from childhood.
f   The writer chooses detail to help the event
come alive for the reader.
g   The text is written in the first person.
h   The text is non-fiction.
i   The text is fiction.
j   The writer tells the story directly to the
reader.
k   The writer uses a narrator to tell the story.
l   The narrator is a character in the story.

2 Use your table to help you list similarities and
differences between the two texts in:

a   purpose and audience
b   writers' perspectives.

 **Find out about the effect of first-person
narration on Cambridge Elevate.**

DEVELOP COMPARISONS: WRITERS' IDEAS

The ideas that a writer presents depend on
purpose, audience and perspective.

In Source C, the writer's purpose is to inform and
entertain her readers. To do this, he presents ideas
and information to make the event come alive for
his readers.

In Source D, the writer is describing an event
that took place in the childhood of an imaginary
character, Jane Eyre. The writer has decided
which ideas to include in the story to interest
and entertain her readers.

ACTIVITY 4

1 With another student, discuss each of the
following statements and decide whether they
are true or false. Give evidence from the texts
to support each of your decisions.

a   Both texts deal with cruelty and ill
treatment by cousins.
b   There is more evidence of ill treatment in
Source D.
c   In both texts, victims are disturbed by the
treatment they are given.
d   Both texts give you information about
other relatives in the family.
e   Both texts give details of the setting
of the story to help the reader imagine
events.
f   Both texts end in an unhappy way.
g   Only one text gives a positive image of
family life.

DEVELOP COMPARISONS: USE OF LANGUAGE

When you write about a writer's use of language you need to:

- identify significant features of language
- work out how and why the features are used in the text
- evaluate their effect on the reader.

Here is an example of one student's commentary on the language used to describe John Reed and his behaviour in Source D. The annotations show you how the comments have been constructed.

The writer uses the adjectives 'large' and 'stout' to describe John Reed. She focuses on his size again when she refers to him as having 'thick lineaments' with 'heavy limbs and large extremities'. This repeated focus on his size helps the reader imagine how he must have towered over her and makes her seem like a helpless victim. Also, the verb 'gorged' makes him seem greedy and the noun phrase 'dingy and unwholesome skin', adds to the reader's impression of him as an unattractive boy. This is reinforced by the reference to his 'dim and bleared eye' and 'flabby cheeks'. The verbs used by the writer in paragraph 2 emphasise his unpleasantness, for example: 'bullied and punished me' 'thrusting out his tongue 'and 'strike'. All together the narrator portrays him convincingly as a stereotypical bully – which is what he is.

identifies feature: adjectives
identifies feature: repetition of idea
considers effect on reader
identifies feature and effect
identifies feature: noun phrase
considers why feature is used
evaluates effect

ACTIVITY 5

When you compare writers' uses of language, you need to consider how each writer uses language for effect and point out similarities and differences between them.

1 Look at this description of the cousins from Source C:

Young cousin Edie and her cautious brothers seem to be pondering whether to punch our heads. We sit down and eat, and the cousins kick us from under the table, from excitement rather than spite. Then we play with their ferrets ....

a What does the adjective 'young' suggest about Edie?

b Why do you think the brothers are described as 'cautious'?

c What image of the brothers is created in the phrase 'pondering whether to punch our heads'?

d How does the following verb 'kick' reinforce the reader's impression of them?

e How does the phrase 'from excitement rather than spite' reflect their true feelings?

f The list of the cousins' activities starts with the personal pronoun 'we'. What does this indicate about their relationship with the visitors?

g What overall impression of the cousins does the writer create?

2 Identify similarities and differences between the ways in which the cousins are presented in the two sources.

3 Write a paragraph in answer to this question:

Compare how the writers present the cousins.

You could begin with this sentence:

The writer of Source D begins by describing John Reed's appearance in detail, whereas Laurie Lee focuses on the behaviour of the cousins.

WRITE A COMPARISON

When you write a comparison of two texts you need to focus on the similarities and differences between them. You need to connect a point made about one text with a point made about the other and develop your comments on them both. Your comparison should be based on the focus of the question, for example:

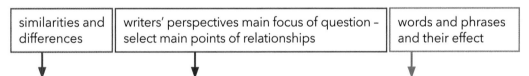

similarities and differences	writers' perspectives main focus of question – select main points of relationships	words and phrases and their effect

Compare the ideas about family relationships and the language used to present them in the two texts you have studied.

A plan for the answer to this question might look like this:

Source C

- **Purpose** – inform, entertain readers, reflect on real-life events
- **Perspective** – first person, adult looking back fondly on childhood
- **Ideas** – good relationship mother/children and between cousins, although a little boisterous
- **Language** – appeals to senses, positive beginning. Para 2 verbs/vocab to create positive impression.

Source D

- **Purpose** – interest/entertain readers, possibly comment on treatment of orphans, shock readers with description of cruelty
- **Perspective** – first person, voice of character in fiction text
- **Ideas** – cruel treatment, older cousin bullying vulnerable girl
- **Language** – adjectives, noun phrases, verbs, focus on bully and victim.

The following paragraphs are the opening of a student's response to the question:

Compare the ideas about family relationships and the language used to present them in the two texts you have studied.

Look at the annotations, which show the skills demonstrated by the student. The highlighted words show you where and how the student has made comparisons between the texts.

Both texts recount a childhood incident using a first-person perspective. This allows the reader to view the events through the eyes of the child narrators. Similarly in both texts, there is bullying or boisterous behaviour from older cousins.

shows understanding of perspective

The first text is taken from an autobiography whose purpose is to inform. The reader can assume that the events are real and that the account is an accurate picture of the relationship between the writer and his cousins. This text contains some reflection as the author looks back on his day, informing readers 'it was a full far-flung and satisfactory day'. The image of their mother teaching them a hymn and the phrase the 'sheep-fold of our wild relations' create an affectionate tone, so the reader can see that an adult perspective is included.

On the other hand, the second text is a work of fiction, the events are imaginary. The writer has chosen to portray family relationships by using the character of Jane Eyre as the narrator. A first-person narrative perspective is used to allow readers to experience events through her eyes. The reader only sees the perspective of a child character. There is no adult voice as in Source C.

focus on main theme of question

Although both texts deal with younger children's relationship with their older cousins, the ideas presented about relationships are very different. In Source C the cousins appear to be unfriendly towards their visitors – 'pondering whether to punch our heads' and 'kick us under the table', but there is no evidence of cruelty, unlike that portrayed in Source D, as we are told this was 'from excitement rather than spite'. Source D begins with a description of the unpleasant appearance of John Reed. This appears to be exaggerated, perhaps because the writer had set out to entertain her readers and wanted to create a strong character for them. Later the reader is told: 'John had not much affection for his mothers and sisters and a strong antipathy to me'. This suggests that relationships in this family are poor and also prepares the reader for the bullying to come. This is a contrast to Source C, where the mother and her sons appear to be enjoying a day out together. The behaviour of the two cousins is described very differently and affects the reader in different ways.

interprets

makes links with rest of text

ACTIVITY 6

1 Continue the answer by comparing how the behaviour of the relatives is described. Aim to show that you can:

a identify significant features of language
b work out how and why the features are used in the text
c evaluate their effect on the reader
d make relevant comparisons.

2 When you have finished, swap your work with that of another student. Annotate each other's work to show where you have met the success criteria listed.

 Use a template to help you assess your work on Cambridge Elevate.

Source E

This extract is taken from a letter that the famous naturalist and geologist Charles Darwin wrote to his sister Caroline in 1835.

 Assess your progress

Read Sources E and F and answer the questions that follow. They will help you assess how well you:

- compare writers' purposes and audiences
- compare writers' ideas and perspectives
- compare writers' use of language and the effects of this
- write comparisons.

 Complete this assignment on Cambridge Elevate.

Dear Caroline

We are now on our road from Concepcion. The papers will have told you about the great Earthquake of the 20th of February. I suppose it certainly is the worst ever experienced in Chili. It is no use attempting to describe the ruins – it is the most awful spectacle I ever beheld. The town of 5
Concepcion is now nothing more than piles and lines of bricks, tiles and timbers – it is absolutely true there is not one house left habitable; some little hovels built of sticks and reeds in the outskirts of the town have not been shaken down and these now are hired by the richest people. The 10
force of the shock must have been immense, the ground is traversed by rents, the solid rocks are shivered, solid buttresses 6–10 feet thick are broken into fragments like so much biscuit. How fortunate it happened at the time of day when many are out of their houses and all active: if the town 15
had been over thrown in the night, very few would have escaped to tell the tale. It is one of the three most interesting spectacles I have beheld since leaving England. It is indeed most wonderful to witness such desolation produced in three minutes of time. 20

Source F

In this extract from an article for Collier's Weekly magazine, the novelist and journalist Jack London gives an account of the aftermath of the 1906 earthquake in San Francisco.

San Francisco is gone. Nothing remains of it but memories and a fringe of dwelling-houses on its outskirts. Its industrial section is wiped out. Its business section is wiped out. Its social and residential section is wiped out. The factories and warehouses,   5 the great stores and newspaper buildings, the hotels and the palaces of the nabobs, are all gone.

Within an hour after the earthquake shock the smoke of San Francisco's burning was a lurid tower visible a hundred miles away. And for three days and nights   10 this lurid tower swayed in the sky, reddening the sun, darkening the day, and filling the land with smoke.

On Wednesday morning at a quarter past five came the earthquake. A minute later the flames were leaping upward. In a dozen different quarters south of Market   15 Street, in the working-class ghetto, and in the factories, fires started. There was no opposing the flames. There was no organization, no communication. All the cunning adjustments of a twentieth century city had been smashed by the earthquake. All the   20 shrewd contrivances and safeguards of man had been thrown out of gear by thirty seconds' twitching of the earth-crust.

1 Write a detailed answer to this question:

Compare how the two writers convey their ideas and views on the destructive power of earthquakes.

Remember to compare:

a   the writers' purposes and audiences

b   ideas about the damage caused by earthquakes in each text

c   the writers' thoughts and feelings about the damage

d   how the writers use language to convey their ideas and influence readers.

Make notes before you write your comparison.

2 When you have finished, ask your teacher or another student to give you feedback on your comparison.

FURTHER PROGRESS

On the letters page of a newspaper such as *The Times*, *The Sunday Times*, *The Telegraph* or *The Guardian*, look for two letters written on the same subject – with opposing views if possible. Compare the letters, pointing out similarities and differences in:

- their ideas and perspectives
- the language in which they express these
- the effects of the above on readers.

 Vocabulary

nabobs: people of notable wealth or status

contrivances: ingenious devices

Unit 7
Evaluate ideas and techniques

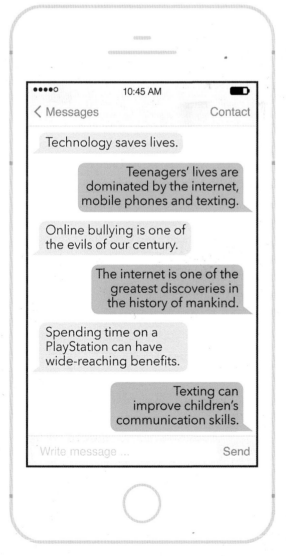

EXPRESS OPINIONS

An important part of responding to texts is expressing your own opinion, saying **what** you think and **why** you think it. You may find that it is easier to give your opinion when you know something about a subject, when you have ideas and information to support it. In this unit, you will improve your skills in selecting details from texts to support opinions.

ACTIVITY 1

1 Work in small groups. Talk about the **subjects** you feel most comfortable giving your opinion on. These might include sport, school, friendships or current affairs.

2 Now talk about **situations** in which you feel least or most comfortable giving your opinion – for example in response to a teacher's question, when talking with family.

3 Consider each of the following statements about the impact of technology on modern life. Discuss which ones you agree with and which ones you disagree with. Give your reasons.

> **10:45 AM**
> < Messages   Contact
>
> Technology saves lives.
>
> Teenagers' lives are dominated by the internet, mobile phones and texting.
>
> Online bullying is one of the evils of our century.
>
> The internet is one of the greatest discoveries in the history of mankind.
>
> Spending time on a PlayStation can have wide-reaching benefits.
>
> Texting can improve children's communication skills.
>
> Write message ...   Send

IDENTIFY VIEWPOINTS

The opinions you gave in Activity 1 were probably based on your own experience and knowledge. When you are asked to give your opinions on a text, you need to study it closely to work out the main ideas and viewpoints.

ACTIVITY 2

1 Read Source A. Make a note of the main points made by the writer.

Source A

Mobile phones are poison in our schools, but don't blame teachers – blame the parents!

Holding out my hand I stare into the surly face of the large, angry teenage girl. 'Give me the phone' I say. Truculently, 15-year-old Lisa glares at me. 'What phone?' she 5 asks belligerently as she stuffs it back into her bag.

At this point I have a choice. I can demand that she hand the phone over; she will refuse. Very few 10 teachers want to physically grapple a mobile phone from a teenager's hand. Girls as well as boys are likely to fly off the handle. And what member of staff would want to deal 15 with the outraged parental complaint that would inevitably follow?

Forget the old-fashioned notion that a parent might actually back a teacher and berate their brazen 20 child. As well as out-of-control pupils, the beleaguered teacher of today also has to tackle mums and dads to whom discipline is often a dirty word. 25

Mobile phones sum up many of the things that are wrong in schools in modern Britain. They have become the scourge of the classroom. That is why many teachers, like myself, will 30

applaud yesterday's announcement by Sir Michael Wilshaw, the Chief Inspector of Schools, that pupils face a ban on mobile phones in school as part of a new Ofsted crackdown 35 on discipline.

Schools will be penalised for failing to tackle persistent low-level disruption in lessons under a tough new inspection regime being 40 introduced next term. This could force heads to forbid mobile phone use by pupils – including texting, taking calls and surfing the web – to avoid being marked down 45 by inspectors.

Teachers will breathe a sigh of relief at the news, not least because mobile phones are often used to bully and intimidate both children 50 and staff.

Given that mobiles cause so much trouble, the question which needs to be asked is, why were they ever allowed in schools in the first place? 55 But colleagues would explain that it would take a brave teacher to run the gauntlet of angry parents who insist their children be contactable at all hours of the day and the night. 60

Sir Michael Wilshaw is absolutely right to target the problem of mobile phones in schools. But he is wrong to focus purely on what teachers and head teachers must do. Parents 65 are the key to the battle.

Adapted from an article in the *Mail Online* by Frances Childs

2 In each of the following cases, select the response that you think best reflects the writer's viewpoint. Give reasons for your choice.

Paragraph 1
a   The teacher does not like teenage girls who disobey her.
b   Mobile phones cause problems for teachers in the classroom.
c   Teachers are unwilling to enter into violent confrontation with pupils.

Paragraph 2
a   Teachers today are frightened of parents.
b   Teachers have problems with students and their parents.
c   Teachers today feel let down by lack of support from parents.

Paragraph 4
a   Mobile phones will definitely be banned in schools.
b   She supports the announcement that Ofsted inspectors will crack down on low-level discipline in the classroom.
c   She thinks there are many things wrong with schools in Britain.

Paragraphs 5 and 6
a   Mobile phones are the cause of much bullying in schools.
b   According to the inspectors, mobile phones cause low-level disruption in schools.
c   Mobile phones should be banned in schools.

Paragraph 8
a   Headteachers must get parents on their side.
b   She agrees with Sir Michael Wilshaw that mobile phones are a problem in schools.
c   It is not a headteacher's job alone to solve the problem.

3 From your careful reading of the article, answer the following questions:

a   From what perspective is this article written?
b   How might this perspective have affected the writer's opinions?

4 With another student, discuss which of the writer's opinions you agree with and which ones you disagree with. Refer to the text to support your reasons.

 Watch a student's views on mobile phones in the classroom on Cambridge Elevate.

INVESTIGATE HOW THE STRUCTURE OF A TEXT INFLUENCES THE READER

The way in which a writer organises ideas and structures a text can influence readers. For example the opening to an article is often where a writer introduces their main point and engages the reader's interest. When you write about structure you are expected to comment on the impact that it has on the reader.

ACTIVITY 3

Answer the following questions to work out how the writer of Source A has structured her ideas to influence readers.

1 Work with another student. Put the paragraph summaries below in the order in which they appear in the article.

a   uses anecdote to introduce main topic
b   focuses on teacher's view of parents
c   gives teachers' reaction to initiative
d   sums up her opinions
e   gives details of Ofsted initiative
f   introduces new information
g   headline reveals main points of article
h   develops anecdote and includes thoughts on parental behaviour.

63

2 In your pairs, talk about:

    a   why the writer might have chosen to begin the article with a personal anecdote

    b   how this might help to get readers on her side

    c   the point at which the article changes focus from pupils and their parents

    d   how the change of focus supports the writer's viewpoint

    e   whether you think the final paragraph would influence readers into accepting her opinion.

EXAMINE SENTENCE STRUCTURES

Another way in which writers influence readers is through their use of sentence structure. Writers often use a range of sentence structures to engage their readers. A short sentence might be used to sum up information or to emphasise a key point. Longer sentences are used to provide additional information or to provide contrasting ideas.

When you analyse and evaluate a writer's use of sentence structures, you are expected to comment on **how** they impact on the reader and **why** you think the writer may have used them.

ACTIVITY 4

Read the examples of students' responses to the writer's use of questions in Source A and the comments about them.

Student A The writer uses questions for effect.

Student A simply makes a statement.

Student B The writer uses questions to engage the reader in her argument.

Student B refers to the writer's purpose in her choice of sentence structure.

Student C When the writer uses questions it is as if she is talking directly to the reader, trying to persuade the reader to agree with her. The reader may feel they want to reply to her when she says of mobile phones, 'Why were they ever allowed in the first place?' I think her use of questions is effective because it engages the reader and makes them consider her points, even if they do not agree with them.

Student C considers the effect on the reader ('as if she is talking directly') and also the possible response ('the reader may feel …'). The writer's purpose is referred to in the phrase, 'trying to persuade the reader'. The student's comments are supported by a quotation from the text. This response analyses and evaluates the use of questions because it focuses closely on the writer's purpose and the reader's reaction. The student concludes by offering an opinion on the use of a particular sentence structure.

1 Using Student C's response as a model, analyse and evaluate the effects of the following sentence structures:

a the writer's use of direct speech in the first paragraph
b the use of the compound sentence using the conjunction 'but' in the headline
c the short sentence at the end of the article.

2 When you have finished, ask another student to check how well you have:

a referred to the writer's purpose
b considered the effect on the reader
c expressed your own opinion.

Then amend your work to improve your response.

EXPLORE THE WRITER'S USE OF LANGUAGE

Sometimes writers use language emotively – that is, to provoke a particular emotion or feeling in the reader. The writer of Source A refers to mobile phones as 'poison in our schools', for example. The word 'poison' could make readers, particularly parents, feel that their children's education is being seriously affected by the use of mobile phones in schools, and this might worry them. The word 'poison' also reveals the writer's disapproval of mobile phones in schools. The use of negative language in this way shows evidence of bias.

ACTIVITY 5

1 Copy and complete the table to help you work out how the writer of Source A has used language to influence her readers and what her use of language reveals about her attitude.

Example	Attitude of writer/desired effect on reader
'out-of-control pupils'	She does not seem to have a high opinion of schoolchildren. Perhaps she wants readers to think that all children are out of control.
'the beleaguered teacher of today has to tackle mums and dads for whom discipline is often a dirty word'	
'it would take a brave teacher to run the gauntlet of angry parents'	
'They [mobile phones] have become the scourge of the classroom'	
'Parents are the key to the battle'	

ASSESS THE EVIDENCE

Writers often support or justify their opinions by using evidence. As a reader, you must examine the evidence carefully and assess whether it is reliable and convincing.

Evidence can take a variety of forms. For example:

- **an account of a personal experience** that has led the reader to form a particular opinion. In Unit 4 Source D, for example, the writer's encounter with a cyclist led her to express negative opinions about all cyclists.
- **statistics** – facts and figures that are based on research.

Sometimes writers make **assertions** – statements of opinion expressed in such a way that readers believe they are facts (e.g. 'girls work harder than boys'). Unless such statements are supported by evidence, they only express the opinion of the writer. When assessing evidence, you need to be aware that a writer may be using assertion.

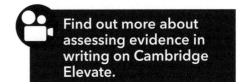

Find out more about assessing evidence in writing on Cambridge Elevate.

ACTIVITY 6

1 Work with another student. Discuss which form of evidence you think would be the most reliable – an account of personal experience or statistics. Give reasons for your choice.

2 Read the following extracts from Source A and answer the questions. Make sure you explain your answers in each case.

> Holding out my hand I stare into the surly face of a large angry teenage girl. 'Give me the phone' I say in as calm a voice as I can muster. Truculently, 15-year-old Lisa glares at me. 'What phone?' she asks belligerently as she stuffs it into her bag.

a Do you think this account of a personal experience is reliable or convincing evidence to support the writer's view that mobile phones should be banned in schools?

b Do you think this evidence could influence readers?

> Many teachers like myself will applaud yesterday's announcement by Sir Michael Wilshaw, the Chief Inspector of Schools, that pupils face a ban on mobile phones in school as part of a new Ofsted crackdown on discipline.

a Which part of the extract includes a fact?

b When the writer says 'Many teachers like myself will applaud yesterday's announcement', is she stating a fact or making an assertion?

c How does she use these words to influence the reader?

Schools will be penalised for failing to tackle persistent low-level disruption in lessons under a tough new inspection regime being introduced next term. This could force heads to forbid mobile phone use by pupils – including texting, taking calls and surfing the web, to avoid being marked down by inspectors.

a Write out the facts in this extract.
b Write out the sentence in which the writer does not use a fact.
c Is the writer accurate when she links disruption in lessons with the use of mobile phones?

EVALUATE A TEXT

In looking closely at this article you have:

- identified the writer's viewpoints and attitudes
- considered how she has structured her ideas to influence her readers
- identified how she has used sentence structure and language to influence her readers
- examined her use of evidence.

Now you are ready to make your evaluation of the text as a whole. When you evaluate a text, you express your opinions on it based on evidence. You comment on the writer's purpose and the possible reader response, as well as analysing features such as the writer's use of language. You should use quotations from the text to support your points, but avoid using long quotations - select individual words and phrases for comment. For example:

The use of the description 'surly face' in the opening line of the text indicates the writer's negative feelings towards teenagers. This negativity is also detected in the rest of the sentence 'the large angry teenage girl.' The use of the verb 'glares' together with the adverbs 'truculently' and 'belligerently' confirms the opinion that the writer is looking for uncomplimentary things to say about the teenager.

 Discover more about the differences between fact and opinion on Cambridge Elevate.

ACTIVITY 7

1 Use everything you have learnt about Source A to help you write a response to this question:

To what extent are the writer's views a fair assessment of the attitude and behaviour of pupils and parents with regard to mobile phones in schools?

In your response you should:

a explain the writer's key points and perspective
b examine the evidence used to support the writer's opinions
c examine the language used by the writer to influence the reader
d state your own opinions clearly
e use evidence from the text and quotations to support your opinions.

2 When you have finished, give your work to another student. Get them to annotate your response to show where you have:

a explained the writer's key points and perspective
b explained whether or not the evidence to support her opinion is convincing
c selected examples from the text to examine her use of language and structure
d made your own judgements in response to the writer's views.

EXAMINE A DIFFERENT PERSPECTIVE

Not all writers share the same perspective. The author of Source A writes from the point of view of a teacher and draws on her experiences with mobile phones in her school. Source B – also about young people and mobile phones – is written from a different viewpoint.

Source B

Why we shouldn't worry about teenagers using mobile phones

Don't be surprised if a new study reveals the benefits of smartphone use.

Like most 12-year-olds, my daughter got her first mobile phone a few months ago – just as she started secondary school. Year 7 is the time when life really opens up for young people: suddenly they're travelling solo to school and going out on their own, meeting up with friends to go shopping or to the park or to the cinema. It made sense to me as a parent, as it does to most parents with children of this age group, to buy her a phone.

Do I worry about her relationship with her phone, not just now but on into the adolescent years that are almost upon her? Yes, I do – and so do many other parents. So I welcome today's news that Imperial College is launching a study into the use of mobiles, focusing on 2,500 year 7 students who will be assessed now and again in two years' time. The study isn't looking at health risks around the use of mobile phones – of brain tumours and so on. [...]

Rather, it's looking at cognitive issues connected with the use of mobiles: such as how the use of phones might affect children's memory or attention span.

I look forward enormously to what the study reveals, but I wonder whether there might be a few shocks in store for people who think mobile phone technology spells doom for today's youngsters, eating up their brain cells with mindless chit-chat and pointless online games. It seems to me that the opposite might be the case: my older daughter, who is 15 and über-connected (even for a 15-year-old), seems to me to have honed her quick-wittedness hand in glove with her mobile phone. Multitasking? Fast thinking? Problem solving? Information gathering? My daughter uses her smartphone for all this and more; and I think you'd agree that all the above are useful, life-enhancing attributes for a teenager.

Another big advantage mobile phones offer young people is

independence, something that they crave and that parents want for them. My 12-year-old can do all sorts of tasks by herself that I, aged 12, would have relied on my parents to do: she can find out cinema times, source clothes she wants in shops, check what time the vet opens so we can get the rabbit's claws clipped. Her world has opened up thanks to her mobile phone, in an entirely positive way, and it will undoubtedly have knock-on effects for her development.

From an article in *The Guardian* by Joanna Moorhead

 Vocabulary

honed: sharpened

ACTIVITY 8

1 Working with another student, list:

  a the points the writer makes about young people and their use of mobile phones

  b the similarities and differences between this article and Source A.

2 What is the writer's perspective in Source B?

3 Look at the following quotations. Explain how each one shows the writer's bias in favour of mobile phones and their use by young people. Comment on her choice of vocabulary and the intended effect on the reader.

  a 'seems to me to have honed her quick-wittedness hand in glove with her mobile phone'

  b 'useful life-enhancing attributes for a teenager'

  c 'Another big advantage mobile phones offer young people is independence'

  d 'Her world has opened up thanks to her mobile phone'

4 How effective do you think the writer is in presenting her opinion? Select examples from the text to support your answer.

TALK ABOUT IT

Having looked at two different texts on mobile phones with different perspectives, you now have the opportunity to put forward your own views.

ACTIVITY 9

You are going to prepare a presentation called 'Mobile phones, the scourge of our century?' You can use evidence from one or both of the texts to support your views, as well as offering your own ideas and opinions.

1 Work with another student. To prepare:

  a discuss your views on the statement

  b plan the order in which you will present your ideas and viewpoints

  c select evidence to support your views

  d decide how you will use language to influence your listeners.

2 When you have prepared and practised your presentation, present it to another pair of students. Ask them to comment on how well you used your evidence and how convincingly you presented the issues and your opinions.

 Assess your progress

Read Source C, making notes on the issues and ideas in the article, then answer the questions that follow. They will help you assess how well you:

- identify viewpoints
- explain how writers structure their ideas to influence readers
- judge the impact of sentence structures and language
- examine how evidence is used to support points
- use quotations to support your views.

 Complete this assignment on Cambridge Elevate.

Source C

Families don't need (much) money to be happy

One of the most insistent lessons my parents tried to drum into me as a child was that money was not important for happiness.

The idea that the best things in life are free is not entirely without substance. Certainly the idea that you need bags of cash to have happy children is absurd. Children have what cannot be bought (although they can be taken away) – imagination, wonder and innocence. {5}

My wife and I often find ourselves pushing our two daughters to get them out the house to go on some often quite expensive jaunt, perhaps to an 'attraction' or a visit to the theatre, zoo or a gallery. {10}

But our children themselves seem to lack this aspiration entirely. In fact, given how hard they are worked at school, all they seem to want when they get home is to slouch around, play computer games or watch TV. Children, given love and stability, a TV, a computer and a couple of friends, need little that costs much. If you are under the age of 12, you can definitely be poor and happy. {15} {20}

But family happiness and money are linked in other ways. A close community and a loving family, whether it be melded or single-parented, can compensate for a lot of material discomfort. It is also the case that a lot of family pleasures are free, whether it's a sandwich in the park, a cycle ride or the many free attractions and events in larger cities. {25}

It's when you get to adulthood that money really starts to matter, though, and particularly when you are parents. Many reasonably well-off families seem to believe that if their children aren't going skiing every year, or getting extravagant Christmas and birthday gifts, they are letting them down. The hope for wealth brings worry, and worry makes the children who witness it unhappy. Greed can ruin a family. {30} {35}

So were my parents right? They were right about children not needing much, but rather more misguided about teenagers. They had, however, the right attitude to themselves – they never cared about luxury, and were content with what little they had. {40}

Adapted from an article in *The Guardian* by Tim Lott

1. Write answers to these questions:

   a What is the text about?

   b What is the writer's perspective?

   c How does the writer try to influence the reader to agree with his point of view?

2. Answer the following question:

   'Tim Lott presents a convincing argument to support the view that families don't need (much) money to be happy.'
   To what extent do you agree with this statement?

   This question tests your ability to:

   - identify the writer's viewpoints
   - examine how he has structured his ideas to influence his reader
   - examine how he uses sentence structures and language to convince the reader
   - assess the evidence he presents
   - give your own opinions supported by evidence from the text.

3. When you have finished, read through your work. Identify where you have shown the skills listed in the bullet points.

FURTHER PROGRESS

Find and read the text 'Stalingrad 1949' by John Steinbeck. Answer the following question:

'John Steinbeck creates a vivid description of a city in the aftermath of war.' To what extent do you agree with this statement?

In your response you should comment on:

- the writer's perspective and viewpoint
- the methods used to influence readers
- your own opinion.

Unit 8
Synthesise information and ideas

Make progress
- discuss the importance of music
- research and make notes on different source materials
- synthesise information and ideas for purpose.

FIND EVIDENCE FROM DIFFERENT SOURCES

When you research a subject, you generally need to consult a range of sources. Your research might involve talking to people, accessing information online or in a book, looking at historical records, watching filmed material and looking at photographs. While doing this, it is helpful to make notes on specific details that are relevant to the subject. You then need to combine your research findings to talk or write about your subject.

ACTIVITY 1

You are going to look at four sources to help your research and make notes on 'The importance of music'.

1 You are going to create Source A yourselves. In small groups, talk about:

a   the kinds of music you listen to
b   when, where and how you listen to music
c   the kinds of music you create
d   what music means to you
e   what you think you gain from listening to and/or creating music.

Keep a record of the main points made by students in your group as a spider diagram.

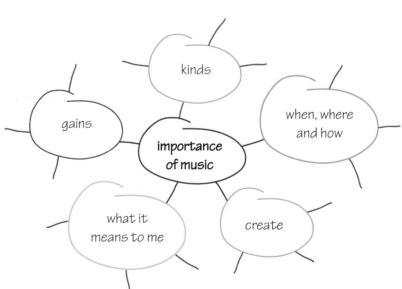

2 Now split into pairs:

a Read Sources B and C, then discuss which points are most relevant to your subject: 'The importance of music'.

b Make your own notes on the points you have selected. These notes are for your own use and there is no 'correct' way of writing them, but the following tips may help in your note-making.

Don't use full sentences.
Many words can also be easily abbreviated, e.g.:

technology → tech
important → imp
negative → -ve / positive → +ve.

You can also use signs:
< less than / > more than
∴ therefore
∵ because
= the same as
→ leads to/becomes.

Source B

The All-Time Top Six Psychological Reasons We Love Music

By Dr Jeremy Dean

What psychological roles does music play in our lives?

Modern technology means it's never been easier to hear exactly the music we want, whenever we want it. But whatever technology we use, the reasons we listen to music are universal.

So what are the universal psychological functions of 5 music? Lonsdale and North (2010) asked 300 young people about their main reasons for listening to music. Here are the answers, in order of importance, from sixth to the number one spot.

6 To learn about others and the world   10
Languishing down at number six was the way in which music teaches us about the world. Music tells us stories about other people and places and it gives us access to new experiences. Music can teach us how other people think and even suggest how we might live.   15

5 Personal identity
In at five is identity. The type of music we like expresses something about ourselves. Even the broadest genres like rock, classical and blues begin 20 to give us a picture of a person. We also seem to discover ourselves through music: it can teach us who we are and where we belong. Through music we can build up and 25 project an image of ourselves.

4 Interpersonal relationships
The fourth most important function of music is its social dimension. Music is a point of conversation. We listen to it while we're with other people and we talk to them 30 about it. It's a way of making a connection.

2= Negative mood management
Tying for the second spot is negative mood management. When we're in a bad mood, music can help us deal with it. When your mood is low, there is something 35 cathartic about listening to sad music. Somehow it helps to know that you're not alone. We use music to relieve tension, express our feelings and escape the realities of everyday life.

2= Diversion   40
Also coming in at number two is diversion. Music relieves the boredom of the commute, or of a lazy Sunday afternoon. It's something to do when we don't know what else to do.

1 Positive mood management   45
Right up at the top of the charts is positive mood management. This is rated people's most important reason for listening to music: making 50 our good moods even better. It entertains us, relaxes us and sets the right emotional tone.

Adapted from
www.spring.org.uk

Source C

Can music make your child cleverer?

Chain reaction: it's been suggested that musical practice can produce nothing short of a 'a full-scale brain upgrade' in children. 5

An extensive body of evidence suggests that if a child is actively involved in music-making for as little as 30 minutes a week, their intelligence, wellbeing and 10 academic performance can be enhanced.

According to peer-reviewed studies, benefits of early engagement with music include 15 improved performance in mathematics and languages; higher levels of IQ; better emotional fluency; greater self-esteem; a more powerful 20 memory; and physical health and fitness.

Musical education may actually change the brain for the better, according to studies 25 carried out at Harvard Medical School. It thickens the corpus callosum, which is a bundle of neural fibres that connects the right and left sides of the brain. 30 This means that communication flows better between the two sides, which has been linked to a higher IQ. Music also enhances parts of the brain that are 35 involved in processing speech, which creates a greater linguistic aptitude; the rhythmic qualities of music may also be linked to mathematical ability. 40

A 2009 study carried out at the University of Zürich found that children with musical training achieved higher grades in every curriculum subject apart from 45 sport, where performance was equal.

In addition to the more concrete benefits, music can boost children's academic performance 50 simply by improving their mood.

In 1996, Professor Sue Hallam, from the Institute of Education at the University of London, conducted a study 55 called The Blur Effect, which demonstrated that children performed better at problem-solving tests when they had been listening to 'Britpop' band Blur, 60 because it made them happier.

Musical systems have been created to enable these benefits to take root. Voces8, a choral group, have designed the Voces8 65 Method, in conjunction with the Institute of Education.

This system includes simple rhythmic and harmonic exercises that have been shown to sharpen 70 the mind. Certain rhythmic exercises have also been proven to help dyslexics.

"Music was a massive part of my life growing up, especially 75 as I am dyslexic," says Dingle Yandell, 32, the bass singer in Voces8. "I am able to visualise a whole score but I've always struggled with the mathematical 80 side. Music has helped me get a grip on that, and on many areas of my life."

Pupils at the Queen Anne school, near Reading, have been 85 practising the method regularly. Caitlin Croke, 16, has been impressed.

"I was always really bad at music," she says. "I'm not taking 90 GCSE music, but doing it in a fun way has really helped. I can actually read sheet music now, and I think my concentration is better in other subjects 95 afterwards."

"It completely changes the mood in a classroom," says John Padley, the school's director of 100 music.

"The children seem to wake up, get energised and focus, and it percolates throughout the school." 105

From an article in The Telegraph *by Jake Wallis Simons*

ACTIVITY 2

Look at the photographs in Source D.

1 Continue working in pairs. Discuss what the photographs suggest to you about the importance of music. Add relevant points to your notes.

BRING YOUR IDEAS AND EVIDENCE TOGETHER

So far you have researched and made notes on 'The importance of music'. You are now going to use your research to help you prepare a presentation or write an essay. Bringing information and ideas together in this way is sometimes called synthesis.

ACTIVITY 3

Source E is an outline of the stages you need to work through in order to plan effectively. Whether you are giving a spoken presentation or writing an essay, there are common elements in the planning.

1 Decide whether you are going to give a presentation or write an essay. Then follow the stages in the plan to synthesise your findings.

 Watch Late Homecoming talk about what music means to them on Cambridge Elevate.

 As you watch Late Homecoming's interview, note down the key points on Cambridge Elevate.

Source D

Source E

The importance of music

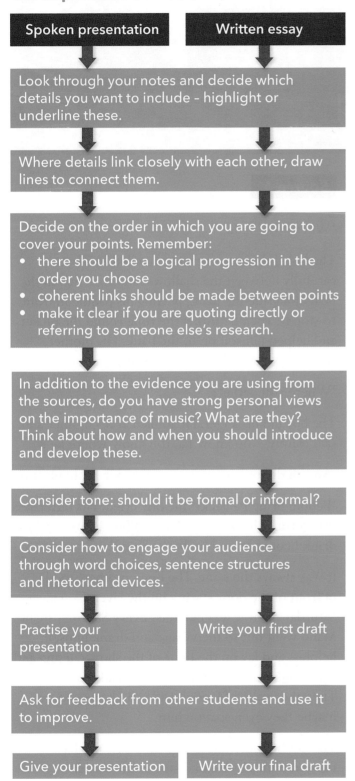

Spoken presentation	Written essay

Look through your notes and decide which details you want to include – highlight or underline these.

Where details link closely with each other, draw lines to connect them.

Decide on the order in which you are going to cover your points. Remember:
- there should be a logical progression in the order you choose
- coherent links should be made between points
- make it clear if you are quoting directly or referring to someone else's research.

In addition to the evidence you are using from the sources, do you have strong personal views on the importance of music? What are they? Think about how and when you should introduce and develop these.

Consider tone: should it be formal or informal?

Consider how to engage your audience through word choices, sentence structures and rhetorical devices.

| Practise your presentation | Write your first draft |

Ask for feedback from other students and use it to improve.

| Give your presentation | Write your final draft |

Assess your progress

In this unit you have brought together, or synthesised, relevant information and ideas from a range of sources to either give a presentation or write an essay. You are now going to research and write about another aspect of music: 'How the way we listen to music has changed over the last 25 years'.

Follow steps a to d:

a Find your own sources to help you research this subject. Remember that your aim is to establish:
- how people listened to music 25 years ago
- the changes that have occurred since that time
- how people listen to music now.

b Make notes on the relevant information and ideas in your sources. Your discussion at the start of this unit might provide useful detail and ideas.

c Use your notes to help you write two or three paragraphs on this subject.

d To add interest to your essay, you could write an additional paragraph predicting the changes that will occur over the next ten years.

Check your answer carefully before sharing it with two or three other students in a group. Decide between you:
- which student has done best
- the qualities of the answer that make it the best.

Complete this assignment on Cambridge Elevate.

FURTHER PROGRESS

Research and synthesis skills are important in many areas of study and in many occupations. Choose a subject that interests you. Find and list a range of sources that can help you to discover more about your chosen subject.

Unit 9
Explore, infer and interpret meaning

Make progress **AO1**
- infer meaning
- explore meaning
- investigate and analyse imagery
- interpret meaning.

THE THINKING READER

Reading is not a passive activity. Writers expect people to be thinking as they read. A writer will not tell you everything; they will leave it to you to work out certain things – to infer meaning, to explore relationships, to make predictions and to draw conclusions. This unit will help you develop these higher-level reading skills.

The following short story, 'Drunkard of the River', is produced in four stages – Sources A–D. Work in pairs, small groups or as a class to talk about the questions posed at the end of each stage.

Source A

'Where you' father?'

The boy did not answer. He paddled his boat carefully between the shallows, and then he ran the boat alongside the bank, putting his paddle in front to stop it. Then he threw the rope round the picket and helped himself on to the bank. His mother stood in front of the door still staring at him. 5

'Where you' father?'

The boy hid his anger. He looked at his mother and said calmly, 'You know Pa. You know where he is.' 10

'And ah did tell you not to come back without 'im?'

'I could bring Pa back?' the boy cried. His bitterness was getting the better of him. 'When Pa went to drink I could bring him back? How?'

It was always the same. The boy's mother stood 15 in front of the door staring up the river. Every Saturday night it was like this. Every Saturday night Mano went out to the village and drank himself helpless and lay on the floor of the shop, cursing and vomiting until the Chinaman was ready to close up. 20 Then they rolled Mano outside and heaven knows, maybe they even spat on him.

The boy's mother stared up the river, her face twisted with anger and distress. She couldn't go up the river now. It would be fire and brimstone 25 if she went. But Mano had to be brought home. She turned to see what the boy was doing. He had packed away the things from the shopping bag and he was now reclining on the couch.

'You have to go for you' father, you know,' she said. 30

'Who?'

'You!'

'Not me!'

'Who you tellin' not me,' she shouted. She was furious now. 'Dammit, you have to go for you' 35 father!'

Sona had risen from the couch on the alert. His mother hardly ever hit him now but he could never tell. It had been a long time since she had looked so angry and had stamped her feet. 40

He rose slowly and reluctantly and as he glanced at her he couldn't understand what was wrong with her. He couldn't see why she bothered about his father at all. For his father was stupid and worthless and made their life miserable. If he could have 45 had his way, Mano would have been out of the house a long time now. His bed would have been the dirty meat-table in front of Assing's shop. That was what he deserved. The rascal! The boy spat through the window. The very thought of his 50 father sickened him.

ACTIVITY 1

1 Use the detail in Source A to explain what you have worked out about:

a Sona's feelings for his father?
b the mother's feelings for Mano?
c the relationship between Sona and his mother?

Support your ideas by referring to the text. Be prepared to challenge each other's viewpoints if you think they are mistaken.

Now read on.

Source B

Yet with Sona's mother it was different. The man she had married and who had turned out badly was still the pillar of her life. Although he had piled up grief after grief, tear after tear, she felt lost and drifting 55 without him. To her he was as mighty as the very river that flowed outside. She remembered that in his young days there was nothing any living man could do that he could not.

In her eyes he was still young. He did not grow old. 60 It was she who had aged. He had only turned out badly. She hated him for the way he drank rum and squandered the little money he worked for. But she did not mind the money so much. It was seeing him drunk. She knew when he staggered back how she 65 would shake with rage and curse him, but even so, how inside she would shake with the joy of having him safe and home.

She wondered what was going on at the shop now. She wondered if he was already drunk and helpless 70 and making a fool of himself.

With Sona, the drunkard's son, this was what stung more than ever. The way Mano, his father, cursed everybody and made a fool of himself. Sometimes he had listened to his father and he had wanted 75 to kick him because he was so ashamed. Often in silence he had shaken his fist and said, 'One day, ah'll – ah'll…'

He had watched his mother put up with sweat and starvation. She was getting skinnier every day, and 80 she looked more like fifty-six than the thirty-six she was. Already her hair was greying. Sometimes he had looked at her and, thinking of his father, he had ground his teeth and had said, 'Beast!' several times to himself. He was in that frame of mind now. 85 Bitter and reluctant, he went to untie the boat.

'If I can't bring 'im, I'll leave 'im,' he said angrily.

'Get somebody to help you!'

He turned to her. 'Nobody wouldn't help me. He insult everybody. Last week Bolai kick 'im.' 90

'Bolai kick 'im? An' what you do?'

His mother was stung with rage and shock. Her eyes were large and red and watery.

The boy casually unwound the rope from the picket. 'What I do?' he said. 'That is he and Bolai business.' 95

His mother burst out crying.

'What ah must do?' the boy said. 'All the time ah say, "Pa, come home, come home, Pa!" You know what he tell me? He say, "Go to hell, yuh little bastard!"'

His mother turned to him. Beads of tears were still 100 streaming down the sides of her face.

'Sona, go for you' father. Go now. You stand up there and watch Bolai kick you' father and you ain't do nothing? He mind you, you know,' she sobbed. 'He is you' father, you ungrateful…' And choking with 105 anger and grief she burst out crying again.

When she raised her head, Sona was paddling towards midstream, scowling, avoiding the shallows of the river.

ACTIVITY 2

Now you are going to talk about your responses to the characters in the story so far. Your ideas may differ from those of others in your group, depending on the details you have picked up and how you assess people in general. There are no 'right' answers, but it is important that you:

- use the detail in the story to explain your views
- listen carefully to what others have to say
- challenge and ask questions.

1 Using evidence from the story so far, discuss what you think and feel about:

   a   Sona

   b   Sona's mother

   c   Sona's father, Mano.

Now read on.

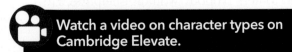
Watch a video on character types on Cambridge Elevate.

Source C

True enough there was trouble in Assing's shop. Mano's routine was well under way. He staggered 110 about the bar dribbling and cursing.

Again and again, the Chinaman spoke to him about his words. Not that he cared about Mano's behaviour. The rum Mano consumed made quite a difference to Assing's account. It safeguarded Mano's 115 freedom of speech in the shop.

But the customers were disgusted. All sorts of things had happened on Saturday nights through Mano's drunkenness. There was no such thing as buying in peace once Mano was there. 120

So now with trouble looming, the arrival of Sona was sweet relief. As Sona walked in, someone pointed out his father between the sugar bags.

'Pa!'

Mano looked up. 'What you come for?' he drawled. 125

'Ma say to come home,' Sona said. He told himself that he mustn't lose control in front of strangers.

'Well!'

'Ma send me for you.'

'You! You' mother send you for me! So you is father 130 now, eh – eh?' In his drunken rage the old man staggered towards his son.

Sona didn't walk back. He never did anything that would make him feel stupid in front of a crowd. But before he realised what was happening his 135 father lunged forward and struck him a blow across his face.

'So you is me father eh? You is me father, now!' He cried, and threw a kick at the boy.

Two or three people bore down on Mano and held 140 him off the boy. Sona put his hands to his belly where his father had just kicked him. Tears came to his eyes. The drunkenness was gripping Mano more and more. He could hardly stand by himself now.

He was struggling to set himself free. The men held 145
on to him. Sona kept out of the way.

'It's a damn shame!' somebody shouted.

'Shame?' Mano drawled. 'An' he is me father now,
'e modder send him for me. Let me go,' he cried,
struggling more than ever. 'I'll kill 'im. So help me 150
God, I'll kill 'im.'

They hadn't much to do to control Mano in this
state. His body was loose and weak now, his bones
seemed to be turning to water. The person who had
cried, 'It's a damn shame!' spoke again. 155

'Why you don't carry 'im home, boy? You can't see
he only making trouble?'

'You'll help me put 'im in the boat?' Sona asked.
He looked calm now. He seemed only concerned
with getting his father out of the shop, and out of 160
all this confusion. Nobody could tell what went on
below the calmness of his face. Nobody could guess
that hate was blazing in his mind.

Four men and Sona lifted Mano and carted him into
the boat. Sona pushed off. After a while he looked 165
back at the bridge. Everything behind him was
swallowed by the darkness. 'Pa,' the boy said. His
father groaned. 'Pa, yuh going home,' Sona said.

The wilderness of mangroves and river spread out
before the boat. They were alone. Sona was alone 170
with Mano, and the river and the mangroves and the
night and the swarms of alligators below. He looked
at his father again. 'Pa, so you kick me up then, eh?'
he said.

ACTIVITY 3

It is not enough simply to read a text. You need
to be thinking and asking questions in order to
explore its meaning. Your questions should act like
an interrogation – they should take you further and
deeper into the text.

1 Discuss the following sequences of questions
to help you discover more about the
characters, their actions and their motivations:

a How is Mano regarded by the Chinaman?
How is Mano regarded by the other
customers?
What are the reasons for the differences
between these?

b This is the first time you have encountered
Mano. How does he behave?
How does he speak?
How does he treat his son?
Why is he like this?
Does his drunkenness excuse his
behaviour?

c How does Sona respond to his father?
What do you learn from Sona's refusal
to 'walk back' (line 134)?
'He looked calm now' (line 160) – is
he calm?
What is he feeling when he pushes the
boat off into the river?
What do you think will happen next?

Now read on.

The boy did not answer. He paddled his
boat carefully between the shallows, and
then he ran the boat alongside the bank,
putting his paddle in front to stop it.

Source D

Far into the night Sona's mother waited. She slept 175
a little on one side, then she turned on the other
side, and at every sound she woke up, straining her
ears. There was no sound of the paddle on the water.
Surely the shops must have closed by now, she
thought. Everything must have closed by this time. 180
She lay anxious and listened until her eyes shut again
in an uneasy sleep.

She was awakened by the creaking of the bedroom
floor. Sona jumped back when she spoke.

'Who that – Mano?' 185

'Is me, Ma,' Sona said.

His bones, too, seemed to be turning liquid. Not
from drunkenness, but from fear. The lion in him
had changed into a lamb. As he spoke his voice
trembled. 190

His mother didn't notice. 'All you now come?' she
said. 'Where Mano?'

The boy didn't answer. In the darkness he took
down his things from the nail-pegs.

'Where Mano?' his mother cried out. 195

'He out there sleeping. He drunk.'

'The monster,' his mother said, getting up and
feeling for the matches.

Sona quickly slipped outside. Fear dazed him now
and he felt dizzy. He looked at the river and he 200
looked back at the house and there was only one
word that kept hitting against his mind: Police!
Police! He knew what would happen. He felt
desperate.

'Mano!' he heard his mother call to the emptiness 205
of the house, 'Mano!'

Panic-stricken, Sona fled into the mangroves and
into the night.

'Drunkard of the River' by Michael Antony,
in *Cricket in the Road and Other Stories*

ACTIVITY 4

1 The writer does not tell us what has happened to Mano, but he has given us clues throughout the story, leading up to the ending and in the ending itself.

   a   What do you think has happened to Mano?
   b   What clues in the story have led you to this conclusion?

2 Now work on your own. In an exam you will be expected to show that you can work out things for yourself – that you can infer meaning. Spend up to 15 minutes writing a detailed answer to the following question:

What have you learnt about Sona's mother from this story?

3 Look again at your completed answer.

   a   Underline any points you have made where you have worked out, or inferred, meaning.
   b   Highlight the evidence from the story that you have used to support your inferences.

4 Compare your answer with that of other students in your group. How well do you think you have done? Give yourself a mark between 1 and 5, where 5 is excellent.

MOTIF AND MOOD

A **motif** is a recurring element in a story that has symbolic significance. In 'Drunkard of the River', the motif is the river itself, running against the background of the story. The writer uses the river as a structural device to link the various parts of the story, and also as a linguistic device to create mood and atmosphere.

ACTIVITY 5

Look back over the story, paying attention to all the references to the river.

1 What mood or atmosphere is created in each of these river references? Choose from the word bank or write down your own ideas.

   a   'He paddled his boat carefully between the shallows, and then he ran the boat alongside the bank, putting his paddle in front to stop it. Then he threw the rope round the picket and helped himself on to the bank.'

   b   'The boy's mother stared up the river, her face twisted with anger and distress. She couldn't go up the river now.'

   c   'When she raised her head, Sona was paddling towards midstream, scowling, avoiding the shallows of the river.'

   d   'The wilderness of mangroves and river spread out before the boat. They were alone. Sona was alone with Mano, and the river and the mangroves and the night and the swarms of alligators below.'

   e   'There was no sound of the paddle on the water.'

threatening	calm	sad	frustrated
controlled	fearful	ominous	angry

2 What does the writer suggest by the use of the image of the river in these sentences?

Although he had piled up grief after grief, tear after tear, she felt lost and drifting without him. To her he was as mighty as the very river that flowed outside.

3 Write a paragraph explaining the use of the river motif in 'Drunkard of the River'.

SENTENCE STRUCTURES

Notice how the writer mixes his sentence structures for maximum effect in this story. In the following example, the annotations show the types of sentences used. Notice the repeated use of short sentences at the end of the paragraph, which help to emphasise Sona's feelings of disgust for his father.

He rose slowly and reluctantly and as he glanced at her he couldn't understand what was wrong with her. He couldn't see why she bothered about his father at all. For his father was stupid and worthless and made their life miserable. If he could have had his way, Mano would have been out of the house a long time now. His bed would have been the dirty meat-table in front of Assing's shop. That was what he deserved. The rascal! The boy spat through the window. The very thought of his father sickened him.

complex

compound

conditional

simple

exclamation

ACTIVITY 6

1 Copy the following extract and annotate it to show the sentence types.

Sona didn't walk back. He never did anything that would make him feel stupid in front of a crowd. But before he realised what was happening, his father lunged forward and struck him a blow across his face.

'So you is me father eh? You is me father, now!' He cried, and threw a kick at the boy.

2 What is the effect of Mano's combined question and exclamation?

Assess your progress

Many stories are built around the important relationships in peoples' lives, whether those relationships are with family, friends or significant strangers. It is the family – Sona, his mother and his father – and the relationships between these three characters that lie at the heart of this story. How much have you worked out about them?

1 In small groups, use your skills in inference, exploration and interpretation to help you with the following:

    a Using evidence from the story and your own responses to the characters, discuss the following key relationships in the story:
- Sona and his mother
- Mano and Sona
- Mano and his wife.

    b Read the following statements and decide if you agree or disagree with each one. Then share your responses and your reasons with other members of your group.
- The mother got what she deserved.
- Mano got what he deserved.
- Sona, if caught, will get what he deserves.

2 Work on your own. Use the points raised during your discussion, and any other ideas you have, to write an answer to this question:

Which character (the mother, Sona or Mano) do you feel most sympathy for? Explain your answer.

Complete this assignment on Cambridge Elevate.

Listen to an audio clip of *The Cat in the Rain* on Cambridge Elevate.

FURTHER PROGRESS

Read more of Michael Anthony's short stories in *Cricket in the Road*, or try his novel *Green Days by the River*.

READING
Unit 10
Develop responses to language and structure

EXPLORE TEXTS

When you read a text, your reaction to it may not be the same as that of other students. In part, this is because words can have different **connotations** for different people. You might associate the word 'steel' with more than just the metal itself: you might think of strength ('nerves of steel') or a lack of feeling ('steely eyes'), for example. It is important to remember that words can have different connotations when exploring meanings in a text.

ACTIVITY 1

Look at these opening lines from a poem:

Tyger Tyger, burning bright,
In the forests of the night

From 'The Tyger' by William Blake

 Listen to a reading of the full poem 'The Tyger' on Cambridge Elevate.

A straightforward explanation of these lines might point out that they describe a tiger whose flame-coloured coat stands out in a dark forest. However, you might also consider other possible meanings.

1 Work with another student. Discuss the following features of the lines from 'The Tyger':

  a the repetition of 'Tyger' – why did the writer choose to repeat this word?

  b the use of the word 'burning' – is it simply to describe the tiger's coat or does it have another meaning?

  c the use of 'bright'– this is usually a positive word, but does it hint at danger here?

  d the rhyme of 'bright' and 'night' – what are some possible connotations of these opposites suggesting light and dark?

2 Some readers may associate a tiger with danger and violence; to others a tiger might suggest beauty or power. Some people consider forests to be frightening, but for others they are places of safety.

  a In your pairs, write the words 'tiger', 'night' and 'burning' at the top of a piece of paper. Beneath each word write three objects, feelings or ideas that you associate with that word.

  b Share the associations you have made with another pair. Discuss the similarities and differences between them.

 Watch a video about exploring poetry on Cambridge Elevate.

3 Read these extracts from students' commentaries on the two lines from the poem. Discuss how well you think each student has explored the lines.

Student A In these two lines the poet is describing a tiger whose bright coat stands out in the forest. It is very dark in the forest, like 'night'.

Student B Using **alliteration**, the poet describes the tiger's coat as 'burning bright'. I think he does this to show how vividly coloured a tiger's coat is, but he is also suggesting how dangerous tigers can be, because flames can hurt you. The tiger stands out in the forest because it is so dark, like night.

Student C The repetition of 'Tyger' at the start of the poem makes the animal seem important. The description that follows – 'burning bright' – may suggest the bright colours of a tiger's coat, but the two words seem more significant than that. 'Burning' suggests fire and the ability to destroy, something which makes it seem as though the poet is focusing on the dangerous, fierce image of the tiger. However, 'bright' is a word with connotations of beauty and clarity. The poet rhymes the word with 'night', which has more negative connotations. It seems as though the tiger represents something clear in the darkness.

DEVELOP EXPLANATION INTO ANALYSIS

When you explain, you show understanding of the meaning of a text and the writer's use of textual detail. When you analyse, you look at the detail of the text more closely and in a more methodical way. Analysis requires you to break down the text into parts to find meaning. To analyse effectively, you should also use your exploration and interpretation skills.

ACTIVITY 2

Read Source A, an extract from a novel describing a hurricane. Do not worry about the highlighted words for the moment.

Here is one student's explanation of the passage:

The writer describes the impact of a terrible hurricane on her island. The passage is full of details of the destruction such as 'tin roofs were on the ground'. This gives the reader a picture of the force of the hurricane, that roofs had been blown off buildings.

Source A

No living person should ever see the underside of a tree. The roots – that gnarled, tangled mess of prongs that plummet unruly into the earth in search of sustenance. As I fled from the schoolhouse after the hurricane had passed, the world was   5
upside down. The fields to my left, to my right, undulated with this black and wretched chaos.

Trees ripped from land that had held them fast for years. Branches that should have been seeking light snuffled now in the dirt – their fruit splattered   10
about like gunshot. Tin roofs were on the ground while the squeaking wheels of carts rotated high in the air, disordered and topsy-turvy. I stumbled through this estranged landscape alarmed as a blind man who can now see.   15

From *Small Island* by Andrea Levy

This explanation shows understanding of the meaning and the use of some textual detail. The quotation 'tin roofs were on the ground' is appropriately selected. In order to improve this answer and demonstrate skills in analysis, this student needs to:

- examine and explore the impact of particular words and phrases
- interpret meaning based on detail
- look for patterns and make connections.

1 In Source A, a student has highlighted some key words that might be grouped together for analysis.

   a What do the words coloured yellow have in common?
   b What do the words coloured green suggest about the hurricane?
   c What do the words coloured blue suggest about the effect of the hurricane on the narrator?

2 Using some of the highlighted words, write a paragraph exploring the effects of words used to describe the force of the hurricane.

3 Now write a paragraph commenting on the effects of the words the narrator uses to describe how she feels about her experiences. Choose two or three words or phrases to quote and explore.

EXPLORE HOW WRITERS CREATE A TONE

A writer's choices of words can indicate their feelings about a subject. Words are chosen and organised to have a particular effect on the reader.

ACTIVITY 3

Look at this headline from a news website:

Horror as couple are attacked by swarm of around 30,000 bees who kill their two horses

From an article in *The Independent* by Rob Williams

1 With another student, discuss your initial ideas about the intended effect of the headline. Is its purpose to:

   a provide factual information about a news story?
   b grab readers' attention by shocking them?
   c amuse readers?

2 The numbers used in the headline – 'couple', 'around 30,000' and 'two' – are facts. What effect might the use of these numbers have on readers?

3 The headline could have been written completely in the **active voice** ('Bees attack couple and kill …'). Instead, the writer chooses the **passive voice** at the start of the sentence – 'couple are attacked'. What is the effect of this choice?

4 What is the purpose of the first word of the headline ('Horror')?

5 What is the effect of using the personal pronoun 'who' in the headline?

Here is what one student wrote in response to the headline:

The headline is intended to attract readers to the news story and get them to read on. The opening, emotive word 'Horror' immediately grabs the reader's attention, and words like 'attacked' and 'killed' suggest a dramatic, horrific story. The use of 'couple' and 'two' compared to the 30,000 bees make the attack seem even more terrifying as the couple and their horses were so outnumbered. The use of the passive voice emphasises the idea that the couple were victims, on the receiving end of a terrifying attack.

The student has looked at details and considered their effects; the writer's intentions have been interpreted, resulting in more than just an explanation of the tone of the passage.

Read Source B, which is a preview of a television programme about bees.

Source B

To bee or not to bee? That is not the question for Martha Kearney. When she's not working for the Bee Bee C, she certainly gets a buzz from the sweet little hairy honeys which occupy her life in Suffolk. Now her hobby is becoming part of her professional 5
life. In *The Wonder of Bees*, a lovely series of four programmes, she investigates the secret lives of these tubby, fluffy insects with the hairclipper buzz, interviews some expert beekeepers and has a first go at making her own wildflower honey. 10

---

1 Work with another student. Discuss the purpose and tone (the writer's attitude towards their subject) of Source B. Consider:

a the use of repetition
b the puns and their effects
c the use of descriptive vocabulary.

2 On your own, write a paragraph commenting on the ways in which the writer attempts to influence the reader to watch the television programme. You should find examples of words and phrases that are characteristic of the text and explore their effects.

3 When you have finished, swap your writing with another student and give them feedback on how well they have explored the tone of the passage.

RESPOND TO EMOTIVE LANGUAGE

Emotive language is language chosen to create an emotional response in the reader. When commenting on emotive language, you need to be precise about its purpose and effects. In Source B, for example, you could describe the word 'lovely' as emotive language, but more precisely it conveys a feeling of warmth and admiration.

Source C

Promises the government made were broken from the start. No more than 10,000 people were relocated, and they were quickly left to fend for themselves. The road was never even finished: it was never paved and it simply stops in the middle of the jungle, at a small town called Labrea beside the Purus River. The highway abides, though, as a red scar through the rainforest and a metaphor for everything that has gone wrong in the Amazon in the past four decades.

From an article in *The Independent* by Robert Penn

ACTIVITY 5

Read Source C, a description of an unfinished road-building project in Brazil.

1 The use of the metaphor 'red scar' to describe the unfinished road is an example of emotive language. Read the responses from students A, B and C and match them to commentaries 1, 2 and 3.

Student A The writer uses emotive language – 'red scar' – to show his strength of feeling about the road.

Student B The writer uses emotive language – 'red scar' – to describe the road. The word 'scar' suggests the pain he feels about the way the Amazon forest has been cut into.

Student C The phrase 'red scar' suggests the hurt the writer feels about the road and the way it has been cut into the Amazon forest. The adjective 'red' may simply describe the colour of the road, but it also makes it seem as though the wound is still fresh, still bleeding. 'Red scar' also suggests that it is not only the writer feeling the pain; it is as though the Amazon forest is a living creature that has been wounded and might also feel pain.

1 This explores the effects of 'red scar'. There is some analysis, as different parts and their relationship are explored: both 'red' and 'scar' are explained and there is some speculation – some suggestion about possible meaning and effect.

2 This identifies emotive language and uses an example from the text. There is awareness that there is strong emotion, but it is not explained.

3 This identifies emotive language, uses an example from the text and provides an explanation of the effect of the quoted phrase – that it can be connected to 'pain'.

 Read the article with all the emotive language removed on Cambridge Elevate.

Source D

One of the most awe-inspiring places I've ever visited is
Ellis Island in New York, in particular the galleried hall
where desperate immigrants exhausted and traumatised
by a harrowing sea voyage were processed once they'd
disembarked. It's immaculate now, the tiled floor   5
polished, the sun streaming through the high windows
through which you can see the Statue of Liberty, but it's
not hard to imagine it packed with desperate humanity
and their battered cardboard suitcases, men in fraying
suits and flat caps, women in stained shawls, grubby-   10
cheeked children with bright eyes. Even in its modern,
sanitised condition you can feel the apprehension in the
air, the hope, the desperation, the fear, all bottled up in
an attempt to be polite and deferential to the brusque
man with the roster book sitting at the tall desk at the   15
end, this person you'd never seen before and would never
see again, who in the space of a few seconds in a noisy,
packed, fetid room had the power to decide your future
and that of your descendants.

From *And Did Those Feet* by Charlie Connelly

EXPLAIN THE EFFECTS OF EMOTIVE LANGUAGE

Writers use emotive language to get an emotional response from their reader. However, they may use other techniques to develop that response.

ACTIVITY 6

Read Source D, which discusses the history of Ellis Island. Then answer the following questions.

1 The experience of immigrants arriving at Ellis Island in New York is described in three long, complex sentences. Explore the ways in which the writer chooses vocabulary to influence his readers' responses. Think about:

  a the use of adjectives and noun phrases
  b the use of contrast
  c the way that details are built up throughout the extract.

2 The writer tells the reader twice about the modern hall that now exists on Ellis Island. Why do you think he does this?

3 The writer is describing his own experience. Why do you think he uses 'you' in this passage? What is the effect?

EXPLORE STRUCTURE

Writers choose to develop their ideas in a particular sequence. In longer texts you need to analyse not just the writer's choice of words and their sentence structure, but also the structure of paragraphs.

ACTIVITY 7

Read the following article from an online newspaper. Note how the writer begins by setting the scene:

The scene on the Seoul subway these days resembles any other modern underground network: throngs of high school students and <u>commuter droids, hunched over, aloof to</u> their surroundings, unable to stop playing with <u>their handheld thingies.</u>

1 The writer could have set the scene factually by explaining that there were a lot of young people with smartphones on an underground train. Instead, he uses descriptive language. How do the underlined phrases reveal the writer's attitude towards the young people and their phones?

Now read the next three paragraphs of the article:

Only here in South Korea – home of Samsung and some of the world's zippiest internet access (both mobile and hardwired) – people take their digital habits to an extreme.

So much so that the government is worried.

Two recent studies plot a rise in the number of South Korean teens at risk for smartphone addiction – a condition that some psychologists formally call nomophobia (for "no mobile phone phobia"): the fear of being without one's phone.

From an article in *Global Post* by Geoffrey Cain

2 How does 'Only here' connect to the previous paragraph? Which statement in the first paragraph is being developed?

3 This article is about 'digital habits' in South Korea. Why did the writer choose to include the detail between the pair of dashes? What is the intended effect on the reader?

4 What are the possible connotations of the word 'habits' in the second paragraph?

5 All the sentences in the first, second and fourth paragraphs are long and complex. The third paragraph is a single short sentence. What effect does this contrast have on the reader?

6 In the second and fourth paragraphs the writer uses the words 'digital habits', 'addiction', 'psychologists' and 'nomophobia'. What connects these four expressions and links to the main idea in the article?

 Watch a video about structure in non-fiction texts on Cambridge Elevate.

UNDERSTAND THE SEQUENCE OF PARAGRAPHS IN TEXTS

In longer texts, both sentence and paragraph order are carefully chosen to influence the reader.

ACTIVITY 8

Read Source E, in which the writer describes a visit to Chernobyl – part of Ukraine that was devastated by a nuclear accident in 1986. The area is still unpopulated because of the dangers of radiation.

Note how the first paragraph sets the scene and ends with 'listen'. This leads into the description of bird sounds in the second paragraph from 'either side of the broad river'. The third paragraph shifts the perspective to 'Below us' and widens the description from the visual to what is felt and smelled.

Source E

The coach stops haphazardly on an empty two-lane bridge, high over the Pripyat River. It's going to be a spectacular sunset. Clumps of yellow 5 stonecrop and wild carnations are pushing up through cracks in the tarmac. In the gathering dusk we lean on rusting railings, looking out over the 10 softly flowing water, and listen.

From the willow brush on either side of the broad river float the soothing sounds of reed bunting, yellowhammer, 15 blackcap, thrush, nightingale, hoopoe, woodlark, tree pippet and an intermittent cuckoo. Paul Goriup, a birding expert, concentrates as he 20 sifts through all the notes. "Thought so!" The fishing-reel whirr of a Savi's warbler, "Hear that squeaking sound? There's a woodcock out there 25 somewhere too."

Below us, fish leap at mosquitoes. The air rising from the water is damp and cool; the familiar smell of pond 30 life doing its thing. Another movement, less distinct, draws us to the gentle wake of a beaver, paddling back to its lodge. I feel tears welling in 35 my eyes. This is Chernobyl in northern Ukraine. The fact that there is wildlife here at all – let alone in such profusion – is deeply moving, a miracle that 40 once seemed beyond all hope of realisation.

From an article in the *Sunday Times* by Isabella Tree

1 Although this piece of writing is about Chernobyl, the writer delays that information until the third paragraph. What are the effects of delaying that detail?

2 In the first paragraph, the phrases 'spectacular sunset', 'yellow stonecrop and wild carnations' and 'softly flowing water' draw attention to the beauty of the scene. What contrasting vocabulary does the writer use to suggest that the scene is not wholly beautiful?

3 What is the writer's purpose in listing birds in one long sentence in the second paragraph? How does she emphasise the beauty of birdsong?

4 The writer describes the pond in informal language ('doing its thing'). Why do you think the writer chose such a colloquial phrase at this point in the text?

5 In the third paragraph the writer says: 'I feel tears welling in my eyes. This is Chernobyl in northern Ukraine.' These sentences could have been written the other way round. Why do you think the writer chose to put them in this order?

Listen to an experience of Chernobyl on Cambridge Elevate.

Complete this assignment on Cambridge Elevate.

Assess your progress

Read Source F, an extract from a novel about a future world of test-tube babies. The following questions will help you assess how well you:

- explore writers' use of language
- analyse and interpret detail
- explore paragraph and whole text structure
- develop detailed and perceptive comments.

1 Write answers to these questions about the writer's use of language:

   a What impression of the Director is given from the way the character speaks?

   b Look at the section of the text from, 'Now bring in' to 'unloaded'. Comment on the effects of the language used by the writer to describe the way the babies are treated.

   c How is language used in the paragraph beginning 'Turned' to create an impression of the babies' experience of this moment?

   d How does the writer use language to add impact to the moment the lever is put down?

2 Write answers to these questions exploring the structure of the passage:

   a Comment on the structure of the following three sentences:

     • 'In silence the nurses obeyed his command.'

     • 'From the ranks of the crawling babies came little squeals of excitement, gurgles and twitterings of pleasure.'

     • 'Shriller and even shriller, a siren shrieked.'

   b Comment on the effect of the way the sentences are sequenced in the paragraph beginning 'Turned'.

   c The writer breaks up the description of the babies' excitement at the books and roses with a short paragraph in which the Director rubs his hands and says 'Excellent!' How might the reader interpret the Director's actions?

   d The extract ends with four short paragraphs. Comment on the effects of the sequence and the writer's decision to separate the text into short paragraphs.

3 Now work with another student. Read each other's answers and discuss how well each of you has answered the questions. Make a note of questions you have answered well and where you need to improve your skills further.

Source F

The nurses stiffened to attention as the DHC came in.

'Set out the books,' he said curtly.

In silence the nurses obeyed his command. Between the rose bowls the books were duly set out – a row of nursery quartos opened invitingly each at some gaily-coloured image of a beast or fish or bird. 5

'Now bring in the children.'

They hurried out of the room and returned in a minute or two, each pushing a kind of tall dumb-waiter laden, on all its four wire-netted shelves, with eight-month-old babies, all exactly alike (a Bokanovsky group, it was evident) and all (since their caste was Delta) dressed in khaki. 10

'Put them down on the floor.'

The infants were unloaded.

'Now turn them so that they can see the flowers and books.'

Turned, the babies at once fell silent, then began to crawl towards those clusters of sleek colours, those shapes so gay and brilliant on the white 15 pages. As they approached, the sun came out of a momentary eclipse behind a cloud. The roses flamed up as though with a sudden passion from within; a new and profound significance seemed to suffuse the shining pages of the books. From the ranks of the crawling babies came little squeals of excitement, gurgles and twitterings of pleasure. 20

The Director rubbed his hands. 'Excellent!' he said. 'It might almost have been done on purpose.'

The swiftest crawlers were already at their goal. Small hands reached out uncertainly, touched, grasped, unpetalling the transfigured roses, crumpling the illuminated pages of the books. The Director waited until 25 all were happily busy. Then, 'Watch carefully,' he said. And, lifting his hand, he gave the signal.

The Head Nurse, who was standing by a switchboard at the other end of the room, pressed down a little lever.

There was a violent explosion. Shriller and even shriller, a siren 30 shrieked. Alarm bells maddeningly sounded.

The children started, screamed; their faces were distorted with terror.

'And now,' the Director shouted (for the noise was deafening), 'now we proceed to rub in the lesson with a mild electric shock.'

From *Brave New World* by Aldous Huxley

FURTHER PROGRESS

Find your own non-fiction text. This could be a passage from a book or an article from a magazine or newspaper. Think carefully about any interesting features of language and structure you can identify in the text. Work out a series of questions that would help other students focus on the effects of language and structure. Prepare the kinds of responses you would expect for each question.

READING
Unit 11
Analyse and evaluate critically

Make progress
- develop your skills in evaluation
- understand the meaning of critical evaluation
- evaluate the organisation of texts
- evaluate the presentation of character.

USE YOUR SKILLS IN EVALUATION

In Unit 7, you learnt that when you evaluate a text you:

- consider the writer's perspective
- examine the language used and its effects on the reader
- express your own opinion
- base your judgements on evidence in the text.

Now you are going to develop your skills in evaluation.

ACTIVITY 1

Read Source A, which is an extract from a short story. Then answer the following questions.

 Work with another student. Discuss these questions:

a   What is described in the opening paragraph?
b   What mood is created in this paragraph? How can you tell?
c   How does the focus change in the second paragraph?
d   What do you learn about Nat Hocken?
e   How does the focus change in each of the following paragraphs?
f   What do you think may happen next? Why do you think this?
g   Do the ideas expressed here make you want to read the rest of the story?

2 In this text the writer uses a **third person** narrative perspective to describe events. The reader is introduced to the birds through Nat's observations about them.

    a   Do you think Nat Hocken enjoys watching the birds? Find evidence from the text to support your answer.

    b   What do you learn about the birds from Nat? Aim to write down four or five pieces of information.

    c   Look again at the final paragraph. What are Nat's thoughts about the birds at this point?

3 Writers use language to create a particular mood. Copy and complete the following table to help you work out the mood created by the writer's description of the birds.

Language feature	Example	Effect
adjectives	• 'The birds flew inland, purposeful, intent …' • • •	• gives the impression that the birds are behaving like human beings • • •
verbs	• 'wheeling, circling in the sky' • • •	• sounds as if the birds are looking for someone or something • • •

4 Now work on your own. Use your responses to Questions 1–3 to answer this question:

How well does the writer set the scene for a story with unsettling events?

In your answer you should:

    a   consider the writer's ideas and perspective
    b   examine the language used and its effects on the reader
    c   express your own opinion
    d   use evidence from the text to support your judgements
    e   comment on anything you find interesting or unusual.

When you have finished, annotate your work to show where you have included the points on the list above.

Source A

On December the third the wind changed overnight and it was winter. Until then the autumn had been mellow, soft. The leaves had lingered on the trees, golden red, and the hedgerows were still green. […]

Nat Hocken, because of a war-time disability, had a pension and did not work full-time at the farm. […] Although he was married, with children, his was a solitary disposition; he liked best to work alone. […] At midday he would pause and eat the pasty his wife had baked for him, and sitting on the cliff's edge would watch the birds. Autumn was the best for this, better than spring. […] Great flocks of them came to the peninsula, restless, uneasy, spending themselves in motion; now wheeling, circling in the sky, now settling to feed on the rich new-turned soil, but even when they fed it was as though they did so without hunger, without desire. Restlessness drove them back to the skies again.

Black and white, jackdaw and gull, mingled in strange partnership, seeking some sort of liberation, never satisfied, never still. Flocks of starlings, rustling like silk, flew to fresh pasture, driven by the same necessity of movement, and the smaller birds […] scattered from tree to hedge as if compelled.

Nat watched them and he watched the sea-birds too. […] That same impulse to flight seized upon them. Crying, whistling, calling they skimmed the placid sea and left the shore. Make haste, make speed, hurry and begone: yet where, and to what purpose? The restless urge of autumn, unsatisfying, sad, had put a spell upon them and they must flock, and wheel, and cry; they must spill themselves of motion before winter came.

Perhaps, thought Nat […] a message comes to the birds in the autumn, like a warning. Winter is coming. Many of them perish. And like people who, apprehensive of death before their time, drive themselves to work or folly, the birds do likewise.

From 'The Birds' by Daphne du Maurier,
in *The Birds and Other Stories*

EVALUATE CRITICALLY: EVALUATE STRUCTURE

Sometimes you may be asked to evaluate one specific feature of a text rather than a range of aspects. To do this, you need to focus closely on the feature and evaluate it critically. This is an important skill to learn. To evaluate critically, you need to:

- examine and analyse the feature
- consider how you respond to it
- consider how other readers might respond to it
- make a balanced judgement about its effectiveness.

To begin with, consider the way in which a writer has structured paragraphs for ideas and effect.

ACTIVITY 2

Read Source B, then answer the questions that follow.

1 Work with another student. Look at each paragraph again and answer the questions.

Paragraph 1
a   How does the writer set the scene for the incident?
b   What do you think will happen next?

Paragraph 2
a   How does the writer raise the reader's fears for the children?
b   Where does she give the reader hope that the children are safe?
c   What is the effect of the final sentence?

Paragraph 3
a   How does this paragraph increase the sense of danger?
b   What is the reader led to expect?

Paragraph 4
a   What might the reader be feeling by the end of this paragraph?

Paragraph 5
a   Do you think this is a 'happy ending'?

2 Discuss and list the reasons why the writer may have chosen to structure her ideas in this way.

 Use a tension graph to plot how the author builds tension through the paragraphs on Cambridge Elevate.

WRITE AN EVALUATION OF STRUCTURE

Think about the following questions about Source B:

How effective is the writer's use of structure in maintaining the reader's attention?

To what extent does the writer use structure to manipulate the reader's emotions?

Both these questions are asking you to write a critical evaluation. To answer these questions well you need to:

- examine and analyse the structure
- consider the effect on yourself and other readers
- make balanced judgements
- support your judgements with appropriate references from the text.

Source B

The children aren't anywhere near the ice-cream van. 'I'll just see where they are,' he says casually, but then breaks into a run. Fran calls something after him, but he can't hear. He's panicking, telling himself not to be so bloody stupid, but there are so many streams and lakes round here, it's no place for a toddler to be on his own. But he's not on his own, he's with Gareth and Miranda. He asks the man in the ice-cream van whether he's seen three children, a fair-haired toddler with an older boy and girl. A woman standing near by, swirling her tongue around an ice-cream cone, points to a path that leads down to the largest lake.

Nick careers down the hill, jumping on the verge to avoid an elderly couple. The path's uneven, shelving down steeply between the roots of trees. A hundred feet below there's a stream, its water blackish brown, flowing over black rocks. Sometimes it flashes white over miniature waterfalls, or opens into deep pools with pebble promontories. Every hundred yards or so wooden bridges span the stream. There's a path on the other side too, narrower than this, bordered by glistening ferns that are almost as wet as the rocks. Nick crosses over and thinks he sees them, two taller figures holding a small boy by the hand. He opens his mouth to call their names, then realizes it's a couple with their child. His children are nowhere to be seen.

The fir trees tower over him. Even the roots are above his head. Only by craning his head back can he see glints of sunlight on the uppermost branches. A warm, dark, wet, enclosed place. It reminds him of the garden at Lob's Hill. All the trees and bushes are evergreens, their dead leaves forming a weed-killing mulch that kills everything else as well.

And then he sees them. Comes round a corner of the twisting path, and sees them, Jasper with his trainers and socks off, paddling; Miranda sitting on a rock sucking out the last drop of ice-cream from the bottom of a cone; Gareth standing on a rock in the middle of the stream, the turbulent water chafing around him.

Nick calls out, and all three children turn towards him, their faces pale in the gloom of the rhododendron bushes. They say nothing and he wonders what they see, what they make of him, this sweaty anxious adult who stands on the bridge above them, looking down.

From Another World by Pat Barker

🔊 **Listen to an audio version of the extract on Cambridge Elevate.**

Read the first three paragraphs of a student's response to the second question ('To what extent does the writer use structure to manipulate the reader's emotions?') and the comments on the features of critical evaluation. Notice that throughout the answer, the student refers to how different readers might respond to this text.

ACTIVITY 3

1 Continue the response to Source B by writing about the remaining paragraphs of text. You should:

a keep your focus on structure

b consider possible reader responses

c make judgements about the writer's skills

d make references to the text to support your points.

2 Share your response with another student. Use the list to help you identify the features of critical evaluation in each response. Annotate both responses, clearly highlighting these features.

Watch a video on narrative structure on Cambridge Elevate.

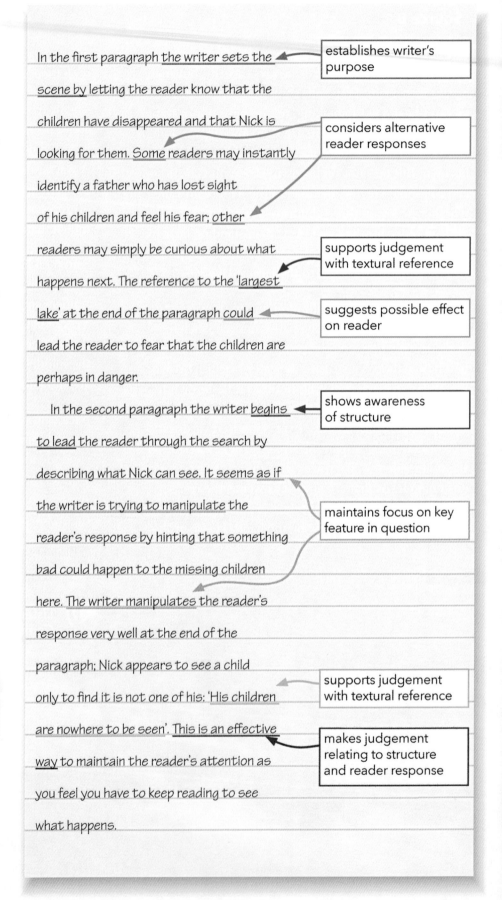

In the first paragraph the writer sets the scene by letting the reader know that the children have disappeared and that Nick is looking for them. Some readers may instantly identify a father who has lost sight of his children and feel his fear; other readers may simply be curious about what happens next. The reference to the 'largest lake' at the end of the paragraph could lead the reader to fear that the children are perhaps in danger.

In the second paragraph the writer begins to lead the reader through the search by describing what Nick can see. It seems as if the writer is trying to manipulate the reader's response by hinting that something bad could happen to the missing children here. The writer manipulates the reader's response very well at the end of the paragraph; Nick appears to see a child only to find it is not one of his: 'His children are nowhere to be seen'. This is an effective way to maintain the reader's attention as you feel you have to keep reading to see what happens.

- establishes writer's purpose
- considers alternative reader responses
- supports judgement with textural reference
- suggests possible effect on reader
- shows awareness of structure
- maintains focus on key feature in question
- supports judgement with textural reference
- makes judgement relating to structure and reader response

EVALUATE CRITICALLY: EVALUATE LANGUAGE

So far you have examined and evaluated critically the **structure** of Source B. Now you will focus the writer's **use of language**.

Read the following examples taken from the work of two students.

The writer conveys Nick's sense of panic in sentences such as 'Nick careers down the hill, jumping on the verge to avoid an elderly couple'. The use of the verb 'careers' suggests that Nick is running very fast and could lose control. This is supported by the information that he has to 'jump to avoid an elderly couple'.

Here the student comments on the writer's choice of words and their effects.

I think the writer's portrayal of Nick's sense of panic is successful because he is shown as a character driven by desperation. He 'careers down the hill' almost like a car out of control. The use of the verb 'careers' may suggest that he is in such a panic he cannot control his movements or his emotions. The fact that he has to 'jump to avoid an elderly couple' is a good way of emphasising his distress – he can barely see what is in front of him. As the reader knows that Nick is so desperate because he has lost his children, this may create sympathy for him.

This is a critical evaluation. The underlining shows you where the student gives their own opinions and explores possible reader responses. This response evaluates the writer's success in presenting Nick's panic.

ACTIVITY 4

1 With another student, decide which of the following questions require critical evaluation. Talk about the reasons for your choice.

 a How does the writer use language to show Nick's panic?
 b How effective is the writer's portrayal of Nick's panic?
 c To what extent does the writer's description of the place lead the reader to imagine the worst?
 d How does the writer create a sense of danger?
 e After reading this extract, one student commented: 'the words made me feel as though I were searching for his children with him.' To what extent do you agree?

Consider Question c. To answer this question well, you need to:

- examine and analyse how the writer describes the place
- evaluate the effect of this description – does it lead the reader to imagine that something bad has happened to the children?

2 Read lines 14–33 again ('The path's uneven' to 'kills everything else as well'). Copy the table and add further examples of description from these lines in the left-hand column.

3 Discuss the effects of your examples with another student, then write an analysis and evaluation for each one in the table.

Example of description	Analysis and explanation of effect
'The path's uneven, shelving down steeply between the roots of trees.'	The word 'uneven' leads the reader to think that it would be easy to slip; the danger of this is emphasised with the alliteration of the words 'shelving' and 'steeply'.
'Its water blackish brown flowing over black rocks'	The repetition in 'blackish brown' and 'black' sets a dismal, dark tone and possibly a sense of foreboding, making the reader expect something bad.

4 Use your notes to help you write an answer to the question:

> **To what extent does the writer's description of the place lead the reader to imagine the worst?**

When you have finished, annotate your work to show where you have:

- examined and analysed the language
- given your opinions
- considered alternative reader response
- used textual details to support your judgement.

EVALUATE PRESENTATION OF CHARACTER

When you evaluate the presentation of a character, you first need to examine how the character is presented. Writers may present characters by:

- placing them in a particular setting
- describing the character's appearance, actions, thoughts and feelings
- using direct speech
- providing contrast with other characters.

You also need to consider the ways in which different readers may respond to the presentation.

ACTIVITY 5

Read Source C, which is an extract from a novel about people in London during the recession.

Source C

Shahid Kamal, who was due to work a shift at the family shop between eight o'clock in the morning and six o'clock in the evening, walked down the street at a brisk clip. He was early, and had several things he could be doing with this extra half-hour: 5
he could have stayed in bed; he could have sat in the café downstairs from his flat reading a book; he could have spent half an hour on the net catching up on the news and his Myspace page and his discussion boards; but instead he chose to take a brisk walk. 10
Five years ago their father had died suddenly in Lahore, struck down by a heart attack at sixty-two, and his brother Ahmed was already beginning to look a little like their dad: paunchy, tired, unfit, indoorsy. Shahid could read the omens and he knew the family 15
body type; now that he was in his thirties he was going to have to take exercise if he was not to turn into another ghee-fattened South Asian with a gut and high blood pressure. So here he was, going the long way round, and at speed. There was lots of 20
traffic on the pavement, most of it people on their way to work, heads down in the cold, most of them carrying briefcases and shoulder bags or handbags. Shahid had no bag, he liked to move unencumbered.

Just before the corner of Pepys Road, Shahid crossed 25
to the other side of the street – to reduce the chance that Ahmed might see him and call him to come and help with the pre-work rush – and turned towards the Common. [...] Commuters came hurrying towards the Tube station from every point of the 30
compass, with cyclists weaving in and out among them. Although he too was heading to work, Shahid was glad he wasn't dragging himself off to some office job. Shahid's view: anybody who had to wear a suit to work died a little inside, every day. 35

From *Capital* by John Lanchester

1 Work with another student. Discuss what the writer tells you about:

   a   Shahid's thoughts and actions
   b   his feelings towards his brother Ahmed
   c   his feelings towards the commuters.

Now think about this question:

The writer portrays Shadid as an outsider. Do you agree?

Read the beginning of a student response to this question, which focuses on the contrast between Shahid and his brother.

I agree with this statement as, from the start, the writer presents Shahid as being different from his family. The contrast between Shahid and his brother is clearly demonstrated in the language used by the writer. Shahid prefers to take a 'brisk' walk rather than arriving too early for work in the family shop. The word 'brisk' suggests he is energetic, unlike his brother Ahmed who is 'paunchy, tired, unfit, indoorsy'. The writer has invented the word 'indoorsy' to imply he rarely goes out as he is too busy working, and 'tired' suggests that he works very hard. Readers may view Ahmed as a loyal son working long hours in the family shop. This is in clear contrast to Shahid, who crosses the street to avoid his brother calling him in to help in the shop. In this sense readers could view Shahid as an outsider, as he is portrayed as someone who does not make an effort to fit in with the family tradition of hard work and devotion to the family business. By including this detail, I think the writer has made it clear that he wants us to believe that Shahid is disloyal. He convinces me that Shahid is an outsider in his family.

> The student evaluates critically, considering the methods used by the writer using phrases such as 'the writer presents' and 'he is portrayed as …'. The effect of language on the reader is clearly demonstrated in phrases such as 'implies' and 'suggests'. The student expresses an opinion using phrases such as 'I agree with', 'is clearly demonstrated' and 'I think'. Reader response is also considered.

2 Continue the answer by focusing on **how** the writer creates contrast between Shahid and the other commuters. Remember to:

   a   consider the methods the writer uses
   b   examine the effects of language on the reader
   c   express your opinion
   d   show that you have considered possible reader response.

When you have finished, annotate your answer to show you have covered each bullet point.

Watch a video on creating characters on Cambridge Elevate.

Source D

Charlie Stowe waited until he heard his mother
snore before he got out of bed. Even then
he moved with caution and tiptoed to the
window. The front of the house was irregular,
so that it was possible to see a light burning in   5
his mother's room. But now all the windows
were dark. A searchlight passed across the sky,
lighting the banks of cloud and probing the dark
deep spaces between, seeking enemy airships.
The wind blew from the sea, and Charlie   10
Stowe could hear behind his mother's snores
the beating of the waves. A draught through
the cracks in the window-frame stirred his
nightshirt. Charlie Stowe was frightened.

But the thought of the tobacconist's shop which   15
his father kept down a dozen wooden stairs
drew him on. He was twelve years old, and
already the boys at the County School mocked
him because he had never smoked a cigarette.
The packets were piled twelve deep below,   20
Gold Flake and Players, De Reszke, Abdulla,
Woodbines, and the little shop lay under a thin
haze of stale smoke which would completely
disguise his crime. That it was a crime to steal
some of his father's stock Charlie Stowe had no   25
doubt, but he did not love his father; his father
was unreal to him, a wraith, pale, thin, and
indefinite, who noticed him only spasmodically
and left even punishment to his mother. For
his mother he felt a passionate demonstrative   30
love; her boisterous presence and her noisy
charity filled the world for him [...] But his
father's affection and dislike were as indefinite
as his movements. Tonight he said he would
be in Norwich, and yet you never knew.   35
Charlie Stowe had no sense of safety as he
crept down the wooden stairs. When they
creaked he clenched his fingers on the collar
of his nightshirt.

From *I Spy* by Graham Greene

Assess your progress

Read Source D and answer the following questions.
They will help you assess how well you:

- understand how to evaluate a text
- critically evaluate structure, language use,
  presentation of place and character.

1 Look at the first paragraph.

  a How does the writer set the scene at the
     beginning of the paragraph?

  b What might the reader be thinking and
     feeling at the end of this paragraph?

  c What might encourage the reader to continue
     reading?

2 Look at the second paragraph.

  a How does the first sentence of this paragraph
     encourage readers to keep reading?

  b List examples of vocabulary intended to
     create suspense.

  c What new element is introduced in this
     paragraph? Does it increase the suspense?

  d How does the language used in the last two
     sentences contribute to the suspense?

3 Use your answers to Questions 1 and 2 to write a
   critical evaluation in response to the question:

**Through his use of language and structure the
writer builds up suspense brilliantly.**

To what extent do you agree?

Remember to:

  a examine and analyse the effects of language
     and structure

  b consider possible reader response

  c give your opinion, making balanced
     judgements

  d support your judgements with appropriate
     textual references.

> ✓ **Complete this
> assignment on
> Cambridge Elevate.**

FURTHER PROGRESS

Read 'The Red Room', a short suspense story by
H.G. Wells. Evaluate the ways in which the writer uses
structure to build up suspense throughout the story.
Evaluate the extent to which his use of language
contributes to the suspense.

Unit 12
Test your progress 2

Complete this test to assess your progress in the skills covered by Units 6-11.

You have **1 hour**.

Route to success:

- Spend 15 minutes closely reading Source A, Source B and the questions.
- The number of marks for each question will give you a clue as to how much time you should spend on each one.
- Remember to refer to the text to support the points you make.

Source A is the opening of a non-fiction book.

Source A

Winter in the Arctic. The forests of fir and spruce are half buried in snow. Their sloping branches are burdened with it. It lies several feet deep all over the ground. The sun, when it comes, appears for only a few brief hours each day, hanging red and sullen 5 just above the horizon before sinking down and disappearing for another eighteen hours or so. And as it vanishes, the bitter cold tightens its grip. There is no sound except for the distant muffled thud as a raft of snow slides off one of the slanting branches to 10 explode in a cloud of white powder on the snowdrift beneath. Few places are more hostile to animal life. Amphibians would freeze solid here. Nor can reptiles tolerate such extreme and continuous cold. Further south, frogs and salamanders, lizards and snakes take 15 shelter beneath the ground and relapse into torpor, their bodily processes suspended until the arrival of spring months later. But here the winter cold is so intense that they would die.

Yet there are animals here. A foot down beneath the 20 surface of the snow a small, entirely white creature the size of a pet hamster scurries along a tunnel. It is a collared lemming. It and other members of its family have excavated a complex home within this snow field. It has different kinds of accommodation. 25 Some are sleeping chambers. Others are dining rooms where the sparse leaves of half-frozen grass still rooted in the earth are exposed and can be cropped. Some of the passage-ways that connect these chambers run along the ground beneath a 30 roof of snow. Others tunnel their way through the snow itself and lead up to the outside world where one of the family may occasionally go to prospect for any vegetable food – a small seed perhaps – that might have recently arrived on the upper 35 surface of the snow.

It costs the lemmings a great deal to survive here. They pay by using some of their precious food to generate heat within their bodies. In order to keep their fuel costs to a minimum, they have to conserve 40 as much heat as they can. And they do that by insulating their bodies with fur. It is dense and fine and covers them entirely except for their eyes.

The ability to generate heat internally is not limited to mammals. Birds, of course, can also do so. 45 They insulate themselves extremely efficiently with feathers. A few reptiles, which absorb their heat directly from the sun, are also able to do so to a limited extent, A female python, coiled protectively around her eggs and unwilling to leave 50 them to go out and bask, can generate some of the warmth they need for development by spasmodic shivers of her muscles. Even fish can do so. Hunters such as shark and tuna, which rely on speed to capture their prey, keep their bodies significantly 55 warmer than the surrounding water. Nonetheless, warm bodies are characteristic of all mammals and losing that warmth, for most, is lethal.

From *The Life of Mammals* by David Attenborough

Read all the questions carefully before starting to answer.

1 Focus on **Source A**. Which four of the following statements are true?

a   Forests of fir and spruce can be found in the Arctic.

b   The sun disappears below the horizon after 18 hours of daylight.

c   Amphibians and reptiles cannot survive the extreme cold of the Arctic.

d   Collared lemmings build houses a foot beneath the surface of the snow.

e   Collared lemmings conserve heat by insulating their bodies with fur.

f   Birds, a few reptiles and some fish can generate heat internally.

g   Hunters of shark and tuna rely on speed to capture their prey.

h   Most mammals survive even if they lose body heat.   **4 marks**

| AO1 This question tests your skill in identifying explicit information. |

2 Look in detail at the first paragraph of **Source A**. How has the writer used language to create an effective image of winter in the Arctic?   **8 marks**

| AO2 This question tests your skill in explaining, commenting on and analysing how a writer uses language to achieve effects and influence readers. |

3 Source A is from the opening of a book about animals. How has the writer structured this opening to capture the interest of the reader?

8 marks

| AO2 This question tests your skills in explaining and analysing how a writer uses structure. |

4 Using details from **Source A** and **Source B**, summarise the difficulties faced by animals and man in the Arctic winter.   **10 marks**

| AO1 This question tests your skills in identifying and interpreting information and selecting and synthesising evidence from two sources. |

5 Compare how the two writers convey their attitudes to the environments they describe in **Source A** and **Source B**.   **10 marks**

| AO3 This question tests your skill in comparing writer's ideas and perspectives. |

6 Which of the two sources (**A** or **B**) do you think most effectively conveys the hardship of the Arctic winter? Explain the reasons for your choice.   **10 marks**

| AO4 This question tests your skill in evaluating texts critically and supporting your evaluation with appropriate textual references. |

Source B is extract from a 19th-century diary.

Source B

May 17th

A clear, beautiful day. Every bright day we lie on a pile of old clothing and sleeping bags outside and bask in the sunlight.

I caught sixteen pounds of shrimps and four pounds of vegetation. Extremely tired and weak afterward. The hunters and myself receive a double ration of the thin shrimp stew. 5

A portion of a can of lard, which had been used as ointment for Elison's wounds, was today issued in equal portions to all. The remainder of the diluted alcohol was also issued. The green buds of saxifrage have been introduced by some in their stews. It has not upset their stomachs and appears to be nutritive. 10

Sunday, May 18th 15

Long shot a large raven at 5 a.m. I had attempted it only two hours earlier, but the bird escaped me. He will be used for shrimp bait. I fished in a storm all forenoon, but caught only ten pounds and about two of vegetation. 20

A vessel could have sailed in Smith Sound today. It was iceless.

To the joy of all, three more issues of alcohol were found in a rubber bag in the boat.

May 19th 25

Fredericks went out at 4 a.m. to cut ice for breakfast. In a moment he returned greatly excited, with the welcome information, "Bear outside." He and Long immediately started in pursuit with their rifles. I followed more leisurely with the shotgun. After 30 an hour's tramp, I turned back, not wishing to break down my strength and compromise the source of our only support – the shrimps.

Fredericks returned at 10 a.m. and Long came in about an hour later. Neither had been able to get 35 within range of the animal. They were thoroughly exhausted by their arduous journey, and had turned back while they had strength enough to reach Camp Clay. When first seen this morning, the bear was standing a few feet from the hut. 40

The large English sledge was cut up for fuel today. Ellis quietly breathed his last at 10:30 a.m. No symptoms of scurvy were apparent. Death was due solely to starvation.

The last issue of diluted alcohol was made today. 45

Sunday, May 25th

Southeasterly wind began blowing at 10 a.m. and continued all day. In the evening it blew a moderate gale. In the heavy drift I was unable to make the customary trip to the shrimping grounds, although 50 the demand for them is great.

We buried Whistler after dinner when the storm was at its height.

Four of us still sleep in the old shanty and are but poorly protected against the storms. But there is no 55 remedy for the matter. Our strength is not equal to the task of getting out the canvas necessary to build a shelter.

My God! This life is horrible; will it never change?

Seal skin thongs cut into small pieces were used in 60 the stew this evening to eke out the scanty supplies of shrimps. Small quantities of the skin were burned to a cinder on the fire and then ravenously devoured.

From *Six Came Back* by David L. Brainard

Complete this assignment on Cambridge Elevate.

In this unit you will read and explore a variety of novel openings.

> **1 What might a writer hope to achieve in their opening paragraphs?**
>
> Work in pairs or small groups.
>
> * What do you think is in a writer's mind when they write the opening words of a novel? The writer may already have spent many months researching and planning ideas or they may be writing the first monthly instalment for publication.
>
> * List the different things a writer might hope to achieve with their opening paragraphs. Share your ideas with other students and add to your list if appropriate.

> **2 What can you work out from opening paragraphs?**
>
> An engaged reader never simply reads the words on a page. They are always thinking about the words and their meaning.
>
> * Read the opening paragraphs of *Ordinary Thunderstorms* in Source A. The annotations show you some of the thoughts and questions of an engaged reader. Are there any you would add?
>
> Work in pairs or small groups.
>
> * Discuss the ways in which this opening does or does not match the points on the list you made.
>
> * Look again at the second paragraph. What do you learn about Adam Kindred? What kind of person do you think he is? What kind of job do you think he has been interviewed for?
>
> * Think again about both paragraphs. What can you work out about the narrator?

Now read Sources B to E, the opening paragraphs of four novels, then do the activities that follow.

Source A

Let us start with the river – all things begin with the river and we shall probably end there, no doubt – but let's wait and see how we go. Soon, in a minute or two, a young man will come and stand by the river's edge, here at Chelsea Bridge, in London.

There he is – look – stepping hesitantly down from a taxi, paying the driver, 5
gazing around him, unthinkingly, glancing over at the bright water (it's a flood tide and the river is unusually high). He's a tall, pale-faced young man, early thirties, even-featured with tired eyes, his short dark hair neatly cut and edged as if fresh from the barber. He is new to the city, a stranger, and his name is Adam Kindred. He has just been interviewed for a job and feels like seeing the 10
river (the interview having been the usual tense encounter, with a lot at stake), answering a vague desire to 'get some air'. The recent interview explains why, beneath his expensive trenchcoat, he is wearing a charcoal-grey suit, a maroon tie with a new white shirt and why he's carrying a glossy solid-looking black briefcase with heavy brass locks and corner trim. He crosses the road, having 15
no idea how his life is about to change in the next few hours – massively, irrevocably – no idea at all.

From *Ordinary Thunderstorms* by William Boyd

That's clever – I'm put in the same place as the narrator.

Sounds ominous.

That's a strange shift in tense – who is he?

I know where I am.

Is he in danger?

It sounds like he's going to be an important character.

All these dashes and brackets make it feel as though the narrator is actually talking to me.

I wonder what's in that case?

I feel as though I'm actually watching him.

Sounds like he's in for a rough time.

Source B

It is a relatively little-known fact that, over the course of a single year, about twenty million letters are delivered to the dead. People forget to stop the mail – those grieving widows and prospective heirs – and so magazine subscriptions remain uncancelled; distant friends unnotified; library fines unpaid. That's twenty million circulars, bank statements, credit cards, love letters, junk mail, greetings, gossip and bills, dropping daily on to doormats or parquet floors, thrust casually 5 through railings, wedged into letter-boxes, accumulating in stairwells, left unwanted on porches and steps, never to reach their addressee. The dead don't care. More importantly, neither do the living. The living just follow their petty concerns, quite unaware that very close by, a miracle is taking place. The dead are coming back to life.

It doesn't take much to raise the dead. A couple of bills; a name; a postcode; nothing that can't 10 be found in any old domestic bin-bag, torn apart (perhaps by foxes) and left on the doorstep like a gift. You can learn a lot from abandoned mail: names, bank details, passwords, e-mail addresses, security codes. With the right combination of personal details you can open up a bank account; hire a car; even apply for a new passport. The dead don't need such things any more. A gift, as I said, just waiting for collection. 15

From *The Lollipop Shoes* by Joanne Harris

Source C

London. Michaelmas term lately over, and the Lord Chancellor sitting in Lincoln's Inn Hall. Implacable November weather. As much mud in the streets as if the waters had but newly retired from the face of the earth, and it would not be wonderful to meet a Megalosaurus, forty feet long or so, waddling like an elephantine lizard up Holborn Hill. Smoke lowering down from chimney-pots, making a soft black drizzle, with flakes of soot in it as big as full-grown snowflakes – gone 5 into mourning, one might imagine, for the death of the sun. Dogs, undistinguishable in mire. Horses, scarcely better; splashed to their very blinkers. Foot passengers, jostling one another's umbrellas in a general infection of ill temper, and losing their foot-hold at street-corners, where tens of thousands of other foot passengers have been slipping and sliding since the day broke (if this day ever broke), adding new deposits to the crust upon crust of mud, sticking at those 10 points tenaciously to the pavement, and accumulating at compound interest.

Fog everywhere. Fog up the river, where it flows among green aits and meadows; fog down the river, where it rolls defiled among the tiers of shipping and the waterside pollutions of a great (and dirty) city. Fog on the Essex marshes, fog on the Kentish heights. Fog creeping into the cabooses of collier-brigs; fog lying out on the yards and hovering in the rigging of great ships; fog drooping on 15 the gunwales of barges and small boats. Fog in the eyes and throats of ancient Greenwich pensioners, wheezing by the firesides of their wards; fog in the stem and bowl of the afternoon pipe of the wrathful skipper, down in his close cabin; fog cruelly pinching the toes and fingers of his shivering little 'prentice boy on deck. Chance people on the bridges peeping over the parapets into a nether sky of fog, with fog all round them, as if they were up in a balloon and hanging in the misty clouds. 20

From *Bleak House* by Charles Dickens

Source D

I became what I am today at the age of twelve, on a frigid overcast day in the winter
of 1975. I remember the precise moment, crouching behind a crumbling mud wall,
peeking into the alley near the frozen creek. That was a long time ago, but it's wrong
what they say about the past, I've learned, about how you can bury it. Because the
past claws its way out. Looking back now, I realize I have been peeking into that   5
deserted alley for the last twenty-six years.

One day last summer, my friend Rahim Khan called from Pakistan. He asked me to
come see him. Standing in the kitchen with the receiver to my ear, I knew it wasn't
just Rahim Khan on the line. It was my past of unatoned sins. After I hung up, I went
for a walk along Spreckels Lake on the northern edge of Golden Gate Park. The   10
early-afternoon sun sparkled on the water where dozens of miniature boats sailed,
propelled by a crisp breeze. Then I glanced up and saw a pair of kites, red with long
blue tails soaring in the sky. They danced high above the trees on the west end of the
park, over the windmills, floating side by side like a pair of eyes looking down on
San Francisco, the city I now call home. And suddenly Hassan's voice whispered in   15
my head: For you, a thousand times over. Hassan the harelipped kite runner.

From *The Kite Runner*
by Khaled Hosseini

Source E

It was a bright cold day in April, and the clocks were striking thirteen.
Winston Smith, his chin nuzzled into his breast in an effort to escape the vile
wind, slipped quickly through the glass doors of Victory Mansions, though not
quickly enough to prevent a swirl of gritty dust from entering along with him.

The hallway smelt of boiled cabbage and old rag mats. At one end of it a   5
coloured poster, too large for indoor display, had been tacked to the wall.
It depicted simply an enormous face, more than a metre wide: the face
of a man of about forty-five, with a heavy black moustache and ruggedly
handsome features. Winston made for the stairs. It was no use trying the lift.
Even at the best of times it was seldom working, and at present the electric   10
current was cut off during daylight hours. It was part of the economy drive
in preparation for Hate Week. The flat was seven flights up, and Winston,
who was thirty-nine and had a varicose ulcer above his right ankle, went
slowly, resting several times on the way. On each landing, opposite the lift-
shaft, the poster with the enormous face gazed from the wall. It was one of   15
those pictures which are so contrived that the eyes follow you about when
you move. BIG BROTHER IS WATCHING YOU, the caption beneath it ran.

From *1984* by George Orwell

❸ Which opening most appeals to you?

Work on your own.

- Read the four openings in Sources B to E. Choose the opening that has the most immediate appeal for you. List the main reasons for your choices.

- Annotate a copy of your chosen opening to show your thoughts and questions. The example of *Ordinary Thunderstorms* (Source A) will help you get started. If you cannot get hold of a copy, list your thoughts and questions on a sheet of paper.

Work in pairs or small groups.

- Share your choice of opening with other students. Explain your experience of reading it closely.

❹ What do you learn about the narrator?

Source B and Source D are both first-person narratives (although we only discover this in the final sentence of Source B). Remember that the narrator is a fictional character, created by the writer to tell the story. The narrator can only tell the reader about their experiences, thoughts and feelings. They cannot relate those of other characters unless directly told about them. The reader needs to build up a picture of the narrator in order to decide what 'really' happens in the story.

Work in pairs.

- What do you learn about the narrators of Sources B and D?

- Talk about how you know these things. Did the narrator tell you them directly or have you used detail to infer them?

- Do you have any reasons to suspect that either of the narrators are not to be trusted?

❺ What do you learn about the setting?

Both Source C and Source E reveal something of the place or setting. Dickens presents a detailed description of London in fog and Orwell, whose book *1984* was set 35 years in the future (first published in 1949), tells us things about the world that the hero, Winston Smith, inhabits.

Work in pairs or small groups.

- Examine how Dickens creates an impression of a fog-bound London.

- What do you learn about Winston Smith's world? What is unusual about it?

❻ Does the opening offer clues about what will happen in the story?

Sometimes writers give clues in their opening paragraphs about what is to follow. Boyd starts with:

Let us start with the river – all things begin with the river and we shall probably end there, no doubt – but let's wait and see how we go.

In the very first sentence he suggests or hints that the story will end with the river. He also hints that something dramatic will happen to Adam Kindred:

He crosses the road, having no idea how his life is about to change in the next few hours – massively, irrevocably – no idea at all.

Work in pairs or small groups.

- Talk about each of the four openings.

- Decide which openings give clues or hint at what will happen in the story.

- Identify the clues and explain what they lead you to expect.

- Share your findings with your class.

7 **How do the writers craft their writing?**

Writers craft their writing in many ways – at its simplest, this refers to the ideas and words they choose and the ways they put them together. However, it extends to how writers structure their ideas, the images they create, the lists, the repetitions, the varied sentence structures, the fragments, the pauses and so on.

Each of these elements affects the others. A short sentence on its own does not create an effect – it is what comes before and after it that gives it its effect, and it is in choosing where to place it that the writer shows his or her craft.

Work in pairs.

- Choose either Source B **and** Source C **or** Source D **and** Source E.

- Read your chosen sources again carefully.

- Talk about the writer's craft in each source. List a range of points, supported by examples, about distinctive features of the writer's craft.

- Choose one of the sources. You are going to give an informal presentation about the writer's craft in your chosen source. Decide:

  – which features you will comment on

  – what you will say about them.

- Work with another pair of students and take it in turn to give your presentation.

8 **Which do you think is the most effective opening?**

Earlier in this section you chose the opening that had the most immediate appeal for you. You have now studied all four openings closely. Have you changed your mind about the most effective opening?

Work on your own.

- Choose the opening that you think is most effective.

- Write an explanation of your choice.

- Aim to include comments on both the content and the writer's craft.

Now work in small groups.

- Read and comment on each others' explanations.

FURTHER PROGRESS

In this section, you have closely studied the openings of five novels. Remember that to be an engaged reader you need to be constantly thinking and asking questions about what you are reading.

Unit 14
Poverty across the centuries

In this section, you will read and explore three texts, from the 19th, 20th and 21st centuries. They cover a range of genres: fiction, literary non-fiction and non-fiction. The three texts are linked by a focus on poverty.

Source A is fiction and was written in the 19th century.

Work in pairs or small groups.

- Read Source A on your own and then share your first impressions of it.

- Talk in more detail about:
  - the image of poverty that the writer creates
  - the methods that the writer uses to create this image
  - the use of dialogue and the impact this has
  - how the writer structures this account
  - the impact the passage has on you and the reasons for this.

Source A

Oliver Twist is apprenticed to an undertaker, Mr Sowerberry. Together, they visit a poor family where the mother has recently died.

They walked on, for some time, through the most crowded and densely inhabited part of the town; and then, striking down a narrow street more dirty and miserable than any they had yet passed through, paused to look for the house which was the object of their search.   5
The houses on either side were high and large, but very old, and tenanted by people of the poorest class: as their neglected appearance would have sufficiently denoted, without the concurrent testimony afforded by the squalid looks of the few men and women who, with folded arms   10
and bodies half doubled, occasionally skulked along. A great many of the tenements had shop-fronts; but these were fast closed, and mouldering away; only the upper rooms being inhabited. Some houses which had become insecure from age and decay, were prevented from falling   15
into the street, by huge beams of wood reared against the walls, and firmly planted in the road; but even these crazy dens seemed to have been selected as the nightly haunts of some houseless wretches, for many of the rough boards which supplied the place of door and window, were   20
wrenched from their positions, to afford an aperture wide enough for the passage of a human body. The kennel was stagnant and filthy. The very rats, which here and there lay putrefying in its rottenness, were hideous with famine.

There was neither knocker nor bell-handle at the open   25
door where Oliver and his master stopped; so; groping his way cautiously through the dark passage, and bidding

Oliver keep close to him and not be afraid,
the undertaker mounted to the top of the first
flight of stairs. Stumbling against a door on the   30
landing, he rapped at it with his knuckles.

It was opened by a young girl of thirteen or
fourteen. The undertaker at once saw enough
of what the room contained, to know it was the
apartment to which he had been directed. He   35
stepped in; Oliver followed him.

There was no fire in the room; but a man was
crouching, mechanically, over the empty stove.
An old woman, too, had drawn a low stool to
the cold hearth, and was sitting beside him.   40
There were some ragged children in another
corner; and in a small recess, opposite the
door, there lay upon the ground, something
covered with an old blanket. Oliver shuddered
as he cast his eyes towards the place, and crept   45
involuntarily closer to his master; for though
it was covered up, the boy felt that it was
a corpse.

The man's face was thin and very pale; his
hair and beard were grizzly; his eyes were   50
bloodshot. The old woman's face was wrinkled;
her two remaining teeth protruded over
her under lip; and her eyes were bright and
piercing. Oliver was afraid to look at either
her or the man. They seemed so like the   55
rats he had seen outside.

"Nobody shall go near her," said the man,
starting fiercely up, as the undertaker
approached the recess. "Keep back!
Damn you, keep back, if you've a life   60
to lose!"

"Nonsense, my good man," said the
undertaker, who was pretty well used
to misery in all its shapes. "Nonsense!"

From *Oliver Twist* by Charles Dickens

113

Source B is literary non-fiction and was written in the 20th century.

Work in pairs or small groups.

- Read Source B on your own and then share your first impressions of it.

- Talk in more detail about:
  - the image of poverty that the writer creates
  - the methods that the writer uses to create this image
  - the use of dialogue and the impact this has
  - how the writer structures this account
  - the impact the passage has on you and the reasons for this
  - how the view of poverty presented in Source B is similar to/different from the view of poverty presented in Source A.

Source B

At about a quarter to six the Irishman led me to the spike. It was a grim, smoky yellow cube of brick, standing in a corner of the workhouse grounds. With its rows of tiny, barred windows, and a high wall and iron gates separating it from the road, it 5 looked much like a prison. Already a long queue of ragged men had formed up, waiting for the gates to open. They were all kinds and ages, the youngest a fresh-faced boy of sixteen, the oldest a doubled-up, toothless mummy of seventy-five. Some were 10 hardened tramps, recognizable by their sticks and billies and dust-darkened faces; some were factory hands out of work, some agricultural labourers, one a clerk in collar and tie, two certainly imbeciles. Seen in the mass, lounging there, they were a 15 disgusting sight; nothing villainous or dangerous, but a graceless, mangy crew, nearly all ragged and palpably underfed. They were friendly, however, and asked no questions. Many offered me tobacco – cigarette-ends, that is. [...] 20

Some time after six the gates opened and we began to file in one at a time. In the yard was an office where an official entered in a ledger our names and trades and ages, also the places we were coming from and going to – this last is intended to keep a 25 check on the movements of tramps. The official also asked us whether we had any money, and every man said no. It is against the law to enter the spike with more than eightpence, and any sum less than this one is supposed to hand over at the gate. But as a 30 rule the tramps prefer to smuggle their money in, tying it tight in a piece of cloth so that it will not chink. [...]

After registering at the office we were led into the spike by an official known as the Tramp Major [...] 35 and a great bawling ruffian of a porter in a blue uniform, who treated us like cattle. The spike consisted simply of a bathroom and lavatory, and for the rest, long double rows of stone cells, perhaps a hundred cells in all. It was a bare, gloomy place 40 of stone and whitewash, unwillingly clean, with a smell which, somehow, I had foreseen from its appearance; a smell of soft soap, Jeyes' fluid and latrines – a cold, discouraging, prisonish smell.

The porter herded us all into the passage, and then 45 told us to come into the bathroom six at a time, to be searched before bathing. The search was for money and tobacco. [...] The old hands had told us that the porter never searched below the knee, so before going in we had all hidden our tobacco in 50 the ankles of our boots. Afterwards, while undressing, we slipped it into our coats, which we were allowed to keep, to serve as pillows.

The scene in the bathroom was extraordinarily repulsive. Fifty dirty, stark-naked men elbowing 55 each other in a room twenty feet square, with only two bath-tubs and two slimy roller towels between them all. I shall never forget the reek of dirty feet. Less than half the tramps actually bathed (I heard them saying that hot water is 'weakening' to the 60 system), but they all washed their faces and feet, and the horrid greasy little clouts known as toerags which they bind round their toes. Fresh water was only allowed for men who were having a complete bath, so men had to bathe in water where others 65 had washed their feet. The porter shoved us to and fro, giving the rough side of his tongue when anyone wasted time.

When we had finished bathing, the porter tied our clothes in bundles and gave us workhouse shirts 70 – grey cotton things of doubtful cleanliness, like abbreviated nightgowns. We were sent along to the cells at once, and presently the porter and the Tramp Major brought our supper across from the workhouse. Each man's ration was a half-pound 75 wedge of bread smeared with margarine, and a pint of bitter sugarless cocoa in a tin billy. Sitting on the floor, we wolfed this in five minutes, and at about seven o'clock the cell doors were locked on the outside, to remain locked till eight in the morning. 80

Each man was allowed to sleep with his mate, the cells being intended to hold two men apiece. I had no mate, and was put in with another solitary man, a thin scrubby-faced fellow with a slight squint. The cell measured eight feet by five by eight high, was 85 made of stone, and had a tiny barred window high up in the wall and a spy-hole in the door, just like a cell in a prison. In it were six blankets, a chamber-pot, a hot-water pipe, and nothing else whatever. I looked round the cell with a vague feeling that 90 there was something missing. Then, with a shock of surprise, I realised what it was, and exclaimed:

'But I say, damn it, where are the beds?'

'*Beds?*' said the other man, surprised. 'There aren't no beds! What yer expect? This is one of them 95 spikes where you sleeps on the floor. Christ! Ain't you got used to that yet?'

From *Down and Out in Paris and London* by George Orwell

115

Source C is non-fiction and was written in the 21st century.

Work in pairs or small groups.

- Read Source C on your own and then share your first impressions of it.

- Talk in more detail about:
  - the image of poverty that the writer creates
  - the methods that the writer uses to create this image
  - the use of quotation and the impact this has
  - how the writer structures this account
  - the impact the passage has on you and the reasons for this
  - how the view of poverty presented in Source C is similar to/different from the view of poverty presented in Sources A and B.

Work in pairs or small groups. You are going to think about the kinds of questions that could be set on these texts in an English Language examination. All the questions target the Assessment Objectives:

AO1:

- Identify and interpret explicit and implicit information and ideas.
- Select and synthesise information from different texts.

AO2: Explain, comment on and analyse how writers use language and structure to achieve effects and influence readers, using relevant subject terminology.

AO3: Compare writers' ideas and perspectives, as well as how these are conveyed across two or more texts.

AO4: Evaluate texts critically and support this with appropriate textual references.

AO1: Identify and interpret explicit and implicit information and ideas

To show your skills in this, you need to identify and interpret appropriate information and ideas in order to answer a question.

Here are two questions that would test these skills. Discuss the answers you would give.

1   Focus on the first paragraph of Source A. List four details that show the poverty of the area being described.

2   Focus only on the first paragraph of Source B. According to this paragraph, which four of the following statements are true?

   a   An Irishman was in charge of the spike.
   b   The spike was in the workhouse grounds.
   c   The spike was a prison.
   d   The gates to the spike were closed.
   e   Men from different backgrounds were waiting outside the spike.
   f   Villains and dangerous people waited outside the spike.
   g   The men respected each other's privacy.

1 **Now focus on Source C. Write a question that tests students on their ability to identify and interpret information and ideas.**

Source C

Today marks the 10th anniversary of Tony Blair's promise to eradicate child poverty by 2020, but about 30% of children remain beneath the breadline.

By midday on Wednesday, Louise Spencer has £6.80 left in her purse to last until Monday, which works out at £1.36 a day to pay for anything she and her two small children might need. She is confident that she will make the money stretch. It's just a question of careful budgeting.

Frugality is an art she has already perfected. This morning she has done the weekly shop, which came in 67p cheaper than the £20 she had set aside. Providing a week's worth of meals for three people for £6.66 a head is easy once you work out how, she says. The gas and electricity payments for the week have already been made, so she knows the children will be warm. The only thing to fear is the unexpected – a broken pushchair, a request to buy her daughter's class photograph.

Louise, 24, doesn't smoke, drink or take drugs and she very rarely goes out with her friends. She spends pretty much all the money she gets in benefits on her children. [...]

According to the official definition, Louise's family are surviving well below the breadline, and Abigail, five, and her son Sean, three, take their place alongside the 3.9 million children in Britain classified as living in poverty. [...]

Poverty in Britain is defined by a relative measure, rather than an absolute one; any household with an income of less than 60% of British median income is classified as in poverty. At the moment, for a single-parent family with two children, the official cut-off line stands at £199 a week, after housing has been paid for; for a two-parent family, it stands at £283.20 a week. [...]

Louise is not inclined to blame the government for her difficulties. She is grateful for the money she gets every week and doesn't think her life would be much enhanced by increased payments. "Money can't always make you happy," she says. "I'm not a greedy person. When you've learned to survive on very little, you can't afford to be greedy."

Instead, she has become adept at making do. When she moved into this flat, after her children's father left her, she had almost nothing. Her mum bought her a secondhand sofa for £30, a charity gave her a washing machine (so old that it barely works). At first sight, the flat gives an impression of profound chaos. Clothes are piled into cardboard boxes in the corner. Belongings are balanced on broken bits of furniture. Saucepans are stacked high on the top of the stove. It's not that she's not house-proud, but being poor gets in the way. There are no cupboards, so everything is shoved into boxes, or spilling out into the open. The children's dolls lie legs poking up into the air on the floor, because buying a toy box has never been the week's most pressing purchase. [...]

Somehow, popular support for tackling child poverty in Britain has never been won, either by the government or by the legion of charities working in this area.

While Live Aid and the campaign to end developing-world debt got hundreds of thousands out into the streets, there has never been much public enthusiasm for pouring money into relieving poverty in our country.

People associate child poverty with distended stomachs in Africa and slum kids in India and find it difficult to engage with the home-grown equivalent, campaigners say. Many still refuse to concede that poverty even exists here, arguing that if children are housed, fed, and have access to free healthcare, they have nothing to complain about. [...]

"We are not suggesting that this is the poverty that you see in Mumbai. Poverty here is not as extreme, but it is still dire," says Martin Narey, chief executive of Barnardo's. "We don't have to choose between helping the developing world and sorting out our own society."

From an article in *The Guardian* by Amelia Gentleman

AO1: Select and synthesise information from different texts

Here you need to select appropriate detail from different sources and use it to answer a question. You are not being asked to compare sources.

Here are two questions that would target this skill. Discuss the answers you would give.

1   Using details from Sources A and B, summarise how people's physical well-being can be affected by poverty.

2   Explain what you have learnt about how society has dealt with its poor over the last 100 years from reading Sources B and C.

❶ Now focus on Sources A and C. Write a question about the living conditions of the poor, which would test students' ability to synthesise information from these two sources.

AO2 (Part 1): Explain, comment on and analyse how writers use language to achieve effects and influence readers, using relevant subject terminology

To demonstrate you have mastered this skill, you must examine and analyse a writer's use of language and show understanding of the intended effect on the reader.

Here are two questions that would target this skill. Discuss the answers you would give.

1   Read this extract from Source A closely:

There was no fire in the room; but a man was crouching, mechanically, over the empty stove. An old woman, too, had drawn a low stool to the cold hearth, and was sitting beside him. There were some ragged children in another corner; and in a small recess, opposite the door, there lay upon the ground, something covered with an old blanket. Oliver shuddered as he cast his eyes towards the place, and crept involuntarily closer to his master; for though it was covered up, the boy felt that it was a corpse.

The man's face was thin and very pale; his hair and beard were grizzly; his eyes were bloodshot. The old woman's face was wrinkled; her two remaining teeth protruded over her under lip; and her eyes were bright and piercing. Oliver was afraid to look at either her or the man. They seemed so like the rats he had seen outside.

"Nobody shall go near her," said the man, starting fiercely up, as the undertaker approached the recess. "Keep back! Damn you, keep back, if you've a life to lose!"

"Nonsense, my good man," said the undertaker, who was pretty well used to misery in all its shapes. "Nonsense!"

How does the writer use language to create sympathy for the family?

2   Focus on the first three paragraphs of Source C. How does the writer use language to help the reader understand the poverty of Louise's family?

1 Now focus on Source B. Write a question that tests students on this assessment objective.

AO2 (Part 2): Explain, comment on and analyse how writers use structure to achieve effects and influence readers, using relevant terminology

For this, you need to examine how a writer has structured a text and show understanding of the intended effect on the reader. Here are two questions that would target this skill. Discuss the answers you would give.

1   Look at Source A. How has Dickens structured this text to have maximum effect on the reader?

2   Look at Source B. How does Orwell use structure to reveal conditions at the spike to the reader?

1 **Now focus on Source C. Think about how the last two paragraphs of the article differ from the earlier part. Write a question that tests students on this assessment objective.**

AO3: Compare writers' ideas and perspectives, as well as how these are conveyed across two or more texts

To do this you must focus on the similarities and/or differences in writers' ideas and perspectives. You must also think about how these are conveyed.

Here is a question that targets this skill. The annotations show you the three elements of the question. Discuss the answer you would give.

	write about the similarities and/or differences

1   Compare how Dickens (Source A) and Gentleman (Source C) present their attitudes to poverty.

the writers' ideas and perspectives

the writer's methods

1 **Copy this question and annotate it to show the three elements of the question:**

Compare how Orwell and Gentleman explore the consequences of poverty.

AO4: Evaluate texts critically and support this with appropriate textual references

Here, you need to consider an aspect or aspects of a text and write a critical evaluation, supporting your opinions with reference to the text.

Here is a question that targets this skill. The annotations show you the three elements of the question. Discuss the answer you would give.

1   'Orwell creates a convincing and effective picture of the tramps in Source B.' Do you agree? Refer to the text to support your points.

> aspect to be considered

> reminder to use detail to support your points

> direction for you to write a critical evaluation

1 **Copy the following question and annotate it to show the three elements of the question:**

'In this extract, Dickens presents the reader with an appalling, sickening and moving image of poverty.' To what extent do you agree with this statement? Explain your answer through reference to the text.

Unit 15

Prepare and give a presentation

Make progress   AO7 AO8 AO9
- consider the importance of speaking and listening
- research and plan a presentation
- practise and develop your skills in presentation
- give a presentation.

VALUE YOUR SKILLS IN SPEAKING AND LISTENING

How important do you think it is to speak effectively and to listen carefully to others? Are these skills as important as your reading and writing skills, for example? Is it as important to be good at speaking as it is to be good at maths? If you never listen carefully, do you ever really learn?

ACTIVITY 1

Read Source A, an article about 'monosyllabic teenagers', then answer these questions.

1 Work in small groups. Discuss the following:

  a What are Peter Hyman's views on the importance of speaking and listening?
  b Are speaking and listening skills only relevant to your English studies?
  c How important are these skills in your life at the moment?
  d How important do you think these skills will be in your future?

 Watch a video about speaking and listening skills in business on Cambridge Elevate.

2 Peter Hyman says that employers are concerned by young people who 'can't string a sentence together'. To what extent do you think this is true of the young people you know?

3 Choose four of the following occupations. Explain why speaking and listening skills are important in each of the occupations you choose.

  a shop assistant
  b university lecturer
  c police officer
  d soldier
  e nurse
  f lawyer
  g plumber
  h driving instructor
  i personal trainer.

 **Watch a video about real-life presentations on Cambridge Elevate.**

Source A

Monosyllabic teenagers 'need speaking lessons' at school

Schools need to provide speaking and listening lessons to prepare teenagers for the world of work

Schools should provide lessons in speaking and debating to put an end to the image of the 'grunting, monosyllabic teenager', according to Tony 5 Blair's* former speechwriter.

Speaking skills should be placed at the heart of the timetable to address concerns from employers that school leavers 'can't string 10 a sentence together', said Peter Hyman.

He insisted that speaking was an 'undervalued area of literacy' which received far less time 15 in the curriculum than reading and writing.

Mr Hyman, who is now head teacher of a taxpayer-funded free school in Newham, east London, 20 said speaking eloquently was 'a moral issue' because it was key to children finding a job.

The comments were made after Ofqual, the qualifications 25 watchdog, said teenagers would no longer be awarded marks for speaking and listening in GCSE English. […]

But in an interview with the 30 Times Educational Supplement, Mr Hyman, head of School 21, insisted clear communication was the 'number one issue' for employers. 35

He said: 'Speaking eloquently is a moral issue because to find

your voice both literally and metaphorically and be able to communicate your ideas and your 40 passions is crucial to how they are going to be a success in the world.

'If you can speak and articulate yourself properly that will happen.

'But it's also the number one 45 issue that employers put in all their surveys: they want good oral communication.

'We've got to dispel the myth of the grunting teenager, the 50 monosyllabic teenager that makes employers say, "I've got this person who I know on paper is quite good, but they can't string a sentence together".' 55

Mr Hyman, who worked for Mr Blair for 10 years and ran his strategic communications unit from 2001 to 2003, said children in his schools were encouraged 60 to talk to each other, question teachers and hold debates.

* Tony Blair: British Prime Minister 1997–2007

From an article in *The Telegraph* by Graeme Paton

SPOKEN LANGUAGE IN YOUR GCSE

As part of your GCSE in English Language, you will be assessed on your skills in presenting information and ideas in a formal setting. You will also need to listen carefully to questions from your audience and to respond to these questions.

The most important starting point for any presentation is your choice of subject matter. If you are interested in your topic, you have a much better chance of interesting your listeners.

 Discover what makes a good presentation on Cambridge Elevate.

ACTIVITY 2

1 Look at these suggestions for presentations that could last for between three and five minutes. In small groups, discuss the possibilities each one offers and then choose the one that interests you most.

a Give a talk to your class on a subject that is of concern to teenagers in general (e.g. global warming, social networking, the right to vote at 16).

b Many schools choose charities to support. Present the case for the charity of your choice to your school governors.

c Give a talk to your class on a subject that you think will entertain them. It could be a subject of personal interest (such as 'comedians of the 21st century') or focus on an extreme and potentially amusing point of view (such as 'bring back village stocks to punish vandals').

DECIDE ON CONTENT

Once you have made your choice, you need to decide on the content of your presentation. What are you going to say? You will probably need to research your subject – three minutes is a long time to fill and you must avoid running out of ideas or repeating the same points.

ACTIVITY 3

1 Note down your aims. Are you hoping to interest, inform, argue, discuss, entertain or persuade your listeners? Bear this in mind when preparing your presentation.

Now research your subject and make notes on what you want to say. Remember, it's the details you include that will make your presentation interesting. Work out how to support the points you make by:

- including relevant facts
- referring to expert opinion.

2 Review your notes. Will the material you have enable you to achieve your aims? If not, do further research.

3 Delivering a presentation requires careful planning. Think about how best to order your material to achieve maximum impact. If you have chosen to do the presentation on the charity, for example, you might decide to keep the most disturbing example of the need for help until last.

ENGAGE YOUR AUDIENCE

Once you have planned your content, you need to think about how to grab and hold your audience's interest. As in your writing, you will need to use a range of vocabulary, images and sentence structures to engage your listeners.

You may decide to use visual aids, such as PowerPoint. When used well, with slides containing key words, clear diagrams and striking photographs, PowerPoint can greatly enhance a presentation. However, there is nothing worse than a presenter turning their back on the audience and reading directly from an overloaded PowerPoint slide.

 Learn more about engaging your audience on Cambridge Elevate.

Read the following presentation openings:

Student A

> Today I'm going to talk about global warming. In my presentation I will tell you about how global warming is affecting us all. I will also tell you about the dangers of global warming and what we need to do to stop global warming.

Student B

> When you got out of bed this morning, did you notice how warm it was for February? Did you think 'Great!', or did you pause to ask 'What's going on here?' Because [pause] you should. High temperatures in February are not great. High temperatures in February mean something's going on.

Student A wastes time telling the audience what they are going to talk about later. The student repeats the words 'global warming' four times, but without any conscious sense of effect.

Student B immediately engages the listeners and makes them think about the subject without naming it. The student uses a vivid example, varies sentence structures and uses repetition consciously for effect.

ACTIVITY 4

1 Look at your notes and plan from Activity 3. List items that might be useful as PowerPoint slides. These might include:

- key words and logos
- short bullet points that sum up detail
- diagrams
- photographs.

Aim to have no less than five and no more than ten.

2 Decide whether these slides would enhance your presentation. If you think they would, then plan their content in more detail.

USE PACE AND INTONATION

Pace and **intonation** make speech sound interesting and convey meaning and emotion. Effective speakers:

- control the pace at which they speak
- pause for effect
- vary their intonation to convey meaning and emotion.

To be an effective speaker, you need to develop these skills. This takes practice.

 Watch a video about pace and intonation to engage your audience on Cambridge Elevate.

ACTIVITY 5

1 Work in pairs. Talk about the different things you could say to engage your audience in the opening sentences of your presentation. Keep notes on the best options.

2 How often do you really listen to yourself speak? By listening to how you say something, you can work out how to vary your pace and your tone for maximum effect. If you can, record the opening of your presentation. Listen to it critically and practise it until you are happy with the result. If you cannot record it, practise it with another student and ask for feedback.

3 Now think about the ending of your presentation. It is always a good idea to finish with a dramatic point or leave your audience with something new to think about.

Now repeat tasks 1 and 2, but this time work on your ending.

CHECK YOUR BODY LANGUAGE

Did you know that the first 30 seconds to two minutes usually make or break the connection between two people when they meet for the first time? Many interviewees are unsuccessful not because of what they say, but because of non-verbal behaviour such as eye contact, posture, facial expressions and gestures.

It is important to be aware of your body language. This puts you in control of the impression you create.

 Find out more about body language on Cambridge Elevate.

 Find out about the importance of eye contact on Cambridge Elevate.

ACTIVITY 6

1 Work in pairs or small groups. Look at the following photographs. For each one, talk about:

a the impression you get of the person
b what it is about the body language that creates this impression.

2 Take it in turns to create exaggerated poses to suit the following situations. Remember to consider posture and facial expressions.

a sitting - appearing interested in what the teacher is saying
b sitting - appearing bored by what the teacher is saying
c standing - meeting someone for the first time who you want to impress
d standing - not paying attention to someone who is talking to you.

3 Now modify your poses so that they still reflect the situation described but are no longer exaggerated. Talk about how you would respond to each of these.

4 As students, you have frequent experience of presentations from your teachers and, perhaps, from visiting speakers. Using this experience, discuss the aspects of body language you think a student should adopt when giving a presentation. Make a list.

STANDARD ENGLISH

The way we speak often depends on where we come from and how well we know the person or people we are talking to. Many of our day-to-day conversations are informal, and the language we use reflects this. We might, for example, speak in local dialect or use slang or shortened words.

The setting for your presentation is formal. This means that you must speak in Standard English, the form of spoken English most commonly used in formal and public situations. Standard English is not limited to a particular area and is recognised across the UK. For most people, Standard English comes naturally. It is the language of news broadcasts, of law courts and of public speeches. It should not be mistaken for speaking 'poshly'. Standard English can be spoken with any accent.

ACTIVITY 6

1 Work in pairs or small groups. Check your understanding of Standard English by speaking the standard form of the following non-standard sentences:

    a   He couldn't of done it 'cause he was with all the other lads.
    b   We was just about to go there.
    c   Look at them cars over there.
    d   When he came in he sees it like 'n and he says it was brill.
    e   Are yous lot goin' out?

2 Talk together about the way you speak and identify examples of non-standard language in your own speech. They might be non-standard because they are slang or part of your local dialect. Decide what the standard version of these is.

ASK AND ANSWER QUESTIONS

Think about the following questions:

Was this an important event in your life?

Can you explain the importance of this event in your life?

The first question requires a simple 'yes' or 'no' answer. Questions like this, which require very short, specific answers are called **closed questions**. They are appropriate when you want to know specific details, such as a person's date of birth or address.

The second question invites a fuller, more detailed answer. This is called an **open question**. Open questions are better when you want to learn more about a subject or a person's ideas, thoughts and feelings. A good listener can help a presenter by asking questions that will prompt the presenter to give more information. This can also be achieved by linking a closed and an open question:

'Was this an important event in your life and, if so, can you explain why?'

ACTIVITY 7

1 Work in pairs. Start by each writing four questions designed to find out as much as possible about your partner's views on school and the reasons for these. Aim to write open questions.

2 Take it in turn to interview each other. You may need to change your questions in light of the responses you get.

3 Discuss together how successful your questions were in prompting detailed responses. Talk about how they could have been improved.

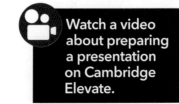
Watch a video about preparing a presentation on Cambridge Elevate.

MAKE YOUR PRESENTATION

Look again at the plan you made for your presentation and for your opening and ending (Activities 3 and 4). Before you proceed, you may want to make changes to this. You may also need to do further research and/or prepare a PowerPoint or other visual aids.

Read the points in the checklist carefully. They will help you to make a good presentation.

CHECKLIST

☐ First and foremost, make sure that you have something interesting to say.

☐ Make sure that any visual aids are relevant and well presented. Do not put too much detail on a slide. If you do, your audience will read it rather than listen to you.

☐ Use simple prompt cards to help you remember your points. Do not read from a script or from slides.

☐ Speak in Standard English. You are demonstrating your presentation skills in a formal setting, so slang and dialect are not appropriate.

☐ Vary your vocabulary and sentence structures. Use rhetorical devices such as rhetorical questions and deliberate repetition to engage your audience or emphasise a point.

☐ Show confidence in your body language and speech. Look directly at your audience and speak fluently without hesitation.

☐ Use pace and intonation to give colour and variety to what you say.

☐ Time your presentation carefully. It should last for no less that three minutes and no more than five minutes.

☐ Practise your presentation. Ask another student to record you and/or comment constructively.

☐ Practise again before giving your presentation.

✔ **Use the checklist on Cambridge Elevate to hone your presentation.**

✔ **Assess your progress**

The following list shows the main elements of an effective presentation. Consider each one carefully and decide how well you did on it. Give yourself a mark from one to five for each. Then write a short commentary on your presentation. Start with what you did well. End with comments on the areas where you feel you were weakest and give suggestions for how you could improve.

✔ interesting content

✔ relevant and well-presented visual aids

✔ effective use of prompt cards

✔ sustained use of Standard English

✔ variety in vocabulary and sentence structures

✔ confidence in body language and speech

✔ use of pace and intonation

✔ efficient timing.

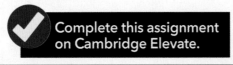 ✔ **Complete this assignment on Cambridge Elevate.**

FURTHER PROGRESS

You can learn a great deal about effective presentations from paying close attention to the presentations given by other students in your class. Make notes on the things that you think are done well and what you need to avoid doing. Use your observations to help you improve your own presentational skills. Remember, it it very likely that you will need these skills in the future – university students are often asked to give a presentation on a particular area of study and good presentational skills are highly valued in many occupations.

Unit 16

Use sentence structures for effect

Make progress (AO6)

- understand the importance of purpose and audience
- revise your knowledge of sentence structures
- use a range of sentence structures to suit your purpose and interest your audience
- appreciate the need for accurate punctuation.

 Watch a video about the features of descriptive writing on Cambridge Elevate.

USE YOUR SKILLS

You have been learning how to write well for many years, building your skills in the areas connected with good writing. Use your knowledge and experience of writing to assess the work of other students.

ACTIVITY 1

The following extracts are from the writing of two students who were asked to describe a park at night.

Student A *The children were playing in the park but some of them wanted to go home because it was getting dark but they couldn't because the gates were locked so they had to keep on playing. One of them called Katie started to cry and decided that she would try and climb over the gates. Two of the others said that they would help her so they walked over to the gates which were very tall and had big clunky locks on them.*

Student B *Night settled reluctantly on the park, masking the trees, the bushes, the flowers and, eventually, the rough soil in a cloak of darkness. All was still. All was silent. The bustle of the day had disappeared. The suited bodies no longer paced the paved routes. The children had long since deserted the swings. Even the drunks had abandoned their empty cans and bottles, stumbling blindly outwards at the gatekeeper's call.*

 S1 climb: find out more about the silent 'b' in Unit 26.

 S2 disappeared: find out more about the prefixes 'dis-' and 'un-' in Unit 26.

1 Work in pairs. Talk about the qualities in the writing in each example. For each student, agree a mark of between 1 and 5 for the following features:

a writing to describe
b range of sentence structures
c vocabulary.

2 Write a short explanation for the marks you have awarded.

3 Compare your marks with those of other students. Have you recognised the same qualities in the writing? Discuss any differences of opinion.

 ## CHOOSE THE TENSE FOR YOUR WRITING

Watch a video about the future of writing on Cambridge Elevate.

The students have both written in the past tense. To form the simple past tense, they have had to change the base form of the verbs they use. This base form is often called the **infinitive**. For example 'to walk' is the infinitive and 'walked' is the simple past tense. Make sure you know these rules for forming the simple past tense:

* The past tense for many verbs is formed by adding 'ed' to the infinitive (e.g. *to* want → wanted).
* If the present tense of the verb ends in an 'e', it is normal to simply add 'd' (e.g. *to* decide → decided; *to* settle → settled).
* If the present tense of the verb ends in a consonant and is preceded by a short vowel sound, it is normal to double the consonant and add 'ed' (e.g. *to* stun → stunned; *to* rot → rotted).

ACTIVITY 2

There are quite a lot of irregular verbs in the English language, where the usual rules for forming the past tense do not apply (e.g. *to* run → ran; *to* sweep → swept). You will know many of these.

1 Test your knowledge by writing the simple past tense for each of the following infinitives. It may help you to think of putting 'he' or 'she' in front of each word first (e.g. begin → he began).

bite	cling	feel	get	lead	ring	swear
become	dig	fight	go	leave	rise	teach
bring	do	find	hang	lose	say	tell
build	drive	fly	have	make	shake	write
catch	eat	forgive	keep	mean	shoot	
choose	fall	freeze	know	pay	sleep	

2 Check your answers with another student. If you have different answers, work together to find the correct one.

WRITE FOR PURPOSE AND AUDIENCE

Look again at the first extract in Activity 1. The student seems to be telling a story, rather than writing a description. The only description given is of 'the big clunky locks' on the gates. By not **describing**, the student was not doing what they had been asked – they were not writing for purpose.

When you write something, always be clear about your purpose. Ask yourself what you are trying to achieve in your writing. You also need to know your audience – the person or people who will be reading your writing.

 Watch a video about writing for a particular purpose on Cambridge Elevate.

ACTIVITY 3

1 Work with another student. Look at these different audiences and discuss how each one might influence the way you write:

a   only you
b   close friends
c   other students who you do not know well
d   people who will be judging you on how you write.

2 Consider each of the following:

a   an email to friends inviting them to a party
b   a letter welcoming Year 1 students to primary school
c   a letter to a newspaper about global warming.

Discuss how the intended audience for each of these might affect the way it was written? Think about:

* the sentence structures
* the vocabulary choices
* the importance of technical accuracy.

3 Students A and B, whose work you read in Activity 1, were writing in an English Language exam. Their audience was the examiner. Which student is most likely to impress the examiner? Why do you think this?

4 Work on your own. Write the first paragraph in response to the following exam task:

Describe a city street at night.

Remember:

* your purpose is to describe a city street at night
* your audience is an examiner who will assess you on your writing skills.

5 Swap your writing with another student. Ask your partner to comment on how well you have written for purpose and audience.

6 Use your partner's comments to help you redraft your paragraph. Think carefully about your range of sentence structures and your vocabulary choices. Check your final draft for technical accuracy.

UNDERSTAND SENTENCE FUNCTIONS

You write in sentences so that your reader can follow your ideas without difficulty. A sentence is a sequence of words that stand together to make a statement, ask a question or give a command:

The culprits hesitated outside the headteacher's study. (statement)

What did he say to them? (question)

Meet me later and I'll tell you. (command)

In its simplest form, a sentence has a subject and a verb. The verb describes the action of the subject. The subject may be stated or implied, for example:

Note that the verb must be complete, or **finite**. If the verb is not complete, then the sentence is not complete:

The culprits hesitated. ✓
The culprits were hesitating. ✓
The culprits hesitating. ✗

ACTIVITY 4

1 Check your understanding of sentence functions (statement, question, command) and of subject and verb, by identifying these elements in the following sentences. Copy and complete the table to record your answers. The first one has been done as an example.

a The culprits hesitated.
b What did he say?
c Meet me later.
d They knew there was no escape.
e Is the headteacher in the study?
f Children sometimes make mistakes.

	Sentence function	Subject	Verb
a	statement	The culprits	hesitated
b			
c			
d			
e			
f			

VARY SENTENCE STRUCTURES

A good writer varies sentence structure to influence the reader. To do this successfully, you need to understand the basics of sentence structure.

At its simplest, a sentence contains one main **clause**, which has a subject and a finite verb:

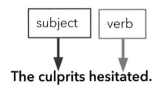

The culprits hesitated.

A **simple sentence** contains one main clause (highlighted blue in the following example). This does not mean it is always short. A simple sentence may be developed to give extra detail:

The five suspected culprits hesitated outside the open door of the headteacher's study.

A **compound sentence** contains two or more main clauses (highlighted blue) linked by the **coordinating conjunctions** 'and', 'or' or 'but' (highlighted yellow):

The culprits hesitated but they knew there was no escape.

The culprits hesitated but they knew their time was up and they shuffled into the study.

ACTIVITY 5

Stories for young children often contain simple sentences so that they are easy to follow.

1 Write five simple sentences to start a story for young children. Your subject could be: the lonely dragon; adventure in the forest; the slimy slug; or something of your own choosing.

2 Highlight the subject and the verb in each of your five sentences.

3 Choose two of your sentences and develop each of them into a compound sentence.

4 Highlight the main clauses and the coordinating conjunctions in your two compound sentences.

A **complex sentence** contains at least one main clause (highlighted blue in the following example) and one **subordinate clause** (highlighted green). The subordinate clause also contains a subject and a verb, but it cannot stand as a sentence on its own; it depends on the main clause to give it complete meaning:

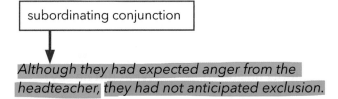

Although they had expected anger from the headteacher, they had not anticipated exclusion.

This could work equally well the other way round:

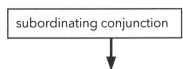

They had not anticipated exclusion, although they had expected anger from the headteacher.

In this example, the two clauses are linked by the **subordinating conjunction** 'although'. Common subordinating conjunctions are 'although', 'if', 'while', 'when', 'since', 'until', 'after'. The subordinating conjunction is usually placed before the subordinate clause. Notice how the comma is used to separate the clauses.

ACTIVITY 6

1 Write two complex sentences that explain to your teacher your view on homework. Annotate the main clause, the subordinate clause and the subordinating conjunction in each sentence.

ACTIVITY 7

Read the following example, which shows how different sentence structures can bring variety, interest and effectiveness to writing:

The five suspected culprits hesitated outside the open door of the headteacher's study. They hesitated but they knew there was no escape. Reluctantly, they shuffled into the study. Although they had expected anger from the headteacher, they had not anticipated exclusion. Their parents would be furious with them!

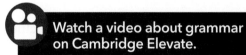

| simple sentence |
| compound sentence |
| simple sentence |
| complex sentence |
| simple sentence |

1 Write a paragraph about what happens next. Your audience is other students. Aim to use a range of sentence structures for effect.

2 Swap your paragraph with that of another student. Annotate the different sentence structures your partner has used and, if appropriate, suggest possible improvements.

Watch a video about grammar on Cambridge Elevate.

USE FRAGMENTS FOR EFFECT

Fragments are words or groups of words that lack the normal main clause structure of a subject and a verb, but which are used as a complete sentence. When used purposefully, fragments can enhance writing, but you should only use them when they suit the purpose.

In the following extract, the writer recalls her arrival at the notorious concentration camp Auschwitz. She was 13 at the time. The fragments are underlined.

Source A

The immense **portals** of the gate open and we march through into an enclosure with tall wire fences. Very tall plain wire fences flanked on both sides by a lower fence of barbed wire.

It is rapidly growing lighter. And colder. Much colder. The eerie light of the watchtowers is growing dimmer. When would we get our things? I need my coat. We keep marching. On and on. [...] It is bitter cold. 5

Clusters of people linger on both sides of the road, beyond the fence. Are they men or women? Shorn heads. Gray dresses. They run to the fence and stare. Blank stares. The blank stares of the insane. They have the appearance of the mentally ill. Impersonal. This is probably an asylum for the mentally ill. Poor souls. 10

The road ends. Our silent, rapid haunted march ends at the entrance of a gray, flat building. In fives we are ordered to file through the entrance. Inside, a long narrow room, very low ceiling. Inside, shocking noises. Shouts, screams. Loud unintelligible screams. 15

20

From *I Have Lived a Thousand Years* by Livia Bitton-Jackson

S3 portals: find out more about forming plurals in Unit 26.

The writer uses fragments effectively to:

- reflect her thought processes as a young girl
- show how she tried to make sense of the harshness and brutality of what was happening around her.

ACTIVITY 8

1 Imagine you have survived a plane crash in a desert. Write a paragraph describing what you see and your thoughts and feelings as you begin to take in the scene around you. Aim to vary your sentence structures and to use fragments effectively in your writing.

2 Work in groups of three or four. Read one another's writing and take a vote on whose is the most effective.

PROGRESS PUNCTUATION

When you write, you need to use punctuation to guide your reader through your words.

1 Here is one student's opening to the task in Activity 7. All the punctuation has been removed. What difficulties do you face when reading it?

---

waves of dizziness washed over me i could feel the heat of the burning midday sun but could make no sense of it memory returned slowly the lightning spark the crisp crack of metal the terror the panic the silence suddenly it was all clear to me i opened my eyes and like a reluctant witness at the gallows i gazed at the horror that surrounded me

---

2 Now read it with the punctuation. Why does the punctuation make it easier for you to read?

Waves of dizziness washed over me. I could feel the heat of the burning midday sun but could make no sense of it. Memory returned slowly. The lightning spark. The crisp crack of metal. The terror. The panic. The silence. Suddenly it was all clear to me. I opened my eyes and, like a reluctant witness at the gallows, I gazed at the horror that surrounded me.

Good punctuation helps the reader through the writing. A useful way of checking your punctuation is to read your work aloud. If you cannot make clear sense of it, your reader will not be able to.

Assess your progress

In this unit you have:

- investigated a range of sentence structures
- learnt that you should use a range of sentence structures to suit your purpose and interest your audience.

1 Write the opening paragraph of a story for another student to read, which starts in a school playground at break time. Describe the scene in the playground and hint that something is about to happen. Use a range of sentence structures to interest your reader.

2 Read your work aloud. Make sure your punctuation guides your reader.

3 Swap your writing with that of another student and use the following to assess each other's work:

✔ Has the writer done what they were asked to?

✔ Is a range of sentence structures used to interest the reader?

✔ Does the punctuation guide the reader?

Use the feedback to help you decide whether you need to make improvements.

Complete this assignment on Cambridge Elevate.

FURTHER PROGRESS

1 Read the first paragraph of Source B in Wider Reading 1 (the opening of *The Lollipop Shoes* by Joanne Harris). Explain how the writer has varied sentence structures to interest and engage the reader.

2 Read the first three lines of Source C in the same section (the opening of *Bleak House* by Charles Dickens). What fragments does Dickens use in these lines? What does he emphasise through their use?

WRITING
Unit 17
Communicate clearly

Make progress (AO5)
- develop ideas to include in a paragraph
- write coherent paragraphs
- punctuate dialogue effectively
- link paragraphs fluently.

USE YOUR SKILLS

You have probably been writing in paragraphs for many years. Make sure you know and understand each of the following basic points about paragraphing before continuing to Activity 1:

- A paragraph is a section of a piece of writing.
- A new paragraph marks a change of focus.
- A new paragraph starts on a new line.
- A new paragraph indicates a change of speaker in a passage of dialogue.
- Paragraphing helps writers organise their thoughts.
- Paragraphing helps readers follow the writer's thoughts.

ACTIVITY 1

Look at the following examples of two students' answers to the question:

To what extent do you think the place in which you grow up shapes the person you become?

Read both extracts carefully, focusing on how the students use and develop their paragraphs.

Student A The place you grow up in has a small impact on the person you become. Other factors are who you associate with and what events happen in your life because, if bad things happen to you, it can often lead you to become resentful and angry.

Also your family make a difference as they influence your decisions and make sure you behave in a certain way. Your Mum and Dad set the rules in your house and you have to follow them or else you end up in trouble. So they have a big impact on the person you become.

Really I don't think the place you grow up has much effect because at the end of the day you are what you choose to be and not who the people around you say you should be.

The place can have a big impact if it's not very nice as this could make …

Student B One way in which I believe the *environment* shapes the person you become is through the opportunities it can offer you. Some areas have sports fields, parks, libraries, restaurants and swimming pools. If you live in a place like this, you will be able to try and experience new things – you might become a keen reader or develop an interest in sport or experiment with foods you've never had before. By having these opportunities you can gain experience, and these experiences can open up new horizons. They could help you decide what you want to do when you are older or could even help you get into a college or university.

137

Depending on if you grew up in a poor or affluent home could also directly influence the person you become. This is because money gives you the opportunity to experience new things. For example, a person who grows up in a poor home may not have the funds to go on holiday and instead may end up sitting at home and watching the television or playing computer games. The person who has the money to travel will see new places and hear different languages being spoken, which gives them . . . .

S1 environment: find out more about commonly misspelt words in Unit 26.

1 Work in pairs. What comments and advice would you give to each student?

2 Now read this information for examiners who assess students' use of paragraphs:

At the lower level, paragraphs will mark some shift in focus. They are likely to be short and undeveloped … Better answers will have well-developed paragraphs with linked ideas.

Decide which student would be marked as 'lower level' and which would be marked as 'better'.

3 Re-read the second and third paragraphs written by Student A. List any ideas that could be used to develop each of these paragraphs.

4 Write one well-developed paragraph with linked ideas that you would include in an answer to the question:

To what extent do you think the place in which you grow up shapes the person you become?

5 Swap your writing with another student. Decide whether it is:

a short and undeveloped
b well-developed and linked.

WRITE COHERENT PARAGRAPHS

Once you can write a well-developed paragraph, the next step is to make sure your paragraphs are **coherent**. This means that the ideas should be closely linked in a logical and effective way. Source A, an extract from a short story, is a good example of a coherent paragraph.

Source A

The watch belonged to my grandfather and it hung on a hook by the head of his bed where he had lain for many long weeks. The face was marked off in Roman numerals, the most elegant figures I had ever seen. The case was 5
of gold, heavy and beautifully chased; and the chain was of gold too, and wonderfully rich and smooth in the hand. The mechanism, when you held the watch to your ear, gave such a deep, steady ticking that you could 10
not imagine its ever going wrong. It was altogether a most magnificent watch and when I sat with my grandfather in the late afternoon, after school, I could not keep my eyes away from it, dreaming that some day I 15
too might own such a watch.

From 'One of the Virtues' in *The Desperadoes and Other Stories* by Stan Barstow

The writer starts by making clear the subject of the paragraph – his grandfather's watch. He then describes its face, its casing and its chain, then considers the inside of the watch, the mechanism. Finally, he sums up all these details when he writes 'It was altogether a magnificent watch'; the last phrase, 'such a watch', emphasises its significance.

ACTIVITY 2

1 Write a coherent paragraph describing a much-loved childhood toy. Follow these six steps:

- Choose the childhood toy.
- List details that will help you describe it.
- List reasons why it was loved.
- Decide how you are going to order and link your ideas.
- Decide how you are going to start and end your paragraph.
- Write your paragraph.

 Use the planning sheet on Cambridge Elevate to help organise your ideas.

2 Read aloud the final sentence of the paragraph about the watch. Notice how the commas are used to separate clauses to help the reader.

It was altogether a most magnificent watch and when I sat with my grandfather in the late afternoon, after school, I could not keep my eyes away from it, dreaming that some day I too might own such a watch.

3 Now read your own writing aloud. If you need to, add commas to separate clauses and help the reader follow your ideas.

4 Swap your writing with another student. Decide whether it is:

a short and undeveloped
b well-developed and linked
c coherent and effective.

 USE PRONOUNS

Look again at the first sentence of the paragraph:

The watch belonged to my grandfather and <u>it</u> hung on a hook by the head of <u>his</u> bed where <u>he</u> had lain for many long weeks.

The underlined words are **pronouns**. They take the place of nouns and help to avoid repetition, as in:

The watch belonged to my grandfather and <u>the watch</u> hung on a hook by the head of <u>my grandfather's</u> bed where <u>my grandfather</u> had lain for many long weeks.

The most common types of pronouns are:

- personal pronouns (I/me, you, he/him, she/her, it, we/us, they/them)
- possessive pronouns (mine, yours, his, hers, its, ours, theirs)
- reflexive pronouns (myself, yourself, himself, herself, itself, yourselves, ourselves, themselves).

139

ACTIVITY 3

Read Source B, an extract from a novel.

Source B

The fat guard had damp patches under his armpits.
He was stood in the doorway to the compartment,
filling it. The compartment already stank of sweat
and now the guard had come in. The window was
stuck fast where the rubber seal had perished and   5
the air seemed to be getting heavier, as if the fat
guard was pressing it against the window with his
massive belly.

'You can't sit in here. First class only.'

'Yeah, well, there's no seats left anywhere else,'   10
said JB.

'You can stand in the aisle,' said the guard.
'This is first class and it'll be full in a minute.'

'Twenty-seven quid this cost me and I've got all
this stuff.'   15

JB pointed to the rack above his head. Two bags
were shoved up there.

'Look, mate, in seven or eight stops there'll be
plenty of room,' said the guard. 'Then you can
stretch out. But for now it's first-class passengers   20
in first-class seats.'

From *Asboville* by Danny Rhodes

1 There are five pronouns in the first paragraph.
Write down the pronouns then, next to each
one, note down which type of pronoun it is.

PUNCTUATE DIALOGUE

Paragraphs are used in dialogue to make the
sequence of speech easy for the reader to follow.
When you want to write the exact thoughts or
words of someone, it is important to use the
correct punctuation.

ACTIVITY 4

1 Copy the following basic rules of punctuating
direct speech. Beside each one, give an
example from Source B.

  a A new paragraph indicates a change of
     speaker.
  b Each piece of speech begins and ends
     with inverted commas.
  c Each new piece of speech starts with a
     capital letter.
  d Every piece of speech ends with a
     punctuation mark.

2 Find the pieces of speech in Source B that end
with a comma. Explain why a comma is used.

3 Write about two people meeting for the first
time on a journey. Include some dialogue in
your writing. Aim to write about 15 lines. Use
the basic rules to check the punctuation of
your dialogue.

 **Watch a video on using dialogue on
Cambridge Elevate.**

CHOOSE PARAGRAPH LENGTH

There is no 'correct' length for a paragraph. If you
have a lot of information to include on a particular
aspect of a subject, then that paragraph will be
long. However, you should try to avoid very long
paragraphs. Very short paragraphs can have a big
impact on your reader, but you should choose
carefully where to place these.

ACTIVITY 5

Read the following extract:

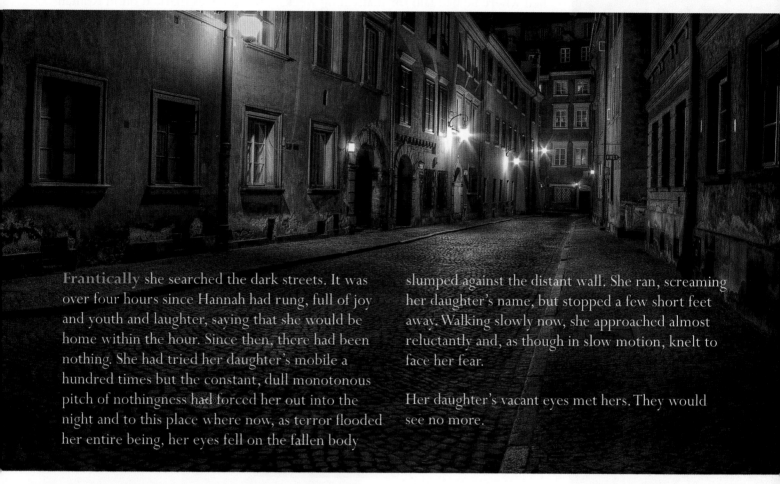

Frantically she searched the dark streets. It was over four hours since Hannah had rung, full of joy and youth and laughter, saying that she would be home within the hour. Since then, there had been nothing. She had tried her daughter's mobile a hundred times but the constant, dull monotonous pitch of nothingness had forced her out into the night and to this place where now, as terror flooded her entire being, her eyes fell on the fallen body slumped against the distant wall. She ran, screaming her daughter's name, but stopped a few short feet away. Walking slowly now, she approached almost reluctantly and, as though in slow motion, knelt to face her fear.

Her daughter's vacant eyes met hers. They would see no more.

 S2 frantically: find out more about changing adjectives to adverbs in Unit 26.

1 The first paragraph contains a lot of detail. Write down what you learn about:

a   why the mother is in the street
b   her relationship with her daughter
c   how she feels at the start and at the end of the paragraph.

2 Why do you think the writer chooses to use only two simple sentences in the second paragraph?

3 Imagine a situation in which someone discovers something wonderful. Create your first long paragraph based on their search.

Create a short second paragraph to show the discovery.

4 Swap your writing with another student. Comment on how well they have used paragraph structure to affect the reader.

LINK PARAGRAPHS FLUENTLY

In good writing, paragraphs are linked fluently. This means that one flows into another naturally and that the connections between them are clear.

In Source A, you read the first paragraph of a short story. Now read Source C, which continues the story. The links between paragraphs have been highlighted.

Source C

The watch belonged to my grandfather and it hung on a hook by the head of his bed where he had lain for many long weeks. The face was marked off in Roman numerals, the most elegant figures I had ever seen. The case was of gold, heavy and beautifully chased; and the chain was of gold too, and wonderfully rich and smooth in the hand. The mechanism, when you held the watch to your ear, gave   5
such a deep, steady ticking that you could not imagine its ever going wrong. It was altogether a most magnificent watch and when I sat with my grandfather in the late afternoon, after school, I could not keep my eyes away from it, dreaming that some day I too might own such a watch.

It was almost a ritual for me to sit with my grandfather for a little while after tea.   10
My mother said he was old and drawing near his time, and it seemed to me that he must be an incredible age. He liked me to read to him from the evening paper while he lay there; his long hands, soft and white from age, fluttered restlessly about over the sheets, like a blind man reading Braille. He had never been much of a reader himself and it was too much of an effort for him now. Possibly   15
because he had had so little education, no one believed in it more, and he was always eager for news of my progress at school. The day I brought home the news of my success in the County Minor Scholarship examination he sent out for half an ounce of twist and found the strength to sit up in bed for a smoke.

'Grammar School next, then Will?' he said, pleased as Punch.   20

'Then college,' I said, seeing the path straight before me. 'Then I shall be a doctor.'

'Aye, that he will, I've no doubt,' my grandfather said. 'But he'll need plenty o' patience afore that day. Patience an' hard work, Will lad.'

Though, as I have said, he had little book learning, I thought sometimes as I sat with my grandfather that he must be one of the wisest men in Yorkshire;   25
and these two qualities — patience and the ability to work hard — were the cornerstones of his philosophy of life.

From 'One of the Virtues' in *The Desperadoes* by Stan Barstow

ACTIVITY 6

In addition to making links between the paragraphs, the writer steadily and fluently builds a picture of his grandfather and his relationship with him.

1 Use your skills in inferring meaning. What different things do you learn about:

   a the kind of man the grandfather is
   b the writer's relationship with him?

PROGRESS PUNCTUATION

In Activity 2, you learnt that commas are used to separate clauses in sentences to help the reader. In Activity 4, you learnt the basic rules of punctuating direct speech.

1 Read the following extract from later in the story. Capital letters and end-of-sentence punctuation have been left in, but commas and paragraphs have been removed. Rewrite the extract with the correct punctuation.

I took down the watch and gave it to him. He gazed at it for some moments winding it up a few turns. When he passed it back to me I held it feeling the weight of it. I reckon he'll be after a watch like that hisself one day eh Will? I smiled shyly for I had not meant to covet the watch so openly. Someday Grandad I said. I could never really imagine the day such a watch could be mine.

Assess your progress

In this unit you have:
- developed ideas in paragraphs
- developed coherent paragraphs
- punctuated dialogue in narrative
- linked paragraphs fluently.

1 Write a passage about a relative of yours in which you show your reader:

   a the kind of person your relative is
   b what your relationship with your relative is like.

You should aim to:
- develop ideas within paragraphs
- use and correctly punctuate dialogue
- make fluent links between your paragraphs.

2 Read through your writing carefully. Check that you have achieved your aims.

3 Swap your writing with that of another student and use the following chart to assess each other's work:

✔ Ideas are developed within paragraphs.

✔ Dialogue is used and correctly punctuated.

✔ Fluent links are made between paragraphs.

Use the feedback to help you decide whether you need to make improvements.

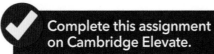
Complete this assignment on Cambridge Elevate.

FURTHER PROGRESS

Read Source A in Wider Reading 1 (the opening to *Ordinary Thunderstorms* by William Boyd). Focus on the writer's use of paragraphs.

1 What does the reader learn from the first paragraph?

2 How does the second paragraph extend and develop the first one?

3 Which pronoun is used in the first sentence of the second paragraph to make a direct link to the first paragraph?

4 What does the final sentence of the second paragraph lead the reader to expect?

Unit 18
Organise information and ideas

Make progress AO5
- use your planning skills
- identify purpose, audience and form
- consider three methods for generating ideas
- plan for paragraphs.

USE YOUR SKILLS

You use planning skills in almost every aspect of your life. You have to plan:

- what to take to school to make sure you have everything you need
- what to take on holiday to make sure you have the right clothes
- what to do at the weekend and who you are going to do it with
- which train or bus you are going to catch to get to a place on time.

ACTIVITY 1

Work in groups of three or four. You are going to plan a Leavers' Party that the majority of your year group would enjoy attending. You will need a few big sheets of paper on which to jot down ideas.

Follow these steps.

1 **Gather ideas:** collect as many ideas as possible about the kind of party you could have. Listen carefully to everyone's suggestions. Agree to consider two or three suggestions in more detail. Use the following prompts to help you think about each suggestion more carefully.

Where will it be? Does it need to be booked in advance?

When will it be? What day of the week? Month? Time?

Will the weather affect its success? If so, what precautions are needed?

What should people wear? How will they get there?

Who will be invited? Will invitations be sent? Should there be a Facebook ban?

What could go wrong? How would you deal with things going wrong?

What will it cost? Will everyone be able to afford it? What if they can't?

Will there be entertainment, food and drink? What will they be?

2 **Plan:** Once you have thought about each suggestion, decide which one will be best for your audience – the students in your year group. Use your ideas to complete details under the following subheadings. If the subheadings do not suit your chosen party, create your own.

- Type of party
- Time and place
- Dress code
- Transport
- Outline of what will happen
- Food, drink and entertainment
- Estimated cost
- Why people will enjoy it.

3 **Present:** Deliver your ideas to your class and be prepared to answer questions. Take a vote on the best-planned party.

IDENTIFY PURPOSE, AUDIENCE AND FORM

When you go into an exam, you have 45 minutes to demonstrate your writing skills. You do not know what the writing task will be, but you can develop planning strategies in advance to help you do your best. The rest of this unit will take you through the process of planning so you can develop the type of planning that suits you best.

First you should identify your purpose, audience and form. Of course, the examiner is always an audience, but there may be another one written into the task.

Task A

Your local council is running a competition. It is asking for an effective description of the best places to visit in your area to promote local tourism.

Write your description.

- **Purpose:** to describe the best places to visit in your area; as the council wants these 'to promote local tourism', it is clear that the description should be a positive one.
- **Audience:** the examiner; members of your local council.
- **Form:** a description.

Sometimes a writing task is linked with a photograph.

Task B

You are going to enter a creative writing competition. Your entry will be judged by a panel of people of your own age.

Write a description suggested by this picture.

- **Purpose:** write a description. Notice that you are not asked to describe the picture itself. It is given as a prompt to help you develop your ideas before you start to write.
- **Audience:** the examiner.
- **Form:** a description.

Task C

Write an article for a school or college website in which you report on a recent school or college event.

- **Purpose:** to report on a recent school or college event.
- **Audience:** the examiner; readers of the school or college website.
- **Form:** an article.

1 Identify the purpose, audience and form of the following writing tasks.

- **a** Write the opening to a story about a family that is forced to move home.
- **b** Write a letter to a teachers' magazine arguing that more could be done to improve the education of young people.
- **c** 'Every area should have a Youth Centre where young people can meet to study together, relax and socialise.' Write an article for a local newspaper in which you explain your point of view on this statement.

GENERATE IDEAS

Once you have identified your purpose, audience and form, you need to generate ideas. The subject you are asked to write about may be something you have never considered and you need to think quickly.

 Watch a video about finding ideas on Cambridge Elevate.

Method 1

Choose key words in the task and ask questions about them. Make a note of your answers.

'**Every area** should have a **Youth Centre** where **young people** can meet to **study together, relax and socialise**.' Write an article for a local newspaper in which you explain **your point of view** on this statement.

Every area: What's my 'area'? What do young people do now? Are all areas the same?

Youth Centre: Do I know any YCs? What might it be like? Where could it be?

young people: What ages? How young? How old? Age limits needed?

study, relax, socialise: All three? Why? Advantages? Problems?

your point of view: Agree? Disagree? Not sure?

Method 2

Brainstorm by placing the subject in the centre of your page and jotting down ideas connected with it. Aim to extend ideas with further detail. For example:

Your local council is running a competition. It is asking for an effective description of the best places to visit in your area to promote local tourism. Write your description.

Remember: Your examiner does not know your area, so you can describe an imagined area.

Method 3

Use a sequence of simple questions to help you develop ideas and build detail. For example:

Write the opening part of a story about a family that is forced to move home.

Who? Reid family – parents, two young children (Katie and Oliver)

What? Moving day; van waiting outside; parents upset

Where? Posh estate; big house; London?

When? Early morning; December; cold; frost on ground; Oliver not well?

Why? Bankruptcy; father didn't tell family; too ashamed; mother bitter about this?

Remember: Only make notes on the questions that help you build your ideas.

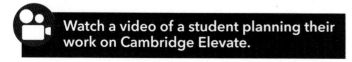
Watch a video of a student planning their work on Cambridge Elevate.

ACTIVITY 3

1 Look again at writing Task B. Spend a few moments looking at the photograph and imagining what it is like to be in this place.

2 Use Method 2 to help you generate ideas for this writing task. Write 'description suggested by picture' in the centre.

3 Talk through your ideas with another student. Ask for feedback on how well you have generated ideas and for further suggestions. If you like the suggestions, add them to your own.

PLAN FOR PARAGRAPHS

A string of loosely connected ideas is not a plan. Before writing, you need to impose some order on your ideas. One way to do this is to plan for paragraphs. Thinking in paragraphs can help you sequence your ideas effectively.

S1 paragraphs: find out more about spelling the 'f' sound in Unit 26.

Look again at the ideas generated using Method 3: 'Write the opening part of a story about a family that is forced to move home.'

> **Who?** Reid family – parents, two young children (Katie and Oliver)
>
> **What?** Moving day; van waiting outside; parents upset
>
> **Where?** Posh estate; big house; London?
>
> **When?** Early morning; December; cold; frost on ground; Oliver not well?
>
> **Why?** Bankruptcy; father didn't tell family; too ashamed; mother bitter about this?

It helps to plan for five paragraphs. Study the following paragraph plan and track the ideas that have been used to help form it.

> **Para 1:** Father waking; thinking over the past; what happened to make him bankrupt – goes downstairs.
>
> **Para 2:** Mother wakes; notices husband gone; looks out window; describe what she sees – everything packed – just waiting for removal men – thinks about the future?
>
> **Para 3:** Parents meet in kitchen: dialogue (remember to paragraph); they argue.
>
> **Para 4:** Katie and Oliver come in – Oliver sick – argument stops – father sorts children – mother walks round empty rooms.
>
> **Para 5:** Removal van pulls up – new life begins? Very short for effect?

By the end of your paragraph plan, you should have a clear route for writing.

Remember:

- A plan for writing does not have to make sense to anyone but you. You will not be marked on your plan.
- You do not have to follow your plan precisely but it will help you to write coherent, linked paragraphs.

ACTIVITY 4

You are going to use the ideas you generated in Activity 3 to help you form a plan for five paragraphs.

1 First, consider the following possibilities. You could:

  a   form your paragraphs around sights, sounds and feelings
  b   journey through the place, moving from the top of the steps to the lighthouse, describing the changing scene
  c   describe the scene from the distant sunset, zooming in over the town and the harbour to the lighthouse or an imagined person
  d   imagine you are looking out from one of the windows and span the scene in front of you from left to right – include a focus on imagined people if you like.

2 Write your paragraph plan. Remember, you do not have to use all your details and you can add new ones as you write.

3 Talk through your plan with another student. Ask for suggestions and add them if you think they will improve your piece of writing.

4 Do you feel confident that you now have a clear route for writing? Assess your confidence with a mark from 1 to 5.

 Watch a video of students discussing each other's work on Cambridge Elevate.

PROGRESS PUNCTUATION

Paragraphing is a feature of punctuation as well as of organisation. You use paragraphs to indicate:

- a shift in focus
- a change of speaker in a dialogue.

Paragraphs help to guide your reader through your writing. There is no fixed or 'correct' length for a paragraph – it can be very short or very long.

Read the following text. Decide where you would place paragraphs.

The sun was gently sinking below the horizon, its muted ruby rays glancing against the soft clouds. 'It's time to go,' she murmured softly. Slowly, they gathered the remnants of their last day together. They drifted aimlessly across the now-deserted beach, the imprints of their feet marking the sand before quickly fading. They moved in unison, both knowing there was nothing more to say or do, no more time to put things right. Darkness fell quietly.

✔ Assess your progress

In this unit you have:

- learnt to identify purpose, audience and form in writing tasks
- practised different methods for generating ideas
- learnt to write a paragraph plan to give you a clear route for writing.

You are going to plan for the following task:

'Write a story in which an unexpected letter arrives'.

1 Use Method 3 to help you generate ideas.

2 Write a plan for five paragraphs.

3 Swap your plan with that of another student and check the following:

  ✔ The plan contains a range of ideas.

  ✔ The plan contains an outline of five paragraphs.

  ✔ The plan provides a clear route for writing.

  Use the feedback to help you decide whether you need to make improvements to your plan.

 Complete this assignment on Cambridge Elevate.

FURTHER PROGRESS

So far, you have covered the basics of planning. You need to continue to develop your planning technique so that in an exam you can plan quickly and efficiently. Look at the following plan, which was written in response to the question:

Describe contrasting areas of a town or city.

The student has developed their planning technique to:

- include a range of detail
- use the zooming-in technique:
  environment → street → home → child
- include descriptive vocabulary that they can use in their writing.

Pleasant		Unpleasant
sun, cloudless skies, beds of purple hyacinths, rainbow with silvers of metallic silver and gold – promising – happy	environment	Skeletal trees – brown, dead leaves; sun trying to unchain herself from dark clouds – ominous – danger threatening
Tree-lined – green hedges – sparkling gates – cars parked exactly – glistening bicycles chained to gates sounds of birds – murmur of happy chatter	street	Litter – last night's debris – broken glass – alleys leading off – groups lurking on corners – battered cars – dull sound of constant traffic
Neatly painted – pastel paints Handkerchief gardens – tidy rows Flowers: colours; vibrant army – white glossy windows – eyes on sunshine world	home	Small flat – broken windows – paint peeling – dead plant in window – remnant of Christmas – reminder of happier times
In garden – white dress – shining hair Picking flower posy for mother – humming nursery rhyme gently – hears ice-cream van calling – runs inside	child	In corner of hut – curled up – frightened – dirty – reaches for only toy – moth-eaten rabbit – hears door slam open – shudders

1 Once you have studied the plan, try using a similar format to plan an answer to the question:

Describe a fair in the daytime and at night.

 Use the planning sheet on Cambridge Elevate to complete this activity.

WRITING
Unit 19
Create tone to influence your readers

USE YOUR SKILLS

For your writing to be effective, it needs to match your purpose and audience. You may at some time need to write a letter of complaint. A letter, sent by post or emailed, can be more effective than a phone call. It can provide proof of exactly what has been said and can be used for further action if needed.

ACTIVITY 1

Work in pairs. Read the following letter of complaint, then use your knowledge of writing for purpose and audience to help you answer these questions.

1 Does the writer make it clear to the bank manager what he is complaining about?

2 Does the writer make it clear what he wants done?

3 Normally, a letter of complaint should be written in Standard English. This is the type of English usually used in public communication and the one you are taught in school. Think about the writer's vocabulary, punctuation and grammar in the letter of complaint. What examples of non-Standard English can you identify?

 Watch a video about the differences between Standard English and non-Standard English on Cambridge Elevate.

4 List three points of advice you would give this writer to help him improve his letter of complaint.

Dear bank manager,

I want to complain. I had to get in touch with my bank about a stupid mistake it made when it said something about me which weren't true and caused me huge problems which I don't really want to go into right now.

I rang the number on the web page and waited ages before I got some young lad on the phone who couldn't be bothered to help. He just gave me another number to ring. I waited ages – again!!! – and then rang off.

Your bank has really cheesed me off. It cost loads of money to phone and I still didn't get an answer. I could of cried. I want to know what you're going to do and how you're going to sort it all out for me.

Yours,

K. Jones

USE THE INFORMAL AND FORMAL REGISTER

The writer of the letter in Activity 1 is angry. This is acceptable if you have a valid complaint. However, the writer does not bear in mind his audience – the bank manager. Generally, the less well you know your audience, the more formal your writing should be. The term **register** is often used to indicate the level of formality in writing.

ACTIVITY 2

Read the following two letters (Sources A and B). As you read, think about the register of each letter.

Source A

Dear Paula,

Thanks ever so much for all the help you've given me over the past few weeks. I've really enjoyed working with you and meeting so many great people. It's made my hols! I've learnt loads and know it will help me a lot in the future.

See you soon.

Still buzzing!!!

Jenny x

Source B

Dear Mrs Kenning,

Thank you for the offer of a part-time job in your office over the summer holiday period.

I am delighted to be able to **accept** this offer and I look forward to meeting you on Saturday, 5th August, to learn more about what the job entails.

Yours sincerely,
Jennifer Atkins

ABC XYZ **S1 accept:** find out more about commonly confused words in Unit 26.

1 The first letter is clearly less formal than the second. Copy Source A and annotate it to show the informal features of the writer's language, thinking about the words and the punctuation. For example:

| first-name terms | shortened form of 'thank you' |

Dear Paula,

Thanks ever so much for all the help you've given me over the past few weeks.

2 The letters were written by the same person to the same person. Can you explain why the way they are written is so different?

 Continue this activity on Cambridge Elevate.

3 Think about the purpose and audience of the following pieces of writing. Place them in order from least formal to most formal:

a a student's paragraph plan for an essay
b a teacher's report on a child for a parent
c a headteacher's welcome letter for Year 7 students
d an Ofsted report on a school for general publication
e a journalist's article on education for a magazine.

4 Check your order with that of another student. Discuss the reasons for any differences.

 ## THE ACTIVE AND PASSIVE VOICES

Most sentences have a subject, a verb and an object.

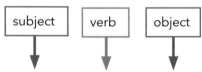

The parents liked the school.

- The subject is the person, group or thing doing the action: 'The parents'.
- The verb is the action itself: 'liked'.
- The object is the person, group or thing that the action is done to: 'the school'.

Even if the sentence is longer, the subject, verb and object remain in the same order:

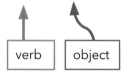

The parents, who were visiting for the first time, liked the school.

In both these examples, 'liked' is an active verb.

Many verbs can be active **or** passive. When the verb is passive, the subject is on the receiving end of the action:

The school was liked by the parents.

Here, the reader learns **what** is liked before learning **who** likes it. The doer (or agent) is identified using 'by': 'by the parents'.

However, often in passive sentences the agent is not identified, for example: 'The school was well liked.' All passive forms are made up using the verb 'be' + the past participle:

The inspector will next consider the pupils' behaviour. → The pupils' behaviour will be considered next by the Inspector.

The headteacher ended the meeting abruptly. → The meeting was ended abruptly by the headteacher.

ACTIVITY 3

1 Change these active sentences into passive ones. Remember to adjust the wording:

a The inspector visited Mr Kerry's classroom twice that morning.
b Regular year assemblies create a strong sense of community.
c Pupils regularly assess their personal progress in every subject.

2 Change these passive sentences into active ones:

a The school is driven forward by challenging and ambitious teachers.
b The needs of all pupils are taken into consideration through careful timetabling.
c Visits to classrooms are made regularly by the headteacher.

3 Rewrite the following in the passive voice:

The student noticed the fire. Immediately, he struck the fire alarm. His quick action saved many lives that day.

 USE THE PASSIVE VOICE

The passive voice is used less frequently than the active voice, but it can be a useful tool.

It can shift emphasis:

The teacher told the disruptive students to leave.

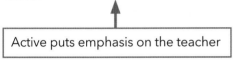

Active puts emphasis on the teacher

The disruptive students were told to leave by the teacher.

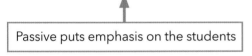

Passive puts emphasis on the students

It can deflect blame:

The governors made a serious mistake.

active

A serious mistake has been made.

passive

It can make something sound less aggressive:

You have made no effort whatsoever with this homework.

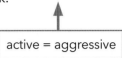

active = aggressive

This homework has not been done to an acceptable standard.

passive = impartial

The passive voice is most commonly used in formal reports where the writer (or speaker) wants to distance themself from the subject:

The school is regarded highly by parents and students. Self-discipline and high levels of achievement are consistently promoted by an experienced and well-qualified teaching staff.

ACTIVITY 4

1 Rewrite these sentences in the passive voice to fit the purpose stated:

   a The audience applauded the choir's outstanding performance. (shift the emphasis)
   b The athlete made a poor decision with serious consequences. (shift the blame)
   c You have not paid for your ticket. (sound less aggressive)

2 Use the passive voice to write four sentences to be included in a formal report on the ICT facilities in your school.

CREATE TONE

The passive voice is generally used in objective reports where there is no evidence of the writer's feelings. Look back to the letters in Activity 2. The tone of both the letters is friendly, even though one is formal and the other informal. The word 'tone' is used to describe a writer's attitude towards the subject and/or the reader. You can create many different tones in writing: serious, comic, friendly, sarcastic, sympathetic, and so on.

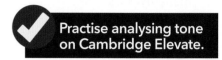

Practise analysing tone on Cambridge Elevate.

Look at how the writer of this paragraph creates a tone of understanding, sympathy and encouragement:

Being a parent is never easy. _Your_ baby will depend on you for everything. That means constant care and affection _twenty-four-seven_. _Many parents_ struggle with sleepless nights, unfinished conversations and lack of money. But, _when the going gets tough_, always remember _there is nothing better than_ the smiles, laughter and love of a happy child.

| empathises with reader |
| addresses reader directly |
| reassures that others have a similar experience |
| informal use of language |
| ends positively |

ACTIVITY 5

Read the following extract:

New parents should not expect an easy ride. A baby depends on its parents for everything: food, clothing, warmth and emotional support. It is not surprising that many parents experience a lack of sleep and a drop in income. Generally speaking, however, most parents resume normal sleeping habits within a year – a small price to pay for a happy child.

1 How would you describe its tone?

2 Copy the extract and write annotations to show how the tone is created.

ACTIVITY 6

Writers create tone through the careful choice of words.

sympathetic

Being a parent is never easy. New parents should not expect an easy ride.

unsympathetic

Many parents struggle with…

understanding

It is not surprising that many parents experience…

understanding   matter of fact

 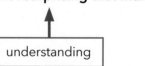 Watch a video about tone on Cambridge Elevate.

1 Imagine this scenario:

A friend is meant to meet you in town and you have planned to have a good day. You turn up on time. You wait an hour but he or she doesn't turn up.

Write three short emails to your friend with three different tones: angry, hurt, anxious.

2 Show your emails to another student. Discuss how you have used words to convey tone in each one.

 Watch a video of two students discussing their responses to this activity on Cambridge Elevate.

USE TONE TO MANIPULATE YOUR READER

The following extract was written by a student preparing a speech for a class debate. The statement to be debated was:

Teenagers today have a better life and a better future than any previous generation.

The tone is informal and sarcastic. Read it closely before examining how the chosen words create tone and manipulate the reader.

I don't wish to sound defeatist, at least not so early in my argument, but the life of teenagers these days is much as it has always been – full of rules, supposedly there to 'protect' you, and restrictive regulations which do little but stunt the growth of personality and kill creativity. Dead.

Let's start with school: that worthy institution sustained by a long line of governments who all went to school and, therefore, believe there is no better thing to impose on the next generation. Of course I think school's a great idea. How else would I spend my days except for sleeping, gaming, reading, socialising, exercising and generally learning more about the world around me? And what about you? What would you do if you didn't have to go to school?

 S2 defeatist: find out more about multi-syllabic words in Unit 26.

ACTIVITY 7

Work with another student. Discuss the following questions.

1 The student starts with 'I don't wish to sound defeatist'. What does 'defeatist' suggest to you? Do you think the student is telling the truth?

2 What are the implications of the underlined words in the following?

   a <u>supposedly</u> there to 'protect' you
   b <u>restrictive</u> regulations
   c stunt the growth of personality and <u>kill</u> creativity. <u>Dead</u>.
   d <u>worthy</u> institution
   e to <u>impose on</u> the next generation.

3 The student writes, 'Of course I think school's a great idea', when they clearly do not. Why do you think they do this?

4 'How else would I spend my days except for sleeping, gaming, reading, socialising, exercising and generally learning more about the world around me?' What does this long list suggest to the reader?

155

5 Think about both paragraphs. How does the student directly encourage the reader to agree with them?

6 Think again about the statement the student was debating:

Teenagers today have a better life and a better future than any previous generation.

Write an opening paragraph to be used in this debate. Aim to:

a convey a positive and cheerful tone
b manipulate your reader into agreeing with you.

PROGRESS PUNCTUATION

You punctuate your writing to guide your reader through the text. Below is the final paragraph of the student's speech. The punctuation has been removed.

1 Read the paragraph first to make sense of it, then rewrite it with the correct punctuation.

so we dont have to go to war or work in the mine or sweep chimneys at a tender age and of course we have technology technology is often hailed as having transformed lives and there is some truth in this new medicines appear every day as do new labour saving devices which make physical effort of any kind unnecessary if youre lucky you will live to 120 and spend your last forty years sitting on a motheaten settee staring at a blank wall with only your plasma screen for company

and that my friend is the real truth of the future awaiting the teenagers of today

Assess your progress

In this unit, you have learnt how to use tone to:

• suit purpose and audience
• manipulate your audience.

You are going to write the text for a speech to be used in a class debate on:

Education should be for life, not just for exams.

You can choose to agree or disagree.

1 Before you write:

✔ Plan your paragraphs.

✔ Think about what tone your wish to adopt to suit your purpose and audience.

✔ Think about how you can create tone and use it to manipulate your audience.

2 Read through what you have written. Check that:

a you have used words to convey tone and manipulate your reader
b your punctuation guides your reader.

3 Ask your teacher or another student to give you feedback on your writing.

Complete this assignment on Cambridge Elevate.

FURTHER PROGRESS

Read the opening four paragraphs of Wider Reading 2 Source C (a newspaper article about poverty in the 21st century).

1 The writer moves seamlessly between the active and the passive voices. Identify the use of each of these in the first four paragraphs.

2 What words would you use to describe the tone of these paragraphs? Explain the reasons for your choices.

WRITING
Unit 20
Extend your vocabulary

Make progress **AO6**
- use your vocabulary knowledge
- extend your vocabulary
- experiment with noun phrases
- use connotative language
- integrate discourse markers.

USE YOUR SKILLS

'Researchers at Harvard University and Google found that the language was expanding by 8,500 words a year in the new millennium.'

There are hundreds of thousands of words in the English language. Although no one can say exactly how many words there are, it is known that the number is growing every day.

- Some words are archaic, which means they are no longer in daily use. You may come across them in texts written a long time ago. Writers may also use archaic words to create a sense of mystery or of the past. For example, Tolkien uses the word 'kine' for cows in *The Hobbit* and 'carven' instead of 'carved'.
- Some words come directly from other languages, such as French – for example 'café', 'baguette', 'genre', 'déjà vu'.
- Some words are very new, although you can often recognise their origins in existing words – for example 'selfie', 'buzzworthy', 'bitcoin'.

You already know tens of thousands of words, but most people do not make full use of their vocabulary range. According to Professor David Crystal:

'An ordinary person, one who has not been to university say, would know about 35,000 [words] quite easily … but a person's active language will always be less than their passive, the difference being about a third.'

To write well, you need a wide vocabulary range. You also need to know how to choose your vocabulary to suit your purpose and audience.

 Find some more examples of archaic words on Cambridge Elevate.

ACTIVITY 1

1 Test your knowledge of vocabulary. Choose words from the box that are similar in meaning to each of the following:

abandon	diminish	haughty
parody	absurd	deduce
impartial	picturesque	abundant
encounter	ironic	significant
adorn	endorse	malignant
vendetta	affluent	foreshadow
mutilate	versatile	

leave	meet	disfigure
harmful	conclude	decorate
scenic	mimicry	important
proud	adaptable	feud
wealthy	approve	ridiculous
neutral	reduce	anticipate
plentiful	mocking	

2 Source A is based on a report in a national newspaper, but some words have been changed. Replace the underlined words with words from the box to make the report more appropriate for its audience.

significantly	published	decreased
reveals	compiled	rarely
decline	launched	
accounted	acceleration	

3 Compare your answers to 1 and 2 with those of another student. How well did you do? Assess your vocabulary range with a mark from 1 (poor) to 5 (very good).

Whatever your mark, you can improve. Aim to learn and use ten new words each week. Keep a record of these in your student notebook.

Source A

People <u>hardly ever</u> use cash nowadays. The most common method of payment is with plastic or by online transfer. This is according to data <u>brought out</u> by Halifax. This data <u>shows</u> that customers' 5 use of cheques and cash has <u>dropped a lot</u> in the past year. Cash transactions <u>were used</u> for 17% of exchanges. The data was <u>taken</u> from research into the spending habits of 'millions' of Halifax 10 customers, the bank said.

The figures come as a new way of paying money to others by mobile phone – via the Paym app – is <u>started up</u>, paving the way for a further <u>increase</u> in the <u>drop</u> in 15 the usage of notes and coins.

BUILD YOUR VOCABULARY

When you have a wide vocabulary, you can choose the best words for your purpose. The English language is rich in synonyms - words that share a similar or related meaning. Look at these synonyms for the adjective 'angry':

ACTIVITY 2

1 The synonyms for 'angry' all have slightly different meanings. Which ones might you choose to describe the following?

   a a teacher who is angry with a student
   b an angry bull
   c an adult who has completely lost control of his temper.

ACTIVITY 3

In your GCSE you will be tested on your use of words and the richness of your vocabulary. This means that to succeed, you have to:

- draw on the wide range of words you know
- learn to use new ones.

1 Work with another student. List as many words as you can that have a similar meaning to the following over-used adjectives. An example of each has been given to start you off:

   a happy (cheerful)
   b sad (dejected)
   c small (insignificant)
   d big (massive)
   e nice (charming).

2 You can find lists of synonyms in a thesaurus – either as a book or online. Use a thesaurus to add to your lists.

3 Look at the underlined words in the following sentences. Which of the words at the end of each sentence do you think would best replace them?

   a There were <u>a lot of</u> weeds in the fields.
   (many / a multitude of / countless / numerous)
   b The boy made a <u>bad</u> mistake.
   (serious / damaging / grave / wicked)
   c She was a <u>good</u> friend.
   (reliable / trustworthy / dependable / excellent)

   d The pupils were <u>told off</u>.
   (rebuked / reprimanded / scolded / lectured)
   e It was a <u>nasty</u> thing to say.
   (disgusting / offensive / foul / malicious)

ACTIVITY 4

When writing dialogue, students often over-use the verb 'to say' (e.g. 'I'll get it,' he said.) There are many other verbs available to show the reader exactly how the words were said:

1 Look at these alternatives for the verb 'to say'. If you do not know any of them, look up their meaning and learn them.

muttered whispered intimated replied
mumbled murmured grumbled sighed
hissed **I'll get it, he …** added
declared announced
responded retorted
asserted uttered enunciated retaliated
answered repeated grunted snarled

2 You can refine the meaning of verbs even further by adding an adverb, for example:

'I'll get it,' he announced <u>grandly</u>.
'I'll get it,' he whispered <u>sheepishly</u>.

Choose five verbs from the list in Question 1 and experiment with using adverbs to refine their meaning.

3 Work in small groups. Share a recent piece of your writing with the students in your group. Talk together about:

   a the range of vocabulary you used
   b how your range could be improved.

USE NOUN PHRASES

A noun phrase is a wider term than 'noun'. It can refer to a single noun, a pronoun or a group of words that functions in the same way as a noun in a sentence.

Noun phrases have a central noun, or 'head', around which all the other words in the phrase cluster. You can test for a noun phrase by checking whether you can swap the words for a pronoun (like 'it'):

it
a row
a row of houses
an isolated row of houses
an isolated row of gaunt four-roomed houses
an isolated row of gaunt four-roomed houses, dark red
an isolated row of gaunt four-roomed houses, dark red, blackened by smoke

The final noun phrase here comes from the novel *The Road to Wigan Pier* by George Orwell. Read Source A, the paragraph from the novel that includes this long noun phrase. Notice how Orwell:

* uses a range of noun phrases to build a detailed picture for the reader
* structures the description by moving from right to left to behind to in front.

Source B

One scene especially lingers in my mind. A frightful patch of waste ground (somehow, up there, a patch of waste ground attains a squalor that would be impossible even in London) trampled bare of grass and littered with newspapers and old saucepans. To the right, an isolated row of gaunt four-roomed houses, dark red, blackened by smoke. To the left an interminable vista of factory chimneys, chimney beyond chimney, fading away into a dim blackish haze. Behind me a railway embankment made of the slag from furnaces. In front, across the patch of waste ground, a cubical building of red and yellow brick, with the sign 'Thomas Grocock, Haulage Contractor'.

5

10

15

From *The Road to Wigan Pier* by George Orwell

ACTIVITY 5

1 Develop your skill in using noun phrases. Follow these steps:

   a Choose a scene that lingers in your mind. It could be a place you have visited, or read about, or imagined.

   b Use Orwell's structure shown in Source B as a model for your writing, starting your sentences as he does with: 'One scene … A … To the right … To the left … Behind me … In front …'.

   c Use noun phrases to build a detailed picture of the scene for your reader.

2 Swap your writing with that of another student. Comment on how successful your partner has been in their use of noun phrases.

ABC XYZ **S1 impossible:** find out more about the suffixes '-able' and '-ible' in Unit 26.

UNDERSTAND DENOTATION AND CONNOTATION

When you need to find the meaning of a word, look in a dictionary.

The dictionary definition identifies the main meaning of the word. This is sometimes called the denotation. However, some words have other meanings associated with them. These associated meanings are sometimes called connotations.

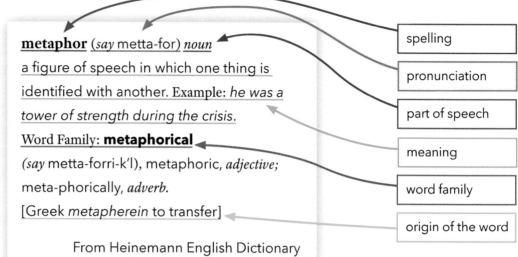

metaphor (*say* metta-for) *noun*
a figure of speech in which one thing is identified with another. Example: *he was a tower of strength during the crisis.*
Word Family: **metaphorical**
(*say* metta-forri-k'l), metaphoric, *adjective;* meta-phorically, *adverb.*
[Greek *metapherein* to transfer]

From Heinemann English Dictionary

spelling
pronunciation
part of speech
meaning
word family
origin of the word

home

denotation	connotation
the place where one lives, belongs	warmth, security and family

Connotations are not always positive:

poppy

denotation	connotation
any of a group of plants with showy red, orange or white flowers	war, death, Remembrance Day, sorrow, loss

You can choose words with connotative meaning to influence your reader.

ACTIVITY 6

Watch a video about using connotation in writing on Cambridge Elevate.

1 Work in pairs. Read the following extracts, which are the opening sentences of three short stories.

   a What connotations do the underlined words have for you?
   b What is suggested to you by the writer's choice of these words?

   On the shores of a distant <u>South Pacific island</u>, she found her <u>home</u>.

   The cold wind whistled icily across the broken <u>tombstones</u>.

   <u>Midnight</u> was fast closing in on the weary group of travellers.

2 Colours often spark associations. Think about the colour red. What ideas, moods and feelings do you associate with this colour? Write a list.

3 How does the use of colour in the following opening sentence of a short story help to add to the sense of movement and energy?

   Beams of yellow light streaked through the curtains, darting and dancing across the walls.

4 Write an opening sentence for a short story for people your own age. Aim to influence your readers by using words that have connotative meaning. Here are a few suggestions that you could build from:

spider's web	snake	black
grey	green	precipice
youths	winter	

5 Read the opening sentences written by two or three other students. Comment on the effect of their use of words that have connotative meaning.

USE EMOTIVE LANGUAGE

You can use words to influence what your readers **feel** as well as what they think. This use of words to target the reader's emotions is called 'emotive language'. In the following example, the writer has chosen words to emphasise the ferocity and danger of volcanoes in order to make the reader feel fear.

> Volcanoes have fascinated and <u>terrorised</u> peoples across the Earth from ancient times to the present day. Named after Vulcan, the Roman god of fire, they have <u>wreaked</u> <u>havoc</u> on the lives of many throughout the history of mankind. From Indonesia to the Caribbean, from Alaska to New Zealand, volcanoes <u>persistently threaten</u> the livelihoods and <u>even</u> the lives of those who live in their <u>dangerous shadows</u>.

 S2 wreaked: find out more about the silent 'w' in Unit 26.

1 Rewrite the following paragraph. Change and add words to show emotive use of language and make the reader feel fear.

Across the world today, somewhere between ten and 20 volcanoes are releasing ash and molten rock from their vents, while many thousands more are a potential danger.

2 Compare your rewrite with that of another student. Which of you has used language most effectively?

 Watch a video about influencing the reader on Cambridge Elevate.

INTEGRATE DISCOURSE MARKERS

Discourse markers are used in writing to guide the reader, to reflect, to connect points and to reinforce and give emphasis. You will know some of the most common discourse markers. Here are a few as a reminder:

therefore	until	alternatively
so	firstly	and
because	moreover	but
then	finally	on the other hand
although	however	

You may have learnt how useful they can be in connecting ideas between sentences and paragraphs. For example:

<u>Firstly</u>, there is a choice of places to stay. <u>Then</u> there is a wide range of things that can be done there. <u>Although</u> your time may be limited, this means that you are never bored. <u>Moreover</u> you can decide how long to stay at each activity.

<u>Alternatively</u> you could go to …

Knowledge of discourse markers helps you to organise ideas, but you need to develop your skill in using them. Read what a senior examiner says:

'Most students use some discourse markers at the start of sentences and paragraphs, but the better ones choose from a range of these and integrate them in their writing.'

Read the following extract from the foreword to David Attenborough's *The Life of Mammals*. The annotations show you how the discourse markers work.

We have a special regard for mammals. We are, <u>after all</u>, mammals ourselves. <u>Indeed</u>, we tend to talk as if mammals are the only kind of animals that exist – <u>until</u>, hard-pressed, we are forced to admit that birds, butterflies and bluebottles are <u>also</u> animals. Mammals, <u>for the most part</u>, have hair <u>and</u> are the only animals that rear their young on milk. <u>Even so</u>, there are a baffling number and variety of them. Over four and a half thousand. <u>And</u> they are more varied in shape and size than any other animal.

From *The Life of Mammals*
by David Attenborough

| reflects |
| connects and extends |
| moves idea forward |
| connects and reinforces |
| connects and develops idea |
| qualifies |
| connects and emphasises |

ACTIVITY 8

1 Choose one of the following opening sentences, or make up your own. Then note down three or four points that could be developed into a paragraph.

   a We have a special regard for the countryside.
   b We have a special regard for the armed forces.
   c We have a special regard for our Olympic medallists.

2 Write your paragraph. Aim to integrate discourse markers, making sure you choose the best ones to suit your purpose.

3 Annotate your writing to show how your chosen discourse markers work.

PROGRESS PUNCTUATION

1 Read the following extract and explain:

    a   why commas are used in each of the four sentences

    b   the use of the dash in the second sentence

    c   the use of the hyphen in 'hard-pressed'.

We are, after all, mammals ourselves. Indeed, we tend to talk as if mammals are the only kind of animals that exist – until, hard-pressed, we are forced to admit that birds, butterflies and bluebottles are also animals. Mammals, for the most part, have hair and are the only animals that rear their young on milk. Even so, there are a baffling number and variety of them.

From *The Life of Mammals* by David Attenborough

2 Look back at the paragraph you wrote in Activity 7. Read it aloud. Check that you have used punctuation correctly and for effect.

Assess your progress

In this unit you have:

- used and increased your vocabulary range
- built noun phrases
- used words to influence the ideas and feelings of your reader
- integrated discourse markers.

1 Write three paragraphs in which you argue for or against one of the following statements:

    a   The school day should start later.

    b   Homework should not be given at weekends.

    c   Year assemblies are a waste of time.

Your audience is your headteacher. Aim to:

- plan your paragraphs
- choose words to suit your purpose and audience
- integrate discourse markers.

2 Read through what you have written. Improve your choice of words if you can and check your punctuation.

3 Ask your teacher or another student to give you feedback on how well you have:

    ✔ planned and developed three paragraphs.

    ✔ used words to suit purpose and audience.

    ✔ integrated discourse markers.

FURTHER PROGRESS

The best way to broaden your vocabulary and to understand how writers use words effectively to suit audience and purpose is to read a range of well-written texts. Investigate the websites of the following newspapers and start to read articles regularly:

- *The Huffington Post*
- *The Telegraph*
- *The Guardian UK.*

Complete this assignment on Cambridge Elevate.

WRITING
Unit 21
Test your progress 3

In Units 16-20 you have learnt to:

- use sentence structures for effect
- communicate clearly and effectively
- organise information and ideas to create coherent texts
- create tone to influence your readers
- use and extend your vocabulary.

Your aim in this test is to demonstrate the best of your writing skills. You will be assessed on your communication, organisation, vocabulary range, use of sentence structures and technical accuracy.

Here are a few reminders of what you need to do:

Communication	<ul><li>write for purpose and audience</li><li>choose information and ideas to interest your reader</li><li>write in Standard English unless using dialogue</li><li>use tone to influence and manipulate your reader.</li></ul>
Organisation	<ul><li>identify purpose, audience and form</li><li>generate ideas and plan for paragraphs</li><li>develop coherent paragraphs and link them fluently</li><li>guide your reader with integrated discourse markers.</li></ul>
Vocabulary, sentence structure and accuracy	<ul><li>choose words to suit purpose and influence readers</li><li>show that you have a wide vocabulary range</li><li>vary sentence structures to interest readers</li><li>use accurate punctuation to guide your reader.</li></ul>

Choose one of the following three tasks. Plan, write and check your answer.

You have 45 minutes.

Either

1   Read Source A. Imagine you were walking home when the storm struck. Describe what you saw, heard and felt.

Or

2   Write a description suggested to you by the picture in Source B.

Or

3   Write a letter to your local Member of Parliament, arguing that more money should be spent on flood defences.

Source A

VIOLENT STORM STRIKES AT MIDNIGHT

A weather system over the Atlantic crashed onto British shores last night, bringing a month's worth of rain in just eight hours.

Winds reached 100 mph and there were reports of flash lightning and even hailstones. Trees have been uprooted, electric supplies halted and damage is widespread …

 Complete this assignment on Cambridge Elevate.

Source B

WRITING
Unit 22
Develop effective description

Make progress AO5 AO6
- appreciate how description is used in different kinds of writing
- use features of descriptive writing for effect
- use varied sentence structures for effect
- explore how to structure descriptions.

USE YOUR SKILLS

Description plays a part in both fiction and non-fiction texts. Writers describe a wide variety of things, such as feelings, places, people, weather and events. Use your reading skills to investigate the use of description in two texts from these different genres.

ACTIVITY 1

The writer of Source A, an extract from non-fiction travel writing, describes a tropical storm with thunder followed by lightning and then rain. To engage the reader, the writer needs to describe these familiar features of weather in interesting ways. Read the extract and discuss the questions that follow in pairs or small groups.

Source A

Towards the end of our trek the hidden sky arrived from beyond the towering canopy, heralding its presence with thunder that sounded like great doors slamming in the clouds and huge boulders rolling in heaven. They rumbled and tumbled with unnatural volume, bigger than any boulders you could ever see. Immense flashes of lightning followed the deafening crashes, enough to make me jump in disbelief. I heard the rain before it reached me, the trees of the forest being so densely packed that drops falling on the canopy took minutes before they reached the ground. But once they'd started to filter through, they came tumbling down into the jungle in a cascade of water that drenched me in seconds.

5

10

15

From Surviving Extremes by Nick Middleton

 Vocabulary

canopy: the thick covering of trees in a jungle

1 The writer's use of the adjective 'towering' to describe the tree covering suggests the enormous size of things in the jungle. Identify other adjectives used by the writer to draw attention to the enormous scale of things.

2 The writer chooses verbs to engage the reader and make the description vivid. Comment on the effects of 'heralding', 'rumbled and tumbled' and 'drenched'.

3 The writer uses a number of noun phrases (e.g. 'The towering canopy'). Identify two noun phrases and comment on their effects.

4 The writer uses the metaphor of 'heralding' in the first sentence to suggest that the sky is like royalty and the thunder is announcing its presence. There are then two similes. Comment on the effects of these two similes.

The writer of Source B, a fiction extract from a novel, describes a hazardous canoe journey.

5 How does the writer use description to help the reader understand the danger of the journey? Think about:

   a interesting uses of verbs
   b uses of similes and noun phrases
   c other features of description that you have noticed.

6 Now think about both texts. What similarities are there in the descriptive techniques used by the writers to engage readers, even though they are from different genres?

Source B

Later the river narrowed once more and the canoe shot forward in the swift current. Ahead of him the surface was broken by rapids; the water seethed and eddied; a low monotone warned him that beyond the rapids was a fall.   5
Dr Messinger began to steer for the bank. The current was running strongly and he exerted his full strength; ten yards from the beginning of the rapids his bows ran in under the bank. There was a dense growth of thorn here, overhanging   10
the river; the canoe slid under them and bit into the beach. Very cautiously, Dr Messinger knelt forward in his place and stretched up to a bough over his head. It was at that moment he came to grief; the stern swung out downstream   15
and, as he snatched at the paddle, the craft was swept broadside into the troubled waters. There it adopted an eccentric course, spinning and tumbling to the falls. Dr Messinger was tipped into the water; it was quite shallow in   20
places and he caught at the rocks but they were worn smooth as ivory and afforded no hold for his hands. He rolled over twice, found himself in deep water and attempted to swim, found himself among boulders again and attempted   25
to grapple with them. Then he reached the falls.

From A Handful of Dust by Evelyn Waugh

USE FEATURES OF DESCRIPTIVE WRITING FOR EFFECT

You can make your descriptive writing distinctive through the words you choose and the way you shape your words into phrases, images and sentences. The same place or person can be described in different ways depending on the effect you want to have on the reader. Look at these examples:

Her blue eyes sparkled.

> This has the effect of making the eyes seem bright and attractive.

Her icy blue eyes sparkled.

> The addition of 'icy' to the noun phrase makes the reader see some coldness in the eyes and suggests a possible danger.

ACTIVITY 2

1 The following sentences all describe the same thing. Focus on the way verbs, adjectives, noun phrases and imagery have been used. For each sentence, write a brief comment about the effects of the writers' language choices.

   a It was raining in Marston.
   b Marston was drowning in torrential rain.
   c The welcome rain fell on Marston.
   d Rain pummelled Marston.
   e The rain, like icy needles, jabbed down on Marston.

Find out about writing techniques on Cambridge Elevate.

2 Now adapt the following sentence in a variety of ways to create a range of different effects:

The waves met the sea wall.

You could add adjectives, make noun phrases, use verbs and imagery to add interest in different ways.

Watch a video about adapting language on Cambridge Elevate.

CREATE TONE AND ATMOSPHERE

Descriptions can be written in a variety of tones to create different atmospheres. Places and people can be described with affection, humour, disgust, sarcasm, anger, and so on.

ACTIVITY 3

Read the following extract, then answer the questions.

Bedraggled breakfast television reporters gamely grappled with umbrellas and held down errant raincoat lapels as they related the sorry tale playing out behind them, raindrops lit by arc lights bulleting past the camera like fireflies on amphetamines. I peeped out of the curtains.

From And Did Those Feet? by Charlie Connelly

1 The writer uses two examples of alliteration near the start of the first sentence. What are the effects of this repeated use of alliteration?

Watch a video about creating atmosphere effectively on Cambridge Elevate.

2 The television reporters are clearly describing some serious weather conditions. What do the following quotations reveal about the writer's attitude towards what he is seeing on the television screen?

a 'the sorry tale behind them'
b 'raindrops lit by arc lights bulleting past the camera like fireflies on amphetamines'.

3 The writer follows the long first sentence with a second short one.

a What is the focus of the first sentence?
b What is the focus of the second sentence?
c What is the effect of the contrast between the two?
d What does the writer's choice of 'peeped' tell you about the way he is feeling?

4 What words would you choose to describe the tone of this extract?

5 Think about a news item you have seen recently that had an effect on you. Write two sentences. Your first sentence should be long and describe what you saw. Your second should be short and show your response to what you saw. Choose words to create tone to show your reader your attitude to the news item.

VARY SENTENCE STRUCTURES IN DESCRIPTIVE WRITING

It is important to use a variety of sentence structures to add interest to your descriptive writing. One way of approaching this is to explore ways of adding information.

ACTIVITY 4

1 In the following examples, the simple sentence 'The house stood out' has been adapted by further information, which has been added in three different ways. Which do you think is the most effective? Why?

a Like a rotten tooth, the house stood out, its grey walls a drab contrast with the gleaming whiteness of the street.
b The house stood out like a rotten tooth, its grey walls a drab contrast with the gleaming whiteness of the street.
c Its grey walls a drab contrast with the gleaming whiteness of the street, the house stood out like a rotten tooth.

2 Think of the simple sentence 'She crossed the road'.

a Add two further pieces of descriptive information. Write the sentence in three different ways.
b Share your sentences with another student. Discuss which sentences you think are most effective and why.

USE SENTENCE STRUCTURES FOR EFFECT

Writers use different types of sentence for different effects. Compressing a lot of information into a single, long sentence, for example, can emphasise the focus of the description:

He was an inch, perhaps two, under six feet, powerfully built, and he advanced straight at you with a slight stoop of the shoulders, head forward, and a fixed from-under stare which made you think of a charging bull.

From *Lord Jim* by Joseph Conrad

Here, details about the size and manner of the character being described are packed into one sentence. This emphasises his power and potentially dangerous nature.

Short sentences can be used to contrast with longer sentences to create particular effects.

 Watch a video about sentence structure in descriptive writing on Cambridge Elevate.

 Watch a video about descriptive methods on Cambridge Elevate.

ACTIVITY 5

Read Source C and answer the questions that follow.

1 The writer builds up a picture of a place, adding details before ending the paragraph with a very short sentence. What 'big' point is the writer emphasising by making that final sentence such a short one?

2 Choose one of these short sentences:

a   He looked away.
b   It was horrible.
c   And then, nothing.

Either: Write one long sentence in which you pack a lot of detail before using the final sentence for contrast and impact.

Or: Write two or three long sentences in which you build up descriptive detail before using a short sentence.

FIND A STRUCTURE FOR YOUR DESCRIPTION

Writers choose words, phrases, images and sentence length to engage the reader and make their descriptions vivid. They also organise and structure their writing to guide and influence the reader.

Source C

The salt is a dried-up sea from the days when the Sahara was a lush, green, fertile landmass. The weather began changing five thousand years ago and now the dried sea is still mined by slaves, criminals and the men from Arouane. In the summer the heat is unbearable so the free people of this town return here. Nothing grows at all in Arouane. Fuel for fires is the rabbit-dropping-sized camel dung for which the children search daily, endlessly. There is one well.

From Geldof in Africa by Bob Geldof

ABC XYZ **S1 well:** find out more about homonyms in Unit 26.

There are many different ways to structure a description. You can structure it:

* chronologically
* from a 'wide angle' to a tighter focus
* as if you are looking down on a scene or seeing something from inside
* around one sense or different senses.

ACTIVITY 6

Read Source D, which is a description of a city, then answer the questions that follow.

Source D

So listen.

Listen, and there is more to hear.

The rattle of a dustbin lid knocked to the floor.

The scrawl and scratch of two hackle-raised cats.

The sudden thundercrash of bottles emptied into crates. The slam-slam of car doors, the changing of gears, the hobbled clip-clop of a slow walk home.

The rippled roll of shutters pulled down on late-night **cafés**, a crackled voice crying street names for taxis, a loud scream that lingers and cracks into laughter, a bang that might just be an old car backfiring, a callbox calling out for an answer, a treeful of birds tricked into morning, a whistle and a shout and a broken glass, a blare of soft music and a blam of hard beats, a barking and yelling and singing and crying and it all swells up all the rumbles and crashings and bangings and slams, all the noise and the rush and the non-stop wonder of the song of the city you can hear if you listen the song . . . .

From If Nobody Speaks of Remarkable Things by Jon McGregor

 S2 cafés: find out more about French words in Unit 26.

1 What is the main focus of the description in Source D?

2 The first paragraph is two words long and the final one is over 100 words long. Why do you think the writer decided to develop his paragraphs in this way?

3 The final paragraph is one very long sentence. Why do you think the writer chose to organise the paragraph this way rather than writing it in several sentences? What effect was he trying to achieve?

4 To organise the long list of sounds, the writer sometimes uses commas to separate them and sometimes uses 'and'. Look at the following two examples of his use of the conjunction 'and':

- 'a whistle and a shout and a broken glass'
- 'all the rumbles and crashings and bangings and slams'

Now read these two comments by students. What do you think of each comment?

Student A I think he uses 'and' here simply to add some variety. If the list was structured only using commas it would be very boring.

Student B I think that by using and repeating 'and' he somehow suggests the noise building up; 'and' makes it seem as though things are accumulating.

---

5 The description is structured around a series of sounds. It opens with a brief instruction: 'So listen.' Attempt a version of this structure.

- **a** Use the following photograph as a prompt for ideas. Start with the instruction: 'So look.'
- **b** Write five more paragraphs. The first three should be short and the fourth slightly longer.
- **c** Your final paragraph should be one long sentence controlled by commas and the use of 'and'.

6 Swap your writing with that of another student. Comment on how well they have:

- **a** structured it so that the paragraphs increase in content
- **b** focused purely on what can be seen
- **c** found a wide vocabulary to describe a range of different sights
- **d** controlled the organisation of the final long paragraph.

BRING IT TOGETHER

Good descriptive writing has a clear whole-text structure. Within that structure it provides interest for the reader by selecting and shaping words in imaginative ways.

ACTIVITY 7

Read Source E, a non-fiction text. While reading, think about the way the writer engages the reader's interest through structure and descriptive language. Then answer these questions:

1 Look at the structure of the article. How does the opening paragraph attract the reader's attention and make them want to read on?

2 In the second paragraph, why does the writer not tell the reader immediately what 'it' was?

Source E

"Look!" he said, and pointed down to where the waves were crashing onto the beach. "Quiet!"

I saw it in an instant. It quite startled me. A huge dark shape was lumbering slowly out of the white water, and was heading, inching, up   5
the beach. First one emerged, then another, and another – until there were maybe fifteen of them, moving slowly and almost painfully up the sloping sand, like wounded soldiers of an invasion force. One of them approached within   10
two metres of us – and once so close, I could see exactly what it was.

A green turtle. I had heard about them – Brazilian green turtles, living on Brazil's Atlantic coast and yet choosing, due to some curious   15
quirk of nature, to lay their eggs three thousand kilometres away on this tiny island in the middle of their ocean.

From an article in *National Geographic Adventure Magazine* by Simon Winchester

3 Why does the writer choose to begin the third paragraph as a new one rather than continuing the previous paragraph?

4 Why do you think he chose to write the following sections in short sentences?

    a 'I saw it in an instant. It quite startled me.'
    b 'A green turtle.'

5 The final paragraph begins with a short (three-word) sentence. What is the effect of writing a contrasting long sentence immediately after this?

6 Look at the writer's choice of vocabulary.

    a How does he use language in interesting ways to describe the turtles moving up the sand?
    b How does he convey his feelings about what he is seeing?

7 Now use this article as a model for your own writing.

    a Write three paragraphs in which you describe an experience of seeing something special or for the first time – real or imagined.
    b Begin with: 'Look!' he said, and pointed …'
    c Then follow the model by writing a second paragraph in which you describe whatever it is you have seen – without naming it.
    d Finally, write a third paragraph in which you disclose what it is you have seen, then add a comment about it.

USE YOUR SKILLS IN EXAMS

As you have seen, good writers describe effectively in both fiction and non-fiction texts. In your exams, you may need to write descriptively in order to:

- bring interest to more factually based, discursive non-fiction writing
- create setting, atmosphere and character in narrative writing
- write a description of a something suggested to you by a photograph.

Write the opening part of a story in which a night-time setting is used to engage the reader.

What kind of writing can I choose? This could be the opening to a ghost story or a horror story, or it could be based on something more down-to-earth.

How I will structure my writing? You might want to end on some scary detail, so you could begin with a wide-angle view and then narrow the focus down to a specific detail. Or you might decide – because it is dark – to focus on sounds rather than what can be seen. You might end with a particularly frightening small sound.

How can I structure paragraphs in effective ways? Separate paragraphs need to describe different aspects of the darkness. You need to think about how to end one paragraph and begin the next.

How can I vary my sentence structures to interest and influence my reader? You need to show that you can write some sentences packed with a lot of detail and contrast these with shorter sentences that have a punchy effect.

How can I vary my vocabulary and use imagery for effect? Think about the tone of your writing and, in particular, about your use of interesting verbs, adjectives, noun phrases and imagery.

Here is part of one student's response to the task:

Something had woken him. He turned and blinked at the pale green numbers on the bedside clock. 3 a.m. Silence. Until, he heard it. Pulling off the covers, he padded groggily to the window, pulled back the heavy patterned curtains and peered out. At nothing. Darkness smothered the yard. But then he heard it.

A faint groaning, or a whining. An animal? He rubbed the glass of the window and at the squeak of skin on glass, the groaning stopped. His eyes growing accustomed to the darkness, he peered through the glass and familiar shapes gradually formed. He could make out the rectangle of the back gate and beside it the two wheelie bins like sinister Daleks in the gloom. And the shed. There was something about the shed.

A minute passed. He became aware of holding his breath. Then he saw it. Out of the blackness at the base of the shed, something moved. A twitch and then, like a small dark cloud forming, it moved out and froze. A fox.

Still holding his breath, he watched as the fox scented the air. Its head nodded, as though to confirm that all was well and out behind it, sliding from beneath the shed, emerged one smaller shape followed immediately by another. Aware of the cold in his room, he shivered and saw the fox staring directly at him. Could it see him? Sense him? Its head nodded again and with a low bark it slid back under the shed followed closely by the two cubs.

 Identify descriptive techniques in a student response on Cambridge Elevate.

ACTIVITY 8

1 Discuss the effectiveness of this piece of writing with another student. Focus on:

a the way it has been paragraphed
b how descriptive details have been presented and structured
c the variety of sentence structures and vocabulary used to engage the reader.

PROGRESS PUNCTUATION

Good punctuation guides a reader through a text. It can also convey tone and, when used well, it can add to the effectiveness of the writing.

1 Consider each of the following. What different meaning is conveyed by the punctuation mark used at the end?

a A faint groaning, or a whining. An animal?
b A faint groaning, or a whining. An animal.
c A faint groaning, or a whining. An animal!

2 Now think about the following sequence of questions: 'Could it see him? Sense him?' What extra dimension is added by the second question?

3 The questions are followed by: 'Its head nodded again'. What does the writer suggest by following the questions in this way?

Assess your progress

In this unit you have:

- used words, phrases and images for effect
- used varied sentence structures to influence your reader
- structured descriptions in order to have an impact on your reader.

Now read this extract and carry out the tasks that follow.

The boy gazed through the misted window. He rubbed his eyes in disbelief and looked again. The scene before him was one he would remember all his life.

---

1 Describe what the boy saw. Before you start writing:

    a   Picture the scene in your mind. It can be real or imagined.

    b   Plan a structure for your description.

    c   Remember to focus on crafting your writing.

2 When you have finished, read through your description and improve it if you can.

3 Ask your teacher or another student for feedback on how well you have:

   ✔ structured your writing

   ✔ used paragraphs effectively

   ✔ varied your sentence structures for effect

   ✔ used an interesting range of vocabulary and imagery.

Complete this assignment on Cambridge Elevate.

Discover ways you can improve your writing on Cambridge Elevate.

Source F

The birds of New York have more or less given up the ghost, and who can blame them? They have been processed by Manhattan and the twentieth century. A standard issue British pigeon would look like a cockatoo among   5 them — a robin redbreast would look like a bird of paradise. The birds of New York are old spivs in dirty macs. They live off charity and welfare handouts. They cough and grumble and flap their arms for warmth. Declassed,   10 they have slipped several links in the chain of being: it's been rough all right. No more songs or plump worms or flights to summer seas. The twentieth has been a bad century for the birds of New York, and they know it.   15

From *Money* by Martin Amis

FURTHER PROGRESS

Read Source F, a description from a novel. The writer focuses on an ordinary aspect of city life – the birds found in New York. However, notice how he describes them in an unusual way, almost as though they are people, and compares them with well-known British birds.

1 Try this type of writing for yourself. Choose a well-known feature of a town or city such as coffee shops, buses or litter, and write a description of it. Take an unusual stance and introduce some 'attitude' to your writing.

Unit 23
Structure narrative

Make progress

- investigate and write story openings and endings
- create characters
- structure dialogue
- describe setting and atmosphere.

USE YOUR SKILLS

There are many different kinds of story - ghost, detective, fantasy, science fiction and so on. Whatever the genre, all stories have to be structured. They must have a beginning and a route to an ending. The writer has to assemble the various parts of the story - the events, the characters, the dialogue, the description - in ways that will interest and engage the reader.

You can structure stories in different ways. The most straightforward way is to put events into a chronological sequence - the order in which they occur. However, sometimes a story can be made more interesting by starting at a later point.

ACTIVITY 1

Read the following notes, which outline a chronological sequence that could form the basis for a story.

Boy and girl have been going out for a long time – go to a dance together – they argue – he leaves – he walks around streets in rain wondering how to make up – he's attacked and badly wounded – she regrets argument and leaves dance to look for him – finds him dying on the pavement.

1 The following statements show some possible starting points. Work with another student and discuss how the story could be sequenced following on from each of these openings.

a   She walked through the blinding rain towards the huddled form.
b   'Well, if you're not happy you know what you can do!' she cried. He turned and walked away.
c   The knife sank deep into his side. His assailant fled into the dark night.

INVESTIGATE STORY OPENINGS

A good story opening will attract the reader's attention and make them want to read on. You can use a range of techniques to achieve this.

 Watch a video about creating effective story openings and endings on Cambridge Elevate.

ACTIVITY 2

Read Sources A to C - a selection of story openings. Then work with another student to answer the questions that follow each one.

Source A

One day some new kids at school were helping the janitor clean up down in the basement where the huge steam heating system was located. They went further and further back into the dark recesses of the basement and found a dusty door that looked like it hadn't been opened in years.

From 'The Skeleton in the Closet'
by Richard and Judy Dockrey Young

1 Source A begins the story in a similar way to the 'Once upon a time …' of many children's stories. The two sentences focus on the setting of the story.

   a Where do you think the story is going to lead?
   b Which details provide the evidence for your answer?

Source B

'I think I **knew** his father,' said my uncle. 'Was he in India during the war?'

I said, 'I've really no idea. I don't know Mark all that well. I only mentioned him because I…'

'That'll be him,' said my uncle, with furrowed brow. 'He was in Calcutta in '43. Man with a limp. Played the trombone. Waiter! Could we have the menu?'

From 'Servants Talk About People'
in Pack of Cards by Penelope Lively

 S1 knew: find out more about the silent 'k' in Unit 26.

2 Source B begins the story in the middle of a conversation.

   a What will the reader want to find out following this brief opening?
   b What can you tell about the uncle from what he says and how he says it?

Source C

The interior of St James's Church, in Havenpool Town, was slowly darkening under the close clouds of a winter afternoon. It was Sunday; service had just ended, the face of the parson in the pulpit was buried in his hands,   5 and the congregation, with a cheerful sigh of release, were rising from their knees to depart.

For the moment the stillness was so complete that the surging of the sea could be heard outside the harbour-bar. Then it was broken   10 by the footsteps of the clerk going towards the west door to open it in the usual manner for the exit of the assembly. Before, however, he had reached the doorway, the latch was lifted from without, and the dark figure of a man in   15 a sailor's garb appeared against the light.

From 'To Please His Wife' in Life's Little Ironies
by Thomas Hardy

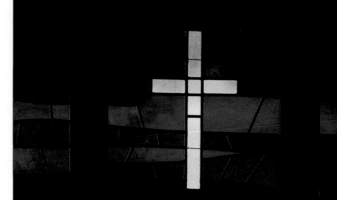

3 Source C begins the story with a setting - a description of the ending of a church service.

   a What contrasts does the writer focus on in the two short paragraphs?

   b How does the writer make the character introduced at the end seem important?

4 Look back at the notes you have made in answer to Questions 1 to 4. List some of the techniques you could use to attract the attention of your readers at the beginning of a story to make them want read on.

ACTIVITY 3

1 Now work on your own. Experiment with writing story openings, using some of the techniques you have identified.

   a Write an opening of only two or three sentences, beginning with a simple 'One day …'. You should introduce something that your reader will want to find out more about.

   b Write an opening that begins in the middle of a conversation. It should be four or five lines long and give your reader some impression of the character of at least one of the speakers.

   c Write two short paragraphs. In the first, describe a setting. In the second, develop that setting but introduce a character who will strike the reader as being significant.

2 Swap your story openings with those of another student. Give each other feedback on:

   a which of the three openings made you want to read on

   b the reasons why

   c any improvements you think could be made.

ACTIVITY 4

Some stories begin in a way that makes the reader want to find out not only what is going to happen next, but also what has led up to the events being described. Read Source D, a longer story opening.

Source D

When Clara Tilling was fifteen and a half she took off all her clothes one morning in school assembly. She walked naked through the lines of girls, past the headmistress at her lectern and the other staff ranged behind her, and out into the entrance lobby. She had   5 left off her bra and pants already, so that all she had to do was unbutton her blouse, remove it and drop it to the floor, and then undo the zipper of her skirt and let that fall. She slipped her feet out of her shoes at the same time and so walked barefoot as well as naked.   10 It all happened very quickly. One or two people giggled and a sort of rustling noise ran through the assembly hall, like a sudden wind among trees. The Head hesitated for a moment – she was reading out the tennis team list – and then went on again, firmly.   15 Clara opened the big glass doors and let herself out.

From 'Clara's Day' in *Pack of Cards* by Penelope Lively

1 The writer describes what is obviously an unusual and shocking event. What can you tell about the narrator's attitude towards the event by the language used to describe it?

2 We are told what Clara did and how she did it.

   a What are we not told?
   b What is the storyteller withholding from the reader?

3 There is only one sentence devoted to the Head. What impression does the narrator give of her?

4 What might have led up to this event?

5 What might follow it to finish the story?

INVESTIGATE STORY ENDINGS

Some stories conclude with a twist – a surprise. Stories that lead up to a surprise need to be structured so that they present the reader with some clues to help them understand the twist at the end. Read Source E, which is a short story.

 Explore some one-word stories on Cambridge Elevate.

Source E

'It's a boy!'

Lifting the child to her breast, she cannot help herself; she remembers.

The candles had flickered, casting broken shadows on the dim walls. Outside, angry black clouds scudded 5 across a steel grey sky. The dark regiments of trees that covered the hillside behind the house were whipped this way and that by a fierce wind. It spat raindrops. The branches of the apple tree slapped hard against the glass of the window to the side of 10 her bed.

'At least think about it,' he had said. 'It's just not possible. We can't afford to keep a child. It doesn't hurt – the doctor has told me …'

She hasn't seen him since that night. Hasn't wanted 15 to see him.

And now. She gazes dreamily down into her baby's eyes – her beautiful child. She will love him and care for him and he will grow into a loving, caring young man. 20

'And what name have you decided on Mrs Newton?'

'Isaac.'

There is a twist at the end of the story, and it is completely imaginary - a fiction made up by the writer. The twist is that the great scientist Isaac Newton might never have been born as his father wanted his mother to terminate the pregnancy.

ACTIVITY 5

1 The story in Source E begins in the present. Identify by line number the points at which it:

   a moves back into the past
   b return to the present.

2 What does the paragraph of description (the third paragraph) add to the story?

3 Write your own short story which begins in the present, moves back in time and then returns to the present. Here is one possible idea, but you could develop your own:

A character is looking in a mirror. Something triggers a memory – a scar? An item of jewellery? The absence of a reflection? The character remembers something before the story returns briefly to the point when it began.

---

4 Read the short stories written by two or three other students in your class. Comment on:

   a how well they have managed the move from present to past and back again
   b their use of descriptive detail to engage you as the reader.

CREATE CHARACTERS

You can use different techniques to create and develop characters. You can describe them and make them behave and talk in particular ways to give your reader an impression of what they are like. Remember that your readers do not need a detailed description of every feature of a character. Focus on features that are significant to your story. It does not really matter what coloured hair a character has unless that colour says something important – vivid purple-dyed hair, for example, might suggest something significant about a character.

ACTIVITY 6

Watch a video about creating characters on Cambridge Elevate.

Read Source F, a description of a character from the beginning of a novel.

Source F

He looked like someone who had seen or known great suffering and hadn't been able to forget it. His large eyes in his large head stuck out further than anyone else's – like they wanted to leave the surface of his face. They made you think of someone who can't get out of the house quickly enough.

Pop Eye wore the same white linen suit every day. His trousers sagged on his bony knees in the sloppy heat. Some days he wore a clown's nose. His nose was already big. He didn't need that red light bulb. But for reasons we couldn't think of he wore the red nose on certain days that may have meant something to him. We never saw him smile. And on those days he wore the clown's nose you found yourself looking away because you never saw such sadness.

From *Mr Pip* by Lloyd Jones

1 The first paragraph of Source F focuses on the character's eyes. The reader is told that they are 'large', but how does the writer use the description of the eyes to tell us something more important about the character?

2 The first two sentences of the second paragraph focus on the character's clothes. What impressions of the character are given by the description of his suit?

3 In the final six sentences, the writer introduces one unusual feature of the character's appearance – the clown's nose. What impressions of the character do you get from this focus on the clown's nose?

4 Attempt your own version of this kind of writing, in which a small number of physical features are described to create an interesting character. Base your description on a relative and think about the following:

a the important aspect of their personality you would like to draw out
b two physical features that you could focus on.

Aim to write two paragraphs, with each paragraph focused on a different feature. Begin your first paragraph with: 'S/he looked like someone who …'.

5 Swap your writing with that of another student. Give each other feedback on:

a how interesting the characters you have created are
b whether you can see any similar techniques used in the passage about Pop Eye.

ACTIVITY 7

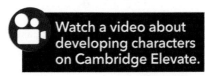

Watch a video about developing characters on Cambridge Elevate.

The ways in which a character talks and behaves can also be used to engage a reader. Writers are often advised to 'show, don't tell'. This means it is best to describe actions and leave the reader to make up their own mind about what these show.

In Source G, a group of Caribbean servicemen are stationed in Yorkshire during the Second World War. They visit a village where the locals have no experience of people of a different colour. The narrator is one of the Caribbean servicemen.

1 What can you infer about the character of the 'middle-aged man' from the things he does?

2 The writer does not tell the reader exactly how the middle-aged man speaks, but we are told he is staring at the young white woman as he speaks his first sentence. What is the writer implying about the middle-aged man's question and his attitude as he asks it?

Source G

A middle-aged man, not in uniform, kept his hands resolutely in his pockets before addressing me. Eyeing intently the young woman, who was by now getting on very nicely with a lucky Fulton – consorting with him as we had been   5
assured no white woman would – this man, not looking on my face as he spoke, asked me, "Why would you leave a nice sunny place to come here if you didn't have to?"

When I said, "To fight for my country, sir," his   10
eyebrows jumped like two caterpillars in a polka.

"Humph. Your country?" he asked without need of an answer. He then took the young woman's arm, guiding her, reluctant as she was, away from Fulton and our group.   15

From Small Island by Andrea Levy

3 Explain how the middle-aged man says 'Humph. Your country?' How do you know how he says these words?

4 When the serviceman answers his question, the narrator describes the middle-aged man's reaction with a simile: 'his eyebrows jumped like two caterpillars in a polka.' What does this description suggest about:

a the middle-aged man's feelings?
b the attitude of the narrator towards the man and the situation?

5 Attempt your own version of this kind of use of action and dialogue to create an impression of a character. Imagine a situation in which there is some kind of confrontation between a figure of authority (a teacher, a police officer, a parent, a ticket inspector or similar) and a young person. Decide:

a from which character's point of view you will relate the incident
b on whose side you want the reader's sympathies to lie
c a few obvious features of the characters (such as age, gender, physical appearance).

When you have a few ideas about these in mind, write a short piece of about 100 words. Use only small amounts of dialogue.

6 Swap your writing with that of another student. Give feedback to each other on:

a what you have 'shown' about your characters
b any similarity of techniques to those in Source G.

 Watch a video about creating credible dialogue on Cambridge Elevate.

 Look at creating credible characters on Cambridge Elevate.

 Generate creative character descriptions on Cambridge Elevate.

STRUCTURE DIALOGUE

Too much dialogue in your narrative writing can limit your chances to show how well you can craft vocabulary for a range of effects. However, dialogue can help break up passages of description and action, and create interesting characters. It is important to learn a variety of ways of presenting dialogue.

ACTIVITY 8

1 Work with another student. Read the following extract. For each use of 'said', make a list of three synonyms that could be used instead – for example the first 'said' could be replaced with 'whispered'.

Mark followed Amir into the alley.

'Are you sure about this?' he said.

'Shut up,' Amir said.

'But …,' Mark said.

'Ssh!' Amir said.

'This is mad,' Mark said.

'Well go home!' Amir said.

2 When writing a dialogue, you do not always need to say who is speaking. Each new paragraph indicates a change in speaker. It does, however, help the reader to track the conversation if you indicate the speaker by name every so often.

Read the extract again and decide where it helps to know or be reminded who the speaker is. Rewrite the dialogue by:

a   removing unnecessary references to the speaker.

b   using synonyms for 'said' where the references are helpful.

ADD DETAIL TO DIALOGUE

As well as avoiding over-use of 'said', you can make your dialogue more interesting by adding descriptive detail.

ACTIVITY 9

Read Source H, then answer the questions that follow.

1 Each time, before Mr Pope speaks, the reader is given some information about his actions and behaviour.

a   How do these descriptions affect the way you respond to his words?

b   What kind of a character is Mr Pope?

2 What does the small descriptive detail 'Nigel sniffed' add to your understanding of how Nigel said 'Yes, please'?

3 Write four or five more paragraphs to continue the extract in Source H. Focus on using small amounts of dialogue interspersed with descriptions of the characters' actions and behaviour.

4 Read through your paragraphs. Use one colour to underline your dialogue and another to underline any descriptive detail you have given.

Source H

Mr Pope opened the bedroom door. Nigel rubbed his eyes on the sleeves of his pyjamas but Mr Pope took no notice of the boy's pathetic state. 'Your mother tells me you want a story,' he announced. Then he closed the door behind him.   5

Nigel sniffed. 'Yes, please,' he said.

Mr Pope smiled slowly. Everything he did was very

slow – stirring his tea, filling his pipe, pushing the lawnmower. 'I'm glad about that,' he said. 'Because I've been thinking for a long time about a story I'd   10
like to tell you.'

'You could have told me in the garden,' said Nigel.

Mr Pope shook his head. 'Oh, no,' he said. 'Oh dear, no. This is a bedtime story. I've had it saved up. Sooner or later, I thought, his Aunty Betty will   15
be ill. Then they'll ask me to baby-sit. I've offered enough times.'

He brought a chair to Nigel's bedside and sat down, his scarred hands spread on his knees. Nigel stared up at him, **fascinated** and slightly afraid.   20

From 'The Baby-sitter' by Alison Prince

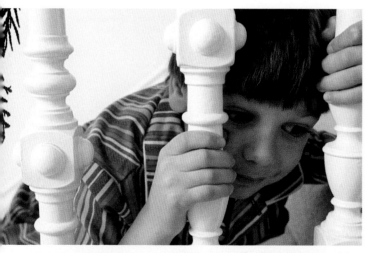

 S2 fascinated: find out more about the letter sequence 'sc' in Unit 26.

CREATE SETTING

The setting of a story is linked with the place, the time and things like the weather. Setting a story well means more than simply giving the readers information. Settings can also create atmosphere.

 Watch a video about creating setting on Cambridge Elevate.

ACTIVITY 10

Read this extract, setting the scene in a novel.

It was Sunday afternoon. The resting horses nibbled the remaining wisps of hay, and they stamped their feet and they bit the wood of the mangers and rattled the halter chains. The afternoon sun sliced in through the cracks of the barn walls and lay in bright lines on the hay. There was the buzz of flies in the air, the lazy afternoon humming.

From outside came the clang of horseshoes on the playing peg and the shouts of men, playing, encouraging, jeering. But in the barn it was quiet and humming and lazy and warm.

From *Of Mice and Men* by John Steinbeck

1 What kind of atmosphere does the phrase 'Sunday afternoon' usually convey?

2 What words does the writer use to create the quiet, peaceful atmosphere in the barn?

3 How does the writer use contrast to emphasise this peacefulness?

4 Although there is a largely peaceful atmosphere in the barn, are there any details that might make a reader infer something different about the atmosphere?

5 Now try to write your own short version of this kind of scene-setting, in which a strong atmosphere is created.

   a Write two short paragraphs in which you create a setting in a town centre on a Saturday night.
   b Try to establish an atmosphere that is lively and happy but in which there is also a hint of possible trouble or danger.
   c Begin your piece: 'It was Saturday night.'

ACTIVITY 11

Read one student's opening to the story based on the following task. Discuss your impressions of it with another student, using the questions as a guide.

Write the opening part of a story about an important meeting.

An important meeting

'You'll be fine. Stop worrying. Give us a twirl.'

He grimaced, running his finger under the too-tight, too-stiff collar of his too-white shirt. 'I'm off.'

'Got your phone?'

'Mum!'

'Just checking. Good luck.'

The bus was strangely on time. He sat upstairs near the back by a window, feeling out of place in his suit. The bus stopped outside the Red Lion, a huge brick-built pub with windows boarded up, the boards covered in graffiti. A grubby 'For Sale' sign lay on the ground by the door. A grey figure limped across the car park, stick in one hand and dog leash in the other. The dog at the end of the leash, an old, stiff-legged Labrador, padded painfully behind. Two lads he vaguely recognised from school were aimlessly scuffing the heels of their trainers against the rust-red brick of the pub wall.

His attention was drawn to the girl who, having boarded, was swaying down the aisle of the now-moving bus. The girl, dressed in blue faded jeans and a white tee shirt, gave him a quick nod of recognition before sitting down next to another girl. She bent close to her friend's ear and the friend turned round, giving him a quick once-over look before turning back. They giggled and he shifted uncomfortably.

The building was only a short walk from the bus stop. It stretched several storeys above the adjacent blocks, its gleaming blue windows reflecting the surroundings as clearly as the screen on an expensive laptop. The gleaming stainless steel and smoked glass revolving door spun silently as a young woman in a dark blue suit, a tan leather briefcase in one hand, emerged and with her free hand signalled for a taxi. As though, it occurred to him, it was nothing. He took a deep breath, ran a clammy hand through his hair and pushed the still-swinging door.

1 There is one main character.

    a   What characteristics does he have?
    b   What details reveal these characteristics?

2 How effective is the opening dialogue? How much like real speech is it?

3 There are two main settings – the view from the bus and the office building.

    a   How have they been contrasted?
    b   What is the writer's purpose in contrasting them?

4 Write a detailed comment for this student, focusing on what they have done well. At the end, offer some advice on how the writing could be improved.

PROGRESS PUNCTUATION

It is important to punctuate dialogue correctly in your writing.

1 Copy the following section of dialogue onto a piece of paper. Annotate it with suggestions about the following:

    a   placing punctuation
    b   the reasons for starting a new paragraph.

Nigel sniffed. 'Yes, please,' he said.

Mr Pope smiled slowly. Everything he did was very slow – stirring his tea, filling his pipe, pushing the lawnmower. 'I'm glad about that,' he said. 'Because I've been thinking for a long time about a story I'd like to tell you.'

'You could have told me in the garden,' said Nigel.

From 'The Baby-sitter' by Alison Prince

2 Write a set of rules instructing Year 7 students on how to punctuate dialogue correctly.

Complete this assignment on Cambridge Elevate.

Assess your progress

In this unit you have learnt to:

- write story openings and endings
- create characters
- structure dialogue
- describe setting and atmosphere.

1 Write a story suggested to you by this photograph.

Before you start writing, think about how you could:

a begin in a way that will engage a reader

b structure your story to reach a conclusion

c describe setting and atmosphere

d introduce and describe any characters.

2 When you have finished, read through your story and improve it if you can.

3 Ask your teacher or another student for feedback on:

✔ the effectiveness of your opening

✔ how well you have structured your story and guided your reader

✔ how well you have used effective detail to describe setting and atmosphere

✔ how well you have made you characters interesting for the reader.

FURTHER PROGRESS

Stories can be shaped in a variety of imaginative ways. Read the following opening to a short story.

The bank robber told his story in little notes to the bank teller. He held the pistol in one hand and gave her the notes with the other. The first note said: ... .

From 'The Bank Robbery' by Steven Schutzman

1 This opening suggests that what follows will be structured around a series of notes.

a What kind of 'back story' will the notes build into? What has led this man to the desperate act of robbing a bank?

b The only other character mentioned in the opening is the bank cashier. She will read the notes. How will she respond to them?

c How might this develop into an unusual story about two people rather than an all-action piece of crime writing?

2 Now continue the story.

WRITING
Unit 24
Present your views

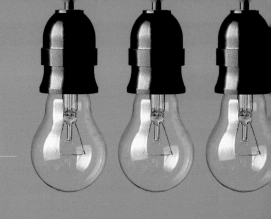

Make progress AO5 AO6
- generate and select ideas
- use discourse markers fluently
- make effective links within and between paragraphs
- vary tone for effect
- structure a balanced argument.

USE YOUR SKILLS

When asked to present your views on a topic you have not thought about before, it is particularly important to generate ideas before starting to write. Having a range of ideas to draw from means that you will not run out of things to say half way through your writing.

ACTIVITY 1

1 Work in small groups. Discuss the following statement and, on a large piece of paper, list ideas you could use to show whether you agree or disagree with it.

Today's young people are the best ever!

You could consider:

a the attitude of young people towards their friends, parents and teachers
b the work ethic of young people in their studies and part-time jobs
c the contributions they make to the wider community in volunteering
d their sporting and creative achievements
e previous generations of young people and the challenges they faced.

2 Think of facts, examples and anecdotes you could use to support some of your ideas. Add these to your list.

3 Share your ideas with another group of students. Add any further suggestions that you think are useful.

LINK IDEAS FLUENTLY

When writing a paragraph, it is important to link ideas so that readers can follow your meaning from one sentence to the next. As discussed in Unit 20, ideas can be linked though the use of discourse markers. These are structural features that help to shape texts. Discourse markers can be used to:

- make links with what has gone before: 'previously'
- make links with what is to come next: 'for example'
- add information: 'moreover', 'furthermore'
- compare or contrast ideas: 'similarly', 'whereas'
- signal an opinion: 'unfortunately'
- emphasise ideas: 'importantly', 'significantly', 'unquestionably'
- conclude: 'to summarise', 'in conclusion'.

You should aim to use a range of discourse markers and integrate them in your work. The very best students integrate them seamlessly so that the discourse markers do not interrupt the flow of the text.

187

ACTIVITY 2

Look at this student response to the question:

Relatives, not friends, have the most influence in our lives. How far do you agree?

Student A <u>In my opinion</u>, relatives have the most influence on our lives and how we choose to live them. I have many reasons for believing this. <u>Firstly</u>, they are the people with whom we had the closest contact in our youngest and most formative years. We relied on them to find out about the world. For example, they taught us the difference between good and bad and how to treat others with respect. Also they showed us how to use our free time sensibly. Furthermore, many young people are interested in sport. Of course this interest is often generated by parents taking children to their first football match or swimming lesson. In addition you need to consider the influence of the relatives in your wider family circle, such as cousins and uncles and aunts.

1 The discourse markers in the first three sentences are underlined. List the discourse markers used in the rest of the paragraph, then compare your list with that of another student.

2 Now read a different student response to the same question. It contains similar ideas but uses discourse markers differently. Identify the discourse markers and note:

  a their position in the sentence
  b the reasons for their use.

Student B The statement that relatives have more influence in our lives than friends is true, but only to a certain extent. Your relatives influence you at home, while your friends influence you when your relatives are not around. Undoubtedly parents are more influential in the early years of their children's lives. Babies and young children rely on their parents for food and shelter. They also rely on them for learning how to talk and to tell the difference between right and wrong. When children go to school, however, they come into contact with other children who may have different sets of values to the ones they are accustomed to.

ABC XYZ **S1 influential:** find out more about the word endings '-tial' and '-cial' in Unit 26.

3 Compare the use of discourse markers in the two student responses. Which student do you think uses discourse markers most fluently?

4 Look back at your ideas on the statement 'Today's young people are the best ever' in Activity 1. Write one paragraph that could be included in an essay discussing this statement.

Remember to:

a link your ideas using a range of discourse markers

b think about where best to position your discourse markers.

5 Annotate your work to show:

a where you have used discourse markers

b the purpose of each discourse marker you have used.

LINK PARAGRAPHS FLUENTLY

You have already learnt that your paragraphs should be linked in a logical way to enable readers to trace the development of ideas throughout your text.

ACTIVITY 3

Read Source A, an article about traffic problems.

1 Answer the following questions to work out how the writer has connected ideas:

a What is the topic of paragraph 1?

b What does the writer reveal about their attitude in paragraph 1?

c How do the words in the opening sentence of paragraph 2 link back to ideas in paragraph 1?

d What new idea is introduced in paragraph 2? How does this idea link back to the topic of paragraph 1?

e What key word appears in paragraph 3 as well as the two preceding paragraphs?

f What link can be made between the final line of paragraph 3 and the title of the article?

2 Look again at the whole text and identify the writer's fluent use of discursive markers.

Source A

Travel doesn't need to cost the earth

What is the worst part of your day? Is it your journey to school or to work? This is an ever-increasing nightmare for most of us. Travelling in the rush hour is exhausting, time-consuming and most of all 5 expensive! The problem, of course, is the traffic. It causes pollution and slows everything down. Traffic on Britain's roads has more than doubled in the past 25 years and nowhere is this more obvious than in our towns and cities during the rush hour. 10

Surely there is a solution to this misery? One town appears to have found it. Hasselt suffered from one of the largest congestion problems in Belgium. This was, however, eliminated with the introduction of free transport into and around the town. In contrast 15 to British towns, the priority in Hasselt was not traffic, but people. Following the introduction of free transport, people reported feeling happier and less stressed.

Public transport in this country is infrequent and 20 unreliable, leading to many of us avoiding it. Free, frequent public transport would guarantee us all our right to mobility —schoolchildren, workers, the disabled, the unemployed, families and young people. Additionally, there would be a decrease in risks to 25 health and traffic chaos would be eliminated. Free public transport would also deliver a dramatic reduction in vehicle emissions which are, inevitably, directly related to the ever-present threat of global warming.

ACTIVITY 4

1 You are going to write three paragraphs giving your views on the following statement:

Public transport should be free for all people under the age of 19.

Before you write:

a   generate a range of ideas and plan your paragraphs
b   think about how you are going to link ideas within and between your paragraphs
c   think of a good title for your writing and how to link your final sentence with it.

Now write your paragraphs

2 Swap your paragraphs with another student. Comment on whether the other student has:

a   effectively developed their views on the topic
b   fluently connected ideas within and between paragraphs
c   linked their final point to the title.

WRITE EFFECTIVE OPENINGS AND ENDINGS

The opening of a text is an important structural feature. In Source A, the writer engages readers by addressing them directly with a question. When you write, aim to engage your reader straight away.

There are many ways in which you can write an opening. You could:

* state your opinion clearly in a way designed to provoke discussion
* offer a balanced opinion on a topic
* give an illustration, referring to specific details
* address your reader directly
* ask a question
* provide an anecdote.

 Watch a video about effective openings and endings in persuasive writing on Cambridge Elevate.

ACTIVITY 5

Below are five openings to essays written by students discussing the advantages and disadvantages of providing free driving lessons in school for Year 11 students. They were writing for students their age.

Student A In my opinion every school student should have the right to driving lessons.

Student B Free driving lessons for 16-year-olds? What a ridiculous idea!

Student C Do you want to learn how to drive before you leave school? I most certainly do!

Student D It's a cold wet night in November and I'm standing alone at a bus stop on an isolated country lane.

Student E In Alaska, young people can apply for a learner's instruction permit from the age of 14 and a half.

1 Rank the openings, with the one you think will most effectively grab the reader's attention first.

2 Share your order with another student. Discuss your choices and the reasons for any differences in your selected orders.

3 Look again at the writing you produced for Activity 4. To broaden your skills in creating effective openings, write three alternative openings to this piece. Tick the one you think is most likely to engage your readers.

CREATE EFFECTIVE ENDINGS

An effective ending is also an important structural feature in a text. It forms the last impression your reader has of your writing. Here are some ideas for finishing your writing effectively:

- Address your readers directly by using a question: 'So now you know where I stand on this issue, how about you?'
- Encourage your readers to share your opinion: 'As sensible people, I know you'll all agree with me when I say …'.
- Make a link with your opening sentence or title.

- Repeat your main idea for emphasis: 'Clearly parents, teachers and students will agree that providing driving lessons for Year 11 students is in everyone's best interest.'
- Use language emotively to appeal to your readers' feelings: 'It's now time for this appalling injustice to end.'
- Vary your sentence structure so that a long and detailed sentence is followed by a short one: 'It's got to stop!'

ACTIVITY 6

1 Look again at the writing you produced for Activity 4. Write two or three alternative endings. Decide which one best suits your piece.

USE TONE FOR EFFECT

Writers sometimes adopt a particular tone in order to get across their views to their readers. Tone can be a very effective weapon in a writer's toolkit.

Read Source B, a letter written by a 16-year-old girl to the editor of *The Times* newspaper. In it, she responds to an article about recent research that suggested that teenagers are not responsible for their mood swings.

Source B

Sir, I am getting **increasingly** annoyed at the barrage of articles about teenagers, and the adults who keep trying to explain our behaviour. ("Moods and Meltdown: What's inside the teenage brain?" March 1st)

I am 16 and a straight-A student, like most of my friends. We are not as irrational and immature as adults seem to think. We've grown up with financial crises and accept that most of us will be unemployed. We no longer flinch at bloody images of war because we've grown up seeing the chaos in the Middle East and elsewhere. Most of us are cynical, and pessimistic because of the environment we've grown up in – which should be explanation enough for our apparent insolence and disrespect, without "experts" having to write articles about it. 15

Has no one ever seen that we are angry at the world we live in? Angry that we will have to clean up your mess, while you hold us in contempt, analysing our responses as though we were another species?

I would like adults to treat us not as strange creatures from another world but as human beings with intelligent thought – a little different from yours, perhaps, but intelligent thought nonetheless. 20

Stop teaching adults how to behave around us, and instead teach them to respect us. 25

Jenni Herd, Kilmarnock, E. Ayrshire

From a letter first published in *The Times*

 S2 increasingly: find out more about prefixes such as 'in-' in Unit 26.

ACTIVITY 7

1 In small groups, discuss your response to Source B with other students.

2 Now work in pairs. Select three words from the box that you think best reflect the tone of the letter. Find an example from the letter to support each of your choices.

polite	passionate	provocative
angry	sad	sarcastic
restrained	aggressive	

3 Jenni Herd's letter is organised into five paragraphs. Identify what each paragraph is about and explain how each one develops and strengthens her argument.

4 Tone is created through:

- the choice of content
- the words and techniques the writer chooses.

To work out how the tone of the letter has been achieved, copy and complete the following table. Give an example of each technique and comment on the effect it has on the reader.

Technique	Example	Effect
selection of detail familiar to the audience	'We've grown up seeing the chaos in the Middle East'	Makes readers think about whether or not they are living in a stable world. It is as if the writer is accusing adults of causing the chaos.
repetition		
addresses audience directly		
rhetorical question		
use of contrast		
vocabulary used emotively		
use of first person plural pronoun 'we'		
punctuation: use of dash		

5 Now work on your own. Write a letter to the editor of *The Times*, explaining why young people have a basic right to be listened to. Follow these steps:

a Gather your ideas and plan your paragraphs.

b Decide on the tone of your letter.

c Use some of the techniques outlined in this section to help create tone.

d Annotate the techniques you have used and their intended effect on your readers.

ACHIEVE STRUCTURE AND BALANCE

Jenni Herd presents a coherent and passionate argument. She writes in the first person and the focus is on her personal viewpoint. A subject can, however, be considered in a more balanced way, where different viewpoints are shown through argument and counter-argument.

Read the opening paragraphs of an article written after research showed that the best place to bring up children was a small village in Devon. The annotations show you how the text has been structured.

Source C

Should we move to the country?

Every parent wants the best for their children, but should that involve moving to the country if you live in a city?

[introduces topic for discussion]

The fact is that both town and country living have benefits for children. No one can deny that the air in the country is cleaner and that there is less pollution. 5 Country dwellers argue that the green space and sense of

[makes first point in favour of one side of the argument]

freedom their children enjoy is an undoubted advantage of living in the country. However, there 10 are many green spaces in towns and cities in the form of parks. Parents who live in cities make a conscious decision to take their children to parks where they can 15 enjoy the same sense of freedom as children who live in the country. It could be argued that a visit to the park as a treat makes children more appreciative of 20 green spaces – more appreciative in fact than their counterparts in the country who probably take this for granted.

[discourse marker used to introduce counter-argument]

[impartial tone, does not express an opinion]

193

ACTIVITY 8

Now read Source D, the rest of the article (paragraphs 3, 4 and 5).

1 Look at paragraph 3.

   a What argument is made in favour of life in the country?

   b How is this counter-argued?

   c What word is used to introduce the counter-argument?

2 Look at paragraph 4.

   a What argument is made in favour of life in the city in paragraph 4?

   b How is this counter-argued?

   c What word is used to introduce the counter-argument?

3 Look at paragraph 5.

   a In what way does the final paragraph act as a summary?

   b What is the effect of the final sentence?

Source D

In these days of fast food and take-aways it must surely be an advantage for a country child not to have instant access to this unhealthy form of food. Country children know exactly where their food comes from; they have seen it 5 growing or have seen animals going to slaughter. What could be healthier? Nevertheless, parents seeking out a healthy diet for their children can do this in a city almost as easily as in the country, as supermarkets and local markets offer a great 10 range of fresh produce.

Town and city dwellers frequently boast about the wealth of sporting activities available to their children from watching live sports fixtures to a wide array of sports clubs. 15

Country children, on the other hand, can test their sense of adventure and desire for challenges by exploring the countryside around them.

So really there are no clear-cut arguments in 20 favour of town or country. Both have their advantages; both have their drawbacks. In the end it comes down to what suits individual families. It's your choice.

4 What words would you use to describe the tone of this article? Support your choices with reference to the article.

PLAN FOR BALANCE

To write a balanced discussion or argument, you need to consider different viewpoints. This requires careful planning. Look at the following plan written by a student preparing to answer this examination question:

'Celebrity culture is a threat to young people's ambition and independence.' To what extent do you agree?

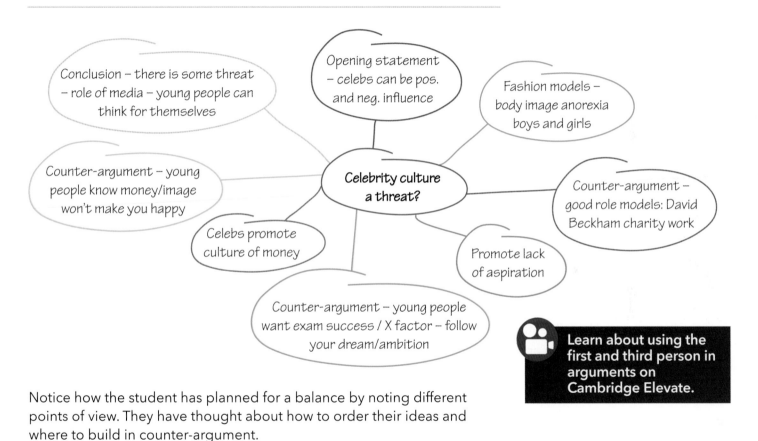

Notice how the student has planned for a balance by noting different points of view. They have thought about how to order their ideas and where to build in counter-argument.

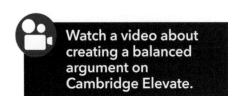

Learn about using the first and third person in arguments on **Cambridge Elevate.**

ACTIVITY 9

1 Write a plan for a structured and balanced piece of discursive writing on the task below. Your audience is other students, teachers and parents.

'Sport is as important as science in education.' To what extent do you agree? Write an article for your school magazine, newsletter or website explaining your views.

2 Work with another student. Talk through your plans. Ask questions and make suggestions for improvement.

Watch a video about creating a balanced argument on **Cambridge Elevate.**

PROGRESS PUNCTUATION

The semi-colon can be used to take the place of a full stop between sentences that are closely linked in meaning. In Source D, the writer uses two semi-colons:

* Country children know exactly where their food comes from; they have seen it growing or have seen animals going to slaughter.
* Both have their advantages; both have their drawbacks.

1 Explain why the use of the semicolon is appropriate in each of the above sentences.

2 The semicolon can also be used to separate items in a list, when the items are too long to be separated by commas. Rewrite the following sentence, adding semicolons as appropriate.

The twins have varied interests: playing games on the internet until the early hours of the morning preparing complex and delicious Mexican dishes using subtle herbs and spices participating in adventure sports such as abseiling and windsurfing.

Assess your progress

In this unit you have learnt to:
* use discourse markers fluently
* make effective links within and between paragraphs
* use tone to influence readers
* plan a balanced argument.

1 Use the plan you produced in Activity 9 to help you write a structured and balanced response to this task:

'Sport is as important as science in education.' To what extent do you agree? Write an article for your school magazine, newsletter or website explaining your views.

2 Ask your teacher or another student for feedback on how well you have:
✔ considered different points of view, using argument and counter-argument
✔ integrated discourse markers and fluently link paragraphs
✔ adopted an impartial tone for a balanced response.

Complete this assignment on Cambridge Elevate.

FURTHER PROGRESS

You write to suit your purpose and audience. These two factors have a direct impact on what you say and how you say it.

1 Think about the following tasks:

a Write a letter to a friend arguing that they should/should not try to go to university.

b Write a letter to your headteacher proposing that the school day should be altered in light of recent research suggesting that young people need more sleep if they are to perform at their best.

What advice would you give a Year 10 student beginning their GCSE English Language course on how to successfully complete each of these tasks?

WRITING
Unit 25
Craft your writing

USE YOUR SKILLS

If you are aiming for the highest grades, you need to show the very best of your writing skills.

In Units 16 to 24 you have developed the skills of writing on which you will be assessed in your English Language exam. But there are still things you can do to make your writing even better.

ACTIVITY 1

Read the opening paragraphs from two students' exam responses. Both students have done well. They were answering this question:

Too many adults put down the teenagers of today. Discuss.

Student A When adults and teachers think of teenagers, I know they think of bad things; Argumentative, moody, selfish and inconsiderate. Well, although this may be true for a small percentage of teenagers, for most of us it is simply describing a stereotype. Most teenagers are not like this at all. Being a teenager, we are neither adults or children, it is a time of uncertainty of character and self, and a search for identity. Adults tend to treat us like children but then they expect us to act in society as polite adults! It is very confusing.

Student B When you look, what *do* you see? A degenerate youth lurking on a street corner, a waste of space, a threat or an insecure man-child, worried about spots and facial hair, expectant and hopeful for the future that lies ahead? How closely do you look? Is it through the eyes of the latest scandalous headline, through the blinkers of your adult self-righteousness, or through the eyes of a person who was once young and who still remembers what it felt like to be waiting on that street corner, waiting for his life to begin?

1 Read the range of comments used by teachers when assessing these students' writing. Decide which comments you would place with Student A and which with Student B.

a   *Generally accurate punctuation.*
b   *Tone manipulates audience.*
c   *Communication is compelling.*
d   *High-level punctuation.*
e   *Wide vocabulary range.*
f   *Fluent linking of sentence forms for effect.*
g   *High-level accuracy in spelling.*
h   *Communication is convincing.*
i   *Tone is matched to audience.*
j   *Sophisticated use of vocabulary.*
k   *Clear linking of sentence forms for effect.*

Did you work out that while Student A's writing is good, Student B's writing is even better?

WHAT YOU WILL BE ASSESSED ON

Your writing is assessed on two assessment objectives (AOs). AO5 is in two parts. The first relates to communication and the second to organisation. AO6 relates to technical skills.

AO5 (Part 1): Communication

You need to:

- communicate clearly, effectively and imaginatively
- select and adapt your tone, style and register for different forms, purposes and audiences.

Communicate imaginatively

One way you can improve your skills in communication is by studying the writing of published authors.

ACTIVITY 2

In Sources A and B, both writers use figurative language to convey their ideas to their readers.

Source A

Eve looked, but all she could see was thousands – *millions* – of golden dust motes drifting in the air as if disturbed by the warm rays from outside mingling with the cold draughts of the hall itself to generate lively breezes that carried glittering particles which wheeled and turned and dazzled like a galaxy of minute, shifting stars.

From *The Secret of Crickley Hall* by James Herbert

Source B

He picked his way gingerly between the graves like a man stepping through a pit of snakes. Yet the only serpents he feared to disturb were those from his own distant past, and surely they were fangless after all this time … .

From 'The Living and the Dead' in *The Desperadoes and Other Stories* by Stan Barstow

1 How does the writer of Source A use imagery to show the reader the beauty of the dust motes (specks)?

2 How does the writer of Source B use imagery to:

a   connect the present with the past
b   inform readers about the man's past?

3 Use language figuratively to create a vivid image of two of the following:

a the changing facial features of someone who has just heard some shocking news
b the way a toddler climbs a staircase
c the atmosphere in a playground just before a fight breaks out
d the moment when a thief steals something in a shop.

4 Share your images in small groups. Talk about what they suggest and how effective they are, then choose the best ones to share with the class.

Use tone to manipulate your reader

ACTIVITY 3

Read Source C, which contains two paragraphs that appear close together in a non-fiction book. In the first paragraph, the writer is discussing hen and stag parties in Blackpool. In the second paragraph, he is writing about the funfair – the Pleasure Beach – also in Blackpool.

1 Work with another student. The writer sustains his tone throughout the two paragraphs. Discuss which of the following words best describe the tone:

angry	sarcastic	cynical
cheerful	friendly	informal
formal	humorous	

2 Tone is created by the content (the things the writer chooses to include) and the words the writer uses. You have selected words to describe the tone. Support each of your choices by reference to the texts.

3 Writers use tone to manipulate their readers. Talk about how you respond to Stuart Maconie's tone. Does it make you more/less likely to agree with him? Why?

4 Now work on your own. Choose a place you know that has changed. Write a paragraph about the changes that have taken place. Use tone to manipulate your reader to agree with your attitude to these changes.

5 Swap your writing with that of another student. Comment on how well they have used tone to manipulate the reader.

Source C

Such nights are a real bone of contention in modern Blackpool. They bring in the dosh and the bar owners love them but there are many in the Blackpool Chamber of Commerce who pine for the good old 5 days when the town's clientele was decent working families who wanted nothing more than a shared TV room for Match of the Day and a choice of Britvic or Sugar Puffs at breakfast. When you've seen a blank-eyed 10 girl in a bridal outfit and L plates urinating in the street, you take their point.

The Pleasure Beach these days promises a more corporate, familial day out. Thanks to the metal detector, I never feel that a 15 Teddy Boy will razor me at any point. It's twenty-nine quid for a wristband that entitles you to ride the 145 attractions all day. If that's not enough, you can stay here at the 'chic, modern' Big Blue Hotel where 20 'each child's bunk bed has its own built-in TV to put an end to fighting for the remote control!' While the kids lie in bed watching TV, slack-jawed with exhaustion and doped on Slush Puppies, Mum and Dad can watch 25 Joe Longthorne do his 'amazingly accurate' vocal impressions at The Paradise Room.

From Pies and Prejudice
by Stuart Maconie

AO5 (Part 2): Organisation

You need to:

- develop, organise and structure your information and ideas
- make fluent links within and between paragraphs
- make effective use of structural and grammatical features.

Develop, organise and structure your information and ideas

The best way to make sure your writing is developed, organised and structured is through efficient planning. You are advised to spend about 45 minutes on your writing in an exam, which should also include four to five minutes for planning.

To plan efficiently, you need to:

- **Identify your form, purpose and audience**

  Form: A story? A description? A letter? An article?

  Purpose: To narrate? To describe? To argue? To discuss? To explain?

  Audience: Judges of a creative writing competition? Readers of a national newspaper? A Member of Parliament? Always your examiner!

- **Generate ideas**

  What are you going to write about? Gather a wide range of ideas from which to select.

- **Plan for paragraphs**

  Sort your ideas into a coherent order. Discard or add ideas as you sort. Plan for five coherent paragraphs, even though you may end up writing more.

ACTIVITY 4

1 You have five minutes. Think about the following task, then follow the three stages of planning to make your plan.

> **Town and city centres are no longer attracting families or adults over the age of 30 on weekend nights. Local councils are considering how to broaden their appeal. Write an article for publication in your local newspaper in which you explain your point of view and offer suggestions.**

2 Work in groups of three or four. Take it in turn to talk through your plans. Be prepared to ask and answer questions to vary and develop ideas.

3 Review your planning techniques. Make a note of ways you could plan more efficiently.

Make fluent links within and between paragraphs

Source D is a longer extract from Stuart Maconie's writing on Blackpool, including one of the paragraphs you read in Activity 3. The fluent links within and between paragraphs have been highlighted.

ACTIVITY 5

2 Look back at the plan you made for writing in Activity 4. Write your first two paragraphs. Aim to fluently link the ideas within and between the two paragraphs.

2 Highlight your writing to show how the ideas are linked.

Make effective use of structural features

Here are some structural features you can introduce into your writing. Which ones you choose will depend on what you are writing and what you want to achieve.

> Linked opening and ending
>
> Contrast
>
> Flash back
>
> Zooming in
>
> Panoramic view
>
> Use of a motif
>
> Intermittent focus on a person, animal or thing

Source D

Today Blackpool has more beds for rent than the whole of Portugal. There is, as the brochures have it, 'accommodation to suit every taste and pocket'. At the top end of the scale are the Paramounts and De Veres 5 with saunas, solariums, gym facilities and 'elegant dining'. At the other end, truer I think to the spirit of the town, are countless little family guest houses and B&Bs tucked down every side street where, and I quote 10 from one's literature, 'Your hosts, Daphne and Shane, guarantee your every comfort and the highest level of customer care. No Stag or Hen Nights.'

Such nights are a real bone of contention 15 in modern Blackpool. They bring in the dosh and the bar owners love them but there are many in the Blackpool Chamber of Commerce who pine for the good old days when the town's clientele was decent 20 working families who wanted nothing more than a shared TV room for *Match of the Day* and a choice of Britvic or Sugar Puffs at breakfast. When you've seen a blank-eyed girl in a bridal outfit and L plates urinating in the 25 street, you take their point.

From Pies and Prejudice by Stuart Maconie

ACTIVITY 6

1 Think about the plan you made for writing in Activity 4. Could you introduce an interesting structural feature to your writing? Perhaps you could make intermittent reference to the thoughts or experiences of:

a one particular family
b a visitor from abroad
c a person who works in a town or city on weekend nights.

2 Look again at the first paragraph you wrote in Activity 5. Rewrite it to include a focus that you can return to throughout your writing.

AO6 Technical Skills

You need to:

- use a range of vocabulary and sentence structures for clarity, purpose and effect
- use a range of sentence structures for clarity, purpose and effect
- spell accurately and punctuate effectively.

Use a range of vocabulary and sentence structures for clarity, purpose and effect

ACTIVITY 7

1 Write the third paragraph of the article you planned in Activity 4. Choose the best words to suit your meaning and show that you can control and vary your sentence structures.

2 Work in small groups. Read one another's paragraphs. Make suggestions for how the choice of words and range of sentence structures for effect could be improved.

Spell accurately and punctuate effectively

The best way to do well in spelling and punctuation in your exam is to:

- know in advance the kind of errors you frequently make
- allow time to read through, check and correct your writing.

ACTIVITY 8

1 Look back through the writing you have done so far this school year. Make a note of any errors you have made in spelling and punctuation. Highlight the errors which you make frequently. If you don't understand the errors, ask your teacher to explain them to you.

2 Look again at the three paragraphs you have written in this unit. Check them for accuracy in spelling and punctuation. Make corrections where needed.

 S1 spelling: find out more about spelling accurately in Unit 26.

CONSIDER EXAMPLES OF STUDENTS' HIGH-QUALITY WRITING

The best writing is convincing and compelling. This means that while reading it, you believe in what you read and want to read on. This does not mean that you cannot write a science-fiction story, for example. It just means that within the context of your story, your reader is convinced.

The following examples are extracts from two students' responses to the task:

Write either a story about or a description of a significant childhood memory.

The first extract is the opening of Student A's answer.

Student A Rather unusually, the most significant moment of my life is one I cannot remember. My story begins in a typical middle-class household, red brick, a menagerie of flowers blooming in a sudden surge to take advantage of the dying bursts of the sun, its final rays of light spreading out like entrails of a wounded soldier. For, you see, this is October, the boundary between the days of sun and the winter months.

A woman – my mother as it happens – sits in a bland living-room of beige furniture where flowery paintings hang inoffensive on the walls. She is watching Fiona Bruce, the lynchpin of the BBC news, and is unaware that in ten minutes I will awaken.

The minutes tick by and my mother gets up and gently walks into the kitchen to quell an insatiable urge for a snack, a morsel of food, anything to fill the seemingly gaping void in her stomach.

She feels faint and calls out as she rests heavily on the worktop. Her husband, a tall, bookish sort of man with the remnants of a failed moustache caught on his lip, immediately abandons his seat facing the television and rushes to support his spouse. She turns and forces out the sentence he was both anticipating and dreading:

'I think it's starting.'

The second extract is the ending of Student B's writing. Before this point, the student had described an idyllic country scene, with meadows of buttercups and daisies. He was walking with his mother and pet dog, Floppy, 'a gentle creature, like a sibling to me and as big as a Shetland pony'. The dog 'tumbled through the undergrowth, snorting loudly with every seed she caught in her damp nostrils' before running off.

Student B Then I heard a sound of unspeakable pain. Where was the dog? I ran to the fence and sighed with relief when I saw her. It was only when she turned that the horror of the scream returned.

An infant rabbit lay between her jaws, screaming. Its little legs kicked for all it was worth, clawing at her nose and eyes. My beloved pet stood motionless until, on seeing me and for fear I would steal her prize, she clamped her jaws together.

The crunch of bones made me scream at her to release the rabbit. I forced my way through the fence, the barbed wire fingers clawing at my skin. I held my dog's head and wrenched at her jaws, the warm animal between them still trembling. At last my mother appeared and pulled my dog away. Her great jaws opened, her tongue wet with brown fur, her teeth withdrawing from the helpless creatures flesh like knives from butter, and the rabbit fell still into my arms.

Behind me as I pulled away, my dog barked and barked, wagging her tail in excitement. My mother pulled her back but did not scold her. What could she do? My dog had acted out of instinct, unaware of her actions. It was too late, and the creature was dying in my arms.

There was a moment of clarity in its wild fear. This small creature, never before in contact with man, lay still. Its eyes bulged and its brown fur ran wet with red blood, hot on my fingers. I kept one arm on its back and the other on its white breast that pulsed with its dying breaths. I could feel myself begin to cry. I could stroke it but I could not take away its pain nor save its life.

On that spring day, so distant yet still so close to me, the rabbit shuddered its flanks, took a last breath and its fidgeting nose stopped snuffling. I lay its limp body onto the grass and cried, the perfect field of yellow and white now stained with crimson.

ACTIVITY 9

The students have chosen very different things to write about, but they both demonstrate high-level writing skills.

1 Work in small groups. For each extract, discuss and identify the qualities of the writing that you think have earned the student high marks. Make a note of these qualities.

2 On your own, decide what you could do to improve your writing. List your 'Aims for improvement'.

✔ Assess your progress

In this unit you have:

- considered the assessment objectives
- investigated the qualities of crafted writing.

Now it's time for you to put what you have learnt into practice.

1 Write **either** a story about **or** a description of a significant childhood memory. You have 45 minutes.

Before you write:

- Spend four to five minutes planning your writing. Think about content and structure.

When you write:

- Link your ideas fluently within and between paragraphs.
- Choose your words and sentence structures for maximum effect on your reader.

After you write:

- Read through what you have written. It helps to say each word aloud or in your head.
- Check that you have expressed your ideas effectively and that your spelling and punctuation is accurate.

2 Ask another student or your teacher for feedback on:

✔ how effectively you have expressed your ideas

✔ how accurate your spelling is

✔ how accurate your punctuation is.

✔ Complete this assignment on Cambridge Elevate.

FURTHER PROGRESS

You already know that extensive reading helps you to improve your own writing. A good way of developing and extending your ideas and the sophistication of your viewpoint is to listen to broadcasted arguments.

Listen to *A Point of View*, a Radio 4 podcast, in which a range of contributors give their reflections on topical issues.

WRITING

Unit 26
Spell with accuracy

The activities in this unit all refer to spellings that you can find throughout the Writing section. You can work through the activities all at once in the order they appear here, or do them as you come across them throughout the other units.

UNIT 16

S1: Silent 'b'

You can hear the 'b' sound in words such as 'but', 'slab' and 'double'. However, 'b' can also be a silent letter – this means that it cannot be heard when the word is pronounced, as in the word 'climb'.

1 Say the following words aloud:

thumb	comb	limb
doubt	bomb	crumb
plumber	subtle	debt
succumb	lamb	tomb

2 Spend two minutes memorising the words. Then close your book and ask another student to test your spelling of them.

S2: Prefixes: 'dis-' and 'un-'

When added to a base word, the prefix 'dis-' can indicate:

- reversal (e.g. appear/disappear)
- negation or lack of (e.g. trust/distrust).

When added to a base word, the prefix 'un-' can indicate:

- reversal (e.g. cover/uncover)
- not or opposite to (e.g. certain/uncertain)
- removal from or release (e.g. chained/unchained).

The correct spelling is formed by simply adding the prefix to the base word. There is no need to do anything else.

1 Attach the correct prefix, 'un-' or dis-', to the following words, making sure you spell them correctly:

similar	natural	service
necessary	credit	scratched
official	grace	

S3: Forming plurals

To form most plurals you simply add 's' to the singular form. For example:

portal → portals   fence → fences   cluster → clusters   head → heads

However, there are some exceptions:

- When the singular form ends in '-s', '-x', '-ch' or '-sh', add '-es' to make it plural. For example:

  dress → dresses   tax → taxes   church → churches   flash → flashes

- If a word ends in '-y' and has a consonant before the last letter, change the 'y' to an 'i' and add 'es'. For example:

  baby → babies   city → cities   sentry → sentries

- If a word ends in '-o' you usually just add '-s'. However, there are a few commonly used words that need '-es' to make them plural:

  hero → heroes   tomato → tomatoes   potato → potatoes

- If a word ends in '-f' or '-fe' you usually change the '-f' or '-fe' to '-ves'. For example:

  wolf → wolves   knife → knives

  But there are a few exceptions, where the plural just takes an 's':

  roof → roofs   chief → chiefs   reef → reefs

There are also a few irregular plurals. For example:

child → children	man → men	formula → formulae
sheep → sheep	mouse → mice	crisis → crises
tooth → teeth	person → people	stimulus → stimuli

1 Using the rules outlined in this section, write the plurals of the following words. There are a few exceptions included in the list:

branch	atlas	takeaway	gas	blotch
holiday	inch	hoax	arch	bully
Christmas	woman	witch	lie	doorman
beach	blush	berry	coach	hippopotamus
radius	comedy	bonus	key	medium
lady	cactus	essay	dish	scissors

2 Check your spellings with another student. If you have different answers, use a dictionary to see who is correct.

UNIT 17

S1: Commonly misspelt words

The student who wrote Source B correctly spells some common words that are often misspelt:

environment	restaurants	holiday
opportunities	experience	different
libraries	interest	

Spelling mistakes with words that you are expected to know can cost you marks in exams. Here are some more commonly misspelt words:

address	favourite	physical
altogether	foreign	privilege
anxious	fulfil	psychology
business	government	recommend
character	guarantee	rhythm
conscience	immediately	separate
definite	marriage	sincerely
disappointed	necessary	skilful
embarrassed	parallel	soldier
exaggerate	parliament	temporary
extraordinary	patience	

1 There are 40 words altogether, including those spelt correctly in Source B.

How many do you know how to spell? Work with another student and test each other.

Write down any words you spell incorrectly and learn the correct spelling.

S2: Changing adjectives to adverbs

Adverbs help to make the meaning of verbs fuller or more precise. Many adverbs are formed by adding 'ly' to an adjective. For example:

reluctant → reluctant*ly*   emotional → emotional*ly*

When adding '-ly' to adjectives that end in a consonant followed by 'y', we change the 'y' to 'i'. For example:

happy → happ*ily*   temporary → temporar*ily*

Some adjectives end in 'ic'. To form the adverb, you need to add 'ally', for example:

frantic → frantic*ally*   basic → basic*ally*

1 Change the following 20 adjectives into adverbs:

quick	romantic	moody
sarcastic	reluctant	nasty
menacing	temporary	rapid
angry	gloomy	sleepy
accidental	historic	emotional
slow	worthy	willing
dreamy	quiet	

2 Check your spellings with another student. If you have different answers, use a dictionary to see who is correct.

UNIT 18

S1: Spelling the 'f' sound

The 'f' sound in a word is usually spelt with 'f' or 'ff': *frost*, *family*, e*ff*ectively. However, it is sometimes spelt with 'ph': paragra*ph*, photogra*ph*. Many words using the 'ph' pattern come from the ancient Greek language.

1 Complete the following words by using 'f', 'ff' or 'ph'.

hy_en	_antom	baili_
gra_ iti	em_asise	para_in
_oreign	tra_ic	brie_ly
_uneral	con_lict	_iloso_y
claustro_obic	al_abet	_rase

2 Test another student on the spelling of words with 'f', 'ff' or 'ph' with a further ten words you have selected.

UNIT 19

S1: Commonly confused words

It is easy to confuse words that sound similar, even when they have different spellings. In her letter, Jennifer Atkins correctly uses the word 'accept'. Many students confuse this word with 'except', which means 'not including'.

1 Work with another student. Look at the following pairs of words, which are often confused.

a Discuss the difference in meaning in each pair of words.

b Use a dictionary if you are not sure.

c Make a note of any pair of words which you often confuse.

advice / advise	currant / current
aloud / allowed	draw / drawer
altar / alter	dual / duel
bazaar / bizarre	ensure / insure
chord / cord	envelop / envelope
coarse / course	pole / poll
complement / compliment	practice / practise
	principal / principle
council / counsel	stationary / stationery
cue / queue	
desert / dessert	storey / story

S2: Syllables

The student uses several multi-syllabic words in this letter. A syllable is a unit of sound. A word might contain one syllable, for example 'least', 'not'; two syllables, for example al/ways, pro/tect; three syllables, for example teen/a/gers, or more.

Breaking a word into syllables and sounding each syllable aloud (or in your head) can help you to spell it correctly.

1 Identify the words in the letter that contain three or more syllables. Write each word and identify the separate syllables with a forward slash. Make sure you know how to spell these words.

UNIT 20

S1: Suffixes: '-able' and '-ible'

In the extract from *The Road to Wigan Pier*, you will find the words 'intermin*able*' and 'imposs*ible*'. There is no clear rule to help you know when to use the correct ending. There are, however, many more words that end in '-able' than in '-ible'.

1 Look at this list of '-ible' words that students often spell incorrectly. Make sure you know their meanings, as well as how to spell them:

audible	sensible	divisible
edible	responsible	negligible
credible	possible	eligible
legible	flexible	fallible
terrible	compatible	gullible
horrible	plausible	compatible
feasible	reversible	
visible	accessible	

S2: Silent 'w'

You can hear the 'w' sound in words such as 'worry', 'way', and 'which'. However, 'w' can also be a silent letter, as in the word 'wreaked'.

The 'w' is most often silent in words that start with 'wr-'. However, there are a few words in which the 'w' is silent within the word – for example 'answer', 'sword', 'two'.

1 Use a dictionary to help you identify and make a list of other words that start with 'wr-'. Make sure you know when to use the silent 'w' in your spelling.

UNIT 22

S1: Homonyms

A **homonym** is one of a group of words that share the same spelling and the same pronunciation but have different meanings. For example:

well (a hole drilled in the ground for water, oil, and so on)
well (in good health)

A **homograph** is one of a group of words that share the same spelling, but not the same pronunciation, and which have different meanings. For example:

minute (a measure of time)
minute (very small)

A **homophone** is one of a group of words that share the same pronunciation but which have different meanings and spellings. For example:

sea (an area of water)
see (to perceive through the eyes)

These three types of words are often grouped together under the general heading of homonyms. There are many homonyms in the English language.

1 For each of the following, write a word that has the same pronunciation but is spelt differently and has a different meaning:

weather	hear	there
mined	which	one

2 What is the meaning of the words 'heat' and 'green' as they are used in Source C? What different meanings do these words have?

S2: Words from France

The English language contains many words of French origin. Most of these retain the French spelling but are pronounced in an English way (e.g. competition). However, some words are spelt and pronounced in the French way (e.g. cliché).

1 Make sure you know the meaning and the spelling of the following commonly used French words:

cliché	bon voyage	liaison
café	chic	silhouette
genre	crèche	
à la carte	déjà vu	

UNIT 23

S1: Silent letters: 'k'

While you can hear the 'k' at the start of words such as 'kettle' and 'keep', it is silent when followed by an 'n'. This means that it cannot be heard in words such as 'knew' and 'know'.

1 Make sure you know how to spell these commonly used words with a silent 'k':

knot	knight	kneel
knuckle	knowledge	knew
knee	knit	knob
knife	knock	known

S2: '-sc-'

Many words contain the sequence of letters 'sc'. Where the 'c' has a hard sound, the spelling is relatively straightforward (e.g. 'screen', 'describe'). However, where the 'c' has a soft sound, the spelling may not be obvious (e.g. 'fascinate').

1 Make sure you know the meaning and spelling of the following words:

abscess	crescendo	obscene
acquiesce	descendant	omniscient
fascism	discipline	muscle
coalesce	effervesce	reminisce
condescend	fluorescent	resuscitate
conscience	luscious	susceptible
convalesce	miscellaneous	

UNIT 24

S1: '-cial' '-tial'

Student B correctly spells the adjective 'influential', which ends in '-tial'. Some adjectives end in '-cial' (e.g. commercial). There is no clear rule governing the use of these word endings. Sometimes a root word will give a clue as to which spelling to choose. For example:

resident → residential   office → official

However, this is not always the case. For example:

benefit → beneficial   palace → palatial

1 Here are some frequently used adjectives ending in '-cial' and '-tial'. Make sure you know their meanings and how to spell them:

commercial	deferential	judicial
provincial	substantial	impartial
circumstantial	financial	spatial
preferential	sacrificial	prejudicial
influential	confidential	
racial	consequential	

S2: Prefixes: 'in-', 'il-', 'ir-', 'im-'

One meaning of the prefix 'in-', when added to a base word, is 'not' or 'the opposite of'. For example:

- 'credible' means that something is believable; 'in credible' means it is not believable
- 'complete' means that something is entire or ended; 'in complete' means it is not.

'In-' is the most common form of this prefix, but there are exceptions:

- If the base word starts with 'r', the prefix is spelt 'ir-'. So if you want to say that something is not rational, you say it is 'irrational'; if something is not regular, you say it is 'irregular'.

- If the base word starts with an 'm' or a 'p', the prefix is spelt 'im-'. So if you want to say someone is not mature, you say they are 'immature'; if something is not perfect, you say it is 'imperfect'.
- The spelling of the prefix 'in-' sometimes changes to match the first letter of the base word. If the base word starts with 'l', the prefix is spelt 'il-'. So if you want to say that something is not legal, you say it is 'illegal'; if something cannot be read and is not legible, you say it is 'illegible'.

1 Attach the prefix 'in-', 'il-', 'ir-' or 'im-' to the following base words to suggest their opposite:

capable	describable	separable
mortal	direct	perfect
possible	logical	personal
responsible	gratitude	legal
literate	reversible	rational
offensive	efficient	consistent
moral	finite	

UNIT 25

S1: Spell accurately

Did you know that some students:

- regularly cross out correct spellings and replace them with incorrect spellings, simply because they lack confidence in their ability to spell correctly?
- believe themselves to be bad spellers even though they spell over 95% of words correctly?
- can spot mistakes in other students' writing which they cannot see in their own?
- limit the marks they could achieve for communication and vocabulary in an exam because they will only use words they are certain they know how to spell?

Read the following extract from one student's exam writing, in which they are discussing the pressures facing young people today.

It's not just school life that is suffocating us; it's also the pressure to 'fit in', 'be cool', and simply just be excepted by people our age. When I first moved to this area I wasent at all confident and if it hadent been for my mother going out of her way to ensure I met girls my age and invited them for tea and sleepovers, I'm not sure how I would have survived. Now, even though I feel secure in myself and my friends, I'm still aware of the weight of pier pressure – a weight that sits heavily on most young people's shoulders. It's pier pressure that often takes us to places we dont really want to go to and that makes us do things we dont really want to do.

The student communicates clearly and quite effectively using a range of vocabulary and punctuation for effect. However, there are two areas in which this student could improve their accuracy:

- The student knows how to use apostrophes for omission in 'I'm' and 'It's', but they need to strengthen their understanding of this and apply it more generally:

  was not → wasn't
  had not → hadn't
  do not → don't

- The student needs to be extra careful with homonyms and ensure they know the meanings of words that sound similar but are spelt differently:

  excepted **or** accepted?   pier **or** peer?

  Look again at samples of your own writing. Identify two areas that you could work on to help you improve your technical accuracy.

WRITING
Unit 27
Test your progress 4

In Units 22–26 you have extended your skills in:

*   using sentence structures to interest and influence your reader
*   communicating effectively and imaginatively
*   structuring your writing to influence your readers
*   adapting tone, register and style to suit your purpose and audience
*   choosing words carefully to demonstrate a wide vocabulary range
*   checking your work to ensure technical accuracy.

This unit contains two tests. Test A is focused on discursive writing. Test B is focused on narrative writing. Your aim in each test is to demonstrate the best of your writing skills. You will be assessed on your communication, organisation, vocabulary range, use of sentence structures and technical accuracy.

Here are a few reminders of what you need to do:

Communication	• write effectively for purpose and audience • engage your reader with interesting ideas • write in fluent Standard English • influence and manipulate your reader.
Organisation	• identify purpose, audience and form • generate ideas and plan for paragraphs • sustain coherence though fluently linked paragraphs • seamlessly integrate discourse markers.
Vocabulary, sentence structure and accuracy	• demonstrate a wide vocabulary range • use language creatively and imaginatively • vary sentence structures to influence readers • achieve high level accuracy in punctuation and spelling.

TEST A

Plan, write and check your answer to one of the questions below.

You have 45 minutes.

At the start: Allow three to five minutes for planning.

While writing: Read through after each paragraph to make sure you are producing a coherent and effective piece of writing.

At the end: Allow three minutes to check your punctuation and spelling.

Either

'It's all too clear that the place in which you grow up has a major impact on the person you become.'

Write an article for a newspaper in which you explain your point of view on this statement.

Or

'Too many young people are wasting their lives on Facebook, Twitter and the like; there must be better things for them to do!'

Write an article for a newspaper in which you explain your point of view on this statement.

TEST B

Plan, write and check your answer to one of the questions below.

You have 45 minutes.

At the start: Allow three to five minutes for planning.

While writing: Read through after each paragraph to make sure you are producing a coherent and effective piece of writing.

At the end: Allow three minutes to check your punctuation and spelling.

You are going to enter a creative writing competition.

Your entry will be judged by a panel of published writers.

Either

Write a story that begins or ends with this sentence:

'As the long day drew to an end, the noises in the corridor faded and the cell doors were locked on the outside.'

Or

Write the opening part of a story suggested to you by this picture.

 Complete this assignment on Cambridge Elevate.

213

Preparing for your exam

It is important that you have practice in taking exam papers before you sit your GCSE exam. This section will give you:

- the practice you need
- the opportunity to look at and assess other students' exam responses
- practical advice.

This section contains two complete sets of practice papers.

SET 1 PRACTICE PAPERS

The first set of practice papers will give you guidance on important things for you to notice and do. These papers will also help you make the most of your time in an exam.

Practice Paper 1: Explorations in creative reading and writing

Sit the paper. Make sure you take note of the expert's advice. You will then have the opportunity to read and assess other students' answers alongside your own, and to make improvements to your responses.

Practice Paper 2: Writers' viewpoints and perspectives

Next sit practice Paper 2 and repeat the process.

SET 2 PRACTICE PAPERS

The second set of practice papers will give you the opportunity to show that you have learnt how to:

- use your time carefully and productively
- read sources and questions closely
- give relevant and appropriately developed answers.

These papers test your skills in the following six assessment objectives:

AO1:
- Identify and interpret explicit and implicit information and ideas.
- Select and synthesise evidence from different texts.

AO2: Explain, comment on and analyse how writers use language and structure to achieve effects and influence readers, using relevant subject terminology to support their views.

AO3: Compare writers' ideas and perspectives, as well as how these are conveyed, across two or more texts.

AO4: Evaluate texts critically and support this with appropriate textual references.

AO5:
- Communicate clearly, effectively and imaginatively, selecting and adapting tone, style and register for different forms, purposes and audiences
- Organise information and ideas, using structural and grammatical features to support coherence and cohesion of texts.

AO6: Use a range of vocabulary and sentence structures for clarity, purpose and effect, with accurate spelling and punctuation.

Set 1 practice Paper 1

Explorations in creative reading and writing

Section A: Reading

In your exam, you will be given an exam paper with an insert. The insert will contain Source A, which will be an extract written in the 20th or the 21st century. You are advised to spend some time reading through the source and thinking about all five of the questions before writing your answers. Use the time to read the source closely and to make notes on the answers you could give to the questions in Section A.

Source A

This extract is from a novel by Margaret Atwood, first published at the beginning of the 21st century. In this section, a character closely examines a photograph that was taken many years before.

The Blind Assassin

She has a single photograph of him. She tucked it into a brown envelope on which she'd written *clippings*, and hid the envelope between the pages of *Perennials for the Rock Garden*, where no one else would ever look.

She's preserved this photo carefully, because it's almost all she has left of him. It's black
5 and white, taken by one of those boxy, cumbersome flash cameras from before the war, with their accordion-pleat nozzles and their well-made leather cases that looked like muzzles, with straps and intricate buckles. The photo is of the two of them together, her and this man, on a picnic. *Picnic* is written on the back, in pencil – not his name or hers, just *picnic*. She knows the names, she doesn't need to write them down.

10 They're sitting under a tree; it might have been an apple tree; she didn't notice the tree much at the time. She's wearing a white blouse with the sleeves rolled to the elbow and a wide skirt tucked around her knees. There must have been a breeze, because of the way the shirt is blowing up against her; or perhaps it wasn't blowing, perhaps it was clinging; perhaps it was hot. It was hot. Holding her hand over the picture, she can still feel the heat coming up from it, like the heat from
15 a sun-warmed stone at midnight.

The man is wearing a light-coloured hat, angled down on his head and partially shading his face. His face appears to be more darkly tanned than hers. She's turned half towards him, and smiling, in a way she can't remember smiling at anyone since. She seems very young in the picture, too young, though she hadn't considered herself too young at the time. He's smiling too – the whiteness
20 of his teeth shows up like a scratched match flaring – but he's holding up his hand, as if to fend her off in play, or else to protect himself from the camera, from the person who must be there, taking the picture; or else to protect himself from those in the future who might be looking at him, who might be looking in at him through this square, lighted window of glazed paper. As if to protect himself from her. As if to protect her. In his outstretched, protecting hand there's the stub end of a cigarette.

25 She retrieves the brown envelope when she's alone, and slides the photo out from among the newspaper clippings. She lies it flat on the table and stares down into it, as if she's peering into a well or pool – searching beyond her own reflection for something else, something she must have dropped or lost, out of reach but still visible, shimmering like a jewel on sand. She examines every detail. His fingers bleached by the flash or the sun's glare; the folds of their clothing; the leaves of
30 the tree, and the small round shapes hanging there – were they apples, after all? The coarse grass in the foreground. The grass was yellow then because the weather had been dry.

Over to one side – you wouldn't see it at first – there's a hand, cut by the margin, scissored off at the wrist, resting on the grass as if discarded. Left to its own devices.

The trace of blown cloud in the brilliant sky, like ice cream smudged on chrome. His
35 smoke-stained fingers. The distant glint of water. All drowned now.

Drowned, but shining.

From *The Blind Assassin* by Margaret Atwood

Have you fully understood the passage? If not, read the questions and then read the passage again.

Section A: Reading

Practice questions

Answer **all** questions in this section.
You are advised to spend about 45 minutes on this section.

0 1   Read again the first part of the source, lines 1 to 9.

List **four** things from this part of the text about the photograph.

[4 marks]

0 2   Look in detail at this extract from lines 16 to 24 of the source:

> The man is wearing a light-coloured hat, angled down on his head and partially shading his face. His face appears to be more darkly tanned than hers. She's turned half towards him, and smiling, in a way she can't remember smiling at anyone since. She seems very young in the picture, too young, though she hadn't considered herself too young at the time. He's smiling too – the whiteness of his teeth shows up like a scratched match flaring – but he's holding up his hand, as if to fend her off in play, or else to protect himself from the camera, from the person who must be there, taking the picture; or else to protect himself from those in the future who might be looking at him, who might be looking in at him through this square, lighted window of glazed paper. As if to protect himself from her. As if to protect her. In his outstretched, protecting hand there's the stub end of a cigarette.

How does the writer use language here to describe the photograph?

You could include the writer's choice of:

- words and phrases
- language features and techniques
- sentence forms.

[8 marks]

Read all the questions before you start to answer Question 1. Use the marks indicated by each question to help you decide how much time to spend on it.

Take note of these – you will not get marks for material taken from outside the stated lines.

This question is worth 4 marks.

Take note of these – you will not get marks for material taken from outside the stated lines.

These are prompts to help you.

Think about how the writer uses words for effect.

This might include features such as repetition, figurative language and punctuation used for effect.

Focus on variations in sentence lengths and structures for effect.

This question is worth 8 marks.

You need to consider the complete passage.

0 3 You now need to think about the **whole** of the source.

This text is from the early part of a novel.

How has the writer structured the text to interest you as a reader?

You could write about:

- what the writer focuses your attention on at the beginning and end
- how the writer develops her ideas
- any other structural features that interest you.

[8 marks]

Structure can be at a whole text level (for example beginnings, endings, shifts in perspective); at a paragraph level (for example topic changes, paragraph cohesion, single sentence paragraphs) or at a sentence level (for example sentence length, sentence variation).

These are prompts to help you.

This question is worth 8 marks.

0 4 Focus on **lines 25 to the end**.

'The writer successfully creates an air of mystery around the photograph.'

To what extent do you agree with this statement?

In your response, you could:

- examine how the writer creates an air of mystery around the photograph
- evaluate the extent to which the writer is successful in doing this
- support your opinions and judgements with quotations from the text.

[20 marks]

Take note of these – you will not get marks for material taken from outside the stated lines.

These are prompts to help you.

This question is worth 20 marks.

Section B: Writing

Practice questions

You are advised to spend about 45 minutes on this section.
Write in full sentences.
You are reminded of the need to plan your answer.
You should leave enough time to check your work at the end.

0 5   You are going to enter a creative writing competition.

Your entry will be judged by a panel of professional writers.

Either:

Write a story in which a photograph plays a significant part.

Or:

Write a description suggested by this photograph:

(24 marks for content and organisation
16 marks for technical accuracy)
[40 marks]

You must also write in Standard English unless you are writing dialogue

Planning helps you structure your writing.

Check your answer for technical accuracy. You can also make other improvements at this stage.

Your audience is professional writers; your audience is also your examiner; you will be assessed on how well you craft your creative writing.

In this practice paper you have a choice of a narrative or descriptive task. In your exam, you may have this choice or you may have two narrative tasks or two descriptive tasks.

Notice how the marks are awarded for your different writing skills.

Section A: Reading

Question 1

She has a single photograph of him. She tucked it into a brown envelope on which she'd written *clippings*, and hid the envelope between the pages of *Perennials for the Rock Garden*, where no one else would ever look.

She's preserved this photo carefully, because it's almost all she has left of him. It's black and white, taken by one of those boxy, cumbersome flash cameras from before the war, with their accordion-pleat nozzles and their well-made leather cases that looked like muzzles, with straps and intricate buckles. The photo is of the two of them together, her and this man, on a picnic. *Picnic* is written on the back, in pencil – not his name or hers, just *picnic*. She knows the names, she doesn't need to write them down.

0 1   Read again the first part of the source, lines 1 to 9.

List **four** things from this part of the text about the photograph.

[4 marks]

This question is designed to assess the first bullet point of AO1: identify and interpret explicit and implicit information and ideas.

It is a relatively straightforward question. It is asking you to identify **four distinct things** about the photograph.

1 Check your answers against the following list and decide how many you identified.

- It is the only one she has of him.
- It was hidden in an envelope between the pages of *Perennials for the Rock Garden*, where no one else would ever look.
- It had been carefully preserved.
- It was almost all she had left of him.
- It was black and white.
- It was taken by one of those boxy, cumbersome flash cameras.
- It was taken from before the war.
- It was of the two of them together on a picnic.
- *Picnic* is written on the back, in pencil.

You may have written something else, such as 'the photograph was very important to the woman'. This is correct, but you will only be awarded the points if you have given evidence from the text to support it – i.e. 'because it was hidden where no one else would ever look' or 'because it was all she had left of him'.

Question 2

0 2   Look in detail at this extract from lines 16 to 24 of the source:

> The man is wearing a light-coloured hat, angled down on his head and partially shading his face. His face appears to be more darkly tanned than hers. She's turned half towards him, and smiling, in a way she can't remember smiling at anyone since. She seems very young in the picture, too young, though she hadn't considered herself too young at the time. He's smiling too – the whiteness of his teeth shows up like a scratched match flaring – but he's holding up his hand, as if to fend her off in play, or else to protect himself from the camera, from the person who must be there, taking the picture; or else to protect himself from those in the future who might be looking at him, who might be looking in at him through this square, lighted window of glazed paper. As if to protect himself from her. As if to protect her. In his outstretched, protecting hand there's the stub end of a cigarette.

How does the writer use language here to describe the photograph?

You could include the writer's choice of:

• words and phrases
• language features and techniques
• sentence forms.

[8 marks]

This question tests AO2 and focuses on the writer's use of language – her phrases, language features, language techniques and sentence forms.

You should:

• show that you understand the writer's use of language
• examine and analyse the effects of the writer's language choices
• select and use relevant quotations
• use appropriate subject terminology to discuss language use.

Here are three students' responses to this question, in order of merit. The comments show you what each student achieves.

Student A

The writer uses adjectives to describe the man. He is wearing a 'light-coloured' hat and his face is 'darkly tanned'. These help the reader imagine what he looks like. A simile is used to describe his teeth. They are compared with 'a scratched match flaring'. This makes them sound very white and bright and maybe a bit dangerous. The writer includes lots of detail about the photograph to describe it. She tells us that the woman is turned towards the man and that he's holding up his hand. She also uses repetition of the word 'protect' to make the reader think that the man is trying to protect the woman to show that he cares about her. There is a range of sentence forms. The writer uses sentences of different lengths to have an effect on the reader and to make it more interesting to read.

- Begins to show understanding of language use.
- Correctly identifies some features.
- Uses some quotations.
- Misunderstands the use of the word 'protect'.
- No example given to support statement.
- Begins to comment on effect.

Student B

The writer uses a range of techniques to describe the photograph. She uses the simile 'like a scratched match flaring' to describe the man's smile. This makes it seem sudden and has connotations of danger. She repeats the word 'young' three times in one sentence to describe the woman, and emphasises this even more by saying twice that she is 'too' young. This makes it seem as though she shouldn't have been there with this man because she wasn't old enough. She also uses repetition later in the paragraph when she repeats the word 'protect' in the sentences: 'As if to protect himself from her. As if to protect her.' These two sentences are structured in very similar ways, but they have a different meaning and the short words 'as if' at the start of each sentence make the reader realise that she doesn't know why the man was holding up his hand

The writer also uses an effective metaphor near the end. She calls the photograph a 'square lighted window'. A window is something that you look through to see something and it is often square. It makes me feel as though I am looking through a window into the world of this man and woman.

- Shows good understanding of writer's use of language.
- Uses correct terms to describe writer's techniques.
- Quotations clearly support points.
- Explains writer's techniques and their effects on the reader.

Student C

- Discerning overview.
- Comments insightfully on language use.
- Closely examines linguistic features.
- Uses quotations effectively.
- Uses correct terminology skilfully.

The writer uses language to describe both what is seen in the photograph and to create an impression of the relationship between the man and the woman in it.

She captures the shading of a black and white photograph through the adjective 'light-coloured' to describe the hat and, although she refers to the 'whiteness' of his teeth, there is no other reference to colour. The use of the simile 'like a scratched match flaring' makes the smile seem temporary and a bit artificial. It also carries a suggestion of danger and makes us wonder if this man is entirely trustworthy. The image of the match is linked with the final reference to 'the stub end of a cigarette'. Smoking in those days may have seemed glamorous but the harsh monosyllabic 'stub end' with its plosive 'b' sound seems intended to detract from any sense of glamour. The emphasis on the youth of the woman, with the repetition of the word 'young' three times in one sentence, also makes the reader wonder if this is some kind of con man.

The writer also uses language to describe how the people are positioned in the photograph. The woman is 'half-turned' towards the man and he's holding up his hand 'as if to fend her off in play'. The use of the words 'as if' suggest that the woman does not know why his hand is held up and this is reinforced by a sequence of reasons all linked with the idea of protection. The word 'protect' is repeated four times and in the final sentence 'protecting' is used to give further emphasis. Sentence structure is used to draw the reader's attention to this even further. The long detailed sentence that starts with 'He's smiling too…' is followed by two short sentences or fragments: 'As if to protect himself from her. As if to protect her.' The close mirroring of these sentences, with the opening emphasis on 'as if', draws the reader's attention to the significant difference in their meaning.

Finally, when describing the people who might be looking at this picture in the future, the writer describes the photograph as a 'square lighted window of glazed paper'. This metaphor effectively creates an image of looking in on other people's lives just as you might look through a window of a house.

2 Which student response most closely matches your own answer? Make notes on how you could improve your answer.

Question 3

| 0 3 | You now need to think about the **whole** of the source.

This text is from the early part of a novel.

How has the writer structured the text to interest you as a reader?

You could write about:

- what the writer focuses your attention on at the beginning and end
- how the writer develops her ideas
- any other structural features that interest you.

[8 marks]

You should:

- show that you understand features of structure
- examine and analyse the effects of the writer's choice of structural features
- select and use relevant examples
- use appropriate subject terminology to discuss structure.

Structural features can be:

- at a whole text level – for example beginnings, endings and perspective shifts
- at a paragraph level – for example topic changes, single-sentence paragraphs
- at a sentence level – for example sentence lengths.

Here is an example of a good response. The annotations show you what the student does well. The underlined words indicate the language the student has used to organise the response and introduce comments on structure.

Student D

The text is structured almost as an investigation. Details relating to a single photograph are revealed gradually across the text. The writer's use of pronouns at the start of sentences is an interesting structural feature across the text. Ten sentences start with the personal pronoun 'she' or 'she's', one with the personal pronoun 'he' and two with the possessive pronoun 'his'. Only one sentence starts with the pronoun 'they'. Although the photograph is of the man and the woman, this deliberate use of pronouns at the start of the sentences places the focus firmly on the woman and her response to it.

✔ Discerning overview.

✔ Effective focus on detail.

✔ Closely examines effect of sentence structure.

The text starts with the simple sentence 'She has a single photograph of him'. In the second, contrasting longer sentence the reader learns that the photograph is hidden as though it is a secret, private thing. The second paragraph also starts with a reference to the photograph. This reinforces the notion of its importance to her: 'it's almost all she has left of him'. This makes the reader think that there is a story behind this man and this photograph. This is followed by a sequence of factual details which are used to give an overview of the photograph – how it was taken, briefly what it shows and also what's written on the back. This is done to suggest she is looking at it in a very objective way.

The link with 'her and this man' is made with the word 'They're' at the start of the third paragraph, but it is not until the fourth paragraph that the reader really finds out more about the man. This and the fifth paragraph are significantly longer than the others. They show the reader what the woman sees, her thoughts and her actions. The increased use of dashes, fragments, for example 'As if to protect her', and even a question, 'were they apples, after all?', are used to reinforce a sense of the woman's thought processes. This use of dashes and fragments is continued in the final three very short paragraphs. New elements of the photograph are revealed but not developed – the hand, cut by the margin, the distant glint of water. It's almost like a series of impressions as though the narrative has been lost, but, nevertheless, images from before are repeated. The 'distant glint of water' reminds the reader of the 'pool or well'; the 'smoke-stained' fingers remind us of the 'stub end'. The final paragraph is just three words: 'Drowned, but shining'. This effectively echoes the final sentence of the previous paragraph and reminds the reader of the earlier reference to 'jewel in the sand'.

Margin annotations:

- ✔ Comments on varied sentence length.
- ✔ Comments on effect.
- ✔ Closely examines effect.
- ✔ Perceptive examination of technique.
- ✔ Detailed and insightful.
- ✔ Explores structural links.

This student:

- starts with a perceptive overview
- comments on structural features
- shows detailed and perceptive understanding of structural features
- examines and analyses the effects of the writer's choice of structural features
- uses examples from the text effectively
- uses appropriate subject terminology.

❸ Assess your own response to this question. Make notes on how you could improve it.

Question 4

---

0 4 Focus on **lines 25 to the end**.

'The writer successfully creates an air of mystery around the photograph.'

To what extent do you agree with this statement?

In your response, you could:

* examine how the writer creates an air of mystery around the photograph
* evaluate the extent to which the writer is successful in doing this
* support your opinions and judgements with quotations from the text.

[20 marks]

This question tests AO4: Evaluate texts critically and support this with appropriate textual references.

You should:

* show that you can evaluate critically
* analyse the effects of a range of the writer's choices
* use examples to explain your judgements
* support your judgements with quotations.

4 Here is a good response to the question. Identify where the student:

* evaluates
* refers to reader response
* explains and analyses effects
* uses examples and quotations to explain and support judgements.

Student E

She only takes the envelope out when she's alone – there's something secretive in the way the writer uses the word 'slides', as if she's anxious, even when alone, that it might be seen. Immediately the reader wonders why this is. She stares at it as if 'searching ... for something else'. She then uses the image of looking into a 'well or pool', where you first see your own reflection but then see through it to what's beneath the surface of the water. Readers will be familiar with this experience and it effectively suggests that the photo holds more than just the surface detail. Whatever she's looking for is precious 'like a jewel on sand'. Although the photograph is very familiar to her, she 'examines every detail'. The reader is caught up in this examination by the further detail that is revealed but still does not know what she is looking for. By describing the woman's actions and her thoughts in this detailed way, the writer helps the reader to understand that there is an unanswered question about this photograph – a mystery that has yet to be solved.

The air of mystery is increased by the reference to the hand and the use of the word 'scissored' in the next paragraph. The meaning here is ambiguous. Was the person to whom the hand belonged a part of the original photograph? Has the photo been deliberately cut to exclude or hide that person? This effectively creates a sense of mystery as to the identity and significance of that person.

The air of mystery is continued. The use of the word 'smudged' makes the reader feel as though nothing is entirely clear. There is a reference again to the smoking habit of the central figure with his 'smoke-stained fingers'. This makes the reader wonder why this detail is important – was it something to do with why the man is no longer around? The writer cleverly manipulates the reader by making subtle links, for example the link between the water of the well and the pool and the reference to the 'distant glint of water'. This is the first time that any mention has been made of water in the picture and yet it immediately sparks the sentence 'All drowned now'. Who are the 'all' that is referred to here? Why and how have they drowned? Have they really 'drowned' or does this simply mean that they are lost in the depths of the photograph? The final paragraph offers no answer. 'Drowned, but shining' simply shows that whatever has been lost is, again, like the jewel, shining and precious.

I agree with the statement made. The writer is successful in creating an air of mystery around the photograph because she raises so many unanswered questions about it and about the woman looking at it.

5 Compare your answer with the sample answer. Make notes on things you could have included to improve your answer.

✓ **Annotate a copy of this response on Cambridge Elevate.**

Section B: Writing

Question 5

> **0 5**   You were asked to write an entry for a creative writing competition, which would be judged by a panel of professional writers. You could:
>
> **Either:**
>
> Write a story in which a photograph plays a significant part.
>
> **Or:**
>
> Write a description suggested by the photograph on the practice paper.
>
> (24 marks for content and organisation
> 16 marks for technical accuracy)
> **[40 marks]**

The same criteria are used to assess both descriptive and narrative writing.
You should:

- communicate clearly, effectively and imaginatively
- choose and adapt your tone, style and register for purpose and audience
- develop, organise and structure your information and ideas
- make fluent links within and between paragraphs
- make effective use of structural features
- use a range of vocabulary for clarity, purpose and effect
- use a range of sentence structures for clarity, purpose and effect
- spell accurately and punctuate effectively.

6 Use these bullet points to help you assess the work of Students F and G. When you have done this, decide which student should get the higher marks. Explain your choice.

7 Use the bullet points to help you assess your own writing. Make notes on how you could improve it.

 Find annotated examples of these responses on Cambridge Elevate.

Student F

<u>Write a story in which a photograph plays a significant part.</u>

The photograph took pride of place on the mantelpiece. I had often dusted it and sometimes, when I was really annoyed, stuck it in a drawer just to annoy him. But now I picked it up and looked at it. It bought back so many memories.

I remembered how it had been a cold, wet night and was getting dark. I was part of a group. I had knew these people for two years now and I knew I was safe. Twenty miles we had to walk to get our adventure medals. We had only compleated ten. By this time things were looking a bit unpredictable. The rain was stoping and starting, the wind would suddenly pick up and then gradualy slow down. Time was not on our side. We had to be back for 11.00 pm and it was now already 6.00 pm. We carried on climbing up the hills and rocks till all of a sudden one of our members out of the group fell.

He fell a few feet and gave out a yell, this was just the beginning of a nightmare. We all rushed down to see how bad he was hurt. He was in pain and it looked as though his ankle was broken.

We all realised at this point that he could not go on. He was dissappointed and so were we. We were all told that if someone was injured that one or two people should stay with that person. I agreed to stay with him while the rest of the group carried on. As soon as the rest of the group reached the next checkpoint they would get someone to find and help us get back to the camp.

I helped him to a suitable position nearby, so he would be comfortable. We expected to see someone about 9.00, only two hours from when the rest of the group carried on. It was now 8.30. Only 30 minutes to go we both thought.

We were both getting really tiered at this point. The darkness was setting in and fog was beginning to settle. We were up high on a huge mountain. It was dangerous and one false move and we could of been off the side.

When it got to 11.30 I decided at this point that we should get prepared to spend the night here as it did not seem like we would be going anywhere. I thought maybe I should go and try and get help but Mark asked me to stay. I didn't really know him all that well but we started to talk properly to each other to pass the time. He told me all about his family and how he was really interested in sport and wanted to be a trainer when he was older. I told him about my Mum and how she had brought us up after Dad died. I also told him that I wanted to go to Uni once I'd finished all my exams. We were almost falling asleep when we heard a sound and suddenly a bright light appeared from nowhere. It was waving around near by and I heard my name being called out from a distance. I felt so relieved. They had finally found us through all the mist and darkness.

I felt really glad and proud that I had stayed with Mark but that wasn't the best bit. After that night we started going out together. The photo that I'm looking at is of him and me on our wedding day over twenty years ago now.

Student G

Write a description suggested by this photograph

The children play. Laughing and joking and teasing and tormenting, their lives carry forward with no regard to the chaos that surrounds them.

Look at that house. No, not just a house. Much more than just a house. That house was once a wondrous world, a refuge, a comfort and a strength. In the kitchen of that house saucepans once bubbled, an oven slowly roasted, a kettle boiled, a fridge hummed, a tap gurgled, a light shone and a cat, loved and well-fed, purred quietly in a corner. Where is that cat now? Where is that house, that home?

'Got you! You're it!'

Voices fill the air. Shrieks and of joy and excitement mask the blood-curdling cries. The children play.

Turn from the house and gaze at that street. No, not just a street. Much more than a street. That street once held the hopes and fears of a small community. In number 19 Mrs Jones raised her children, anxiously watched their first steps, followed them to school and back, tearfully waved them farewell as they ventured into the world. At number 32, Mr Saunders would sit at his window, gazing at the world through tattered net curtains, dreaming of his past. A knock at the door would return him to the present and the kindly offer of a home-baked cake and a cup of warm, refreshing tea. At 26, John Manning would carefully dismantle and reassemble an engine in the front room to the dismay of his wife and the destruction of the carpet.

'That's not fair! I saw it first.'

Two small boys argue over a damaged toy, rescued from the rubble, unlike its owner. They start to fight but are quickly distracted by the fun still to be had. Children like to play.

Cast your eyes up to the sky. The sun shines brightly now, revealing no hint of what has been. Close your eyes and picture the dark night. Hear the murmuring of planes approaching over the Channel. Listen, as the murmurings turn to thunder, and see the frantic dazzle of search lights criss-crossing the sky in a futile attempt to blind the pilots of death. Shiver, as the planes drop their deadly cargo and tremble, as the target is hit.

The toy is a fire engine. Bought by a doting Dad, it once rolled across a tiled kitchen followed excitedly by a stumbling toddler. Now, it offers just a brief diversion.

The night draws in and the children grow tired. One by one, they wave farewell to their friends and wander back to their homes in the distant streets. Their stomachs growl with hunger and they look forward to the dinner which will be on the table almost as soon as they get home. They will not notice the blackout curtains pulled tight, nor the strained faces of their parents, nor the packed cases in the hallway ready for an emergency exit.

The toy fire engine lies once again in the rubble.

Will the children play with it tomorrow?

Writers' viewpoints and perspectives

Section A: Reading

Insert

You are advised to spend some time reading through the sources and all five questions you have to answer.

You should make sure you leave sufficient time to check your answers.

- **Source A:** A magazine article called *Social notebook*.

- **Source B:** 'The Sunday Morning Markets': an extract from a book called *London Labour and the London Poor*.

> In your exam you will be given an exam paper with an insert. The insert will contain two sources – A and B. One of these will have been written in the 19th century. You are advised to spend some time reading through the sources and thinking about all five of the questions before writing your answers.

Source A:

Social notebook
by Paul Barker, 20 February 1996

The bridge carrying the M25 southwards into Kent juts up, like an awkward insect, beyond the dumpy dome and ready-made cornices of the Thurrock Lakeside shopping centre. The centre and the retail park next to it occupy about two million square feet. Three-and-a-half million people live within 30 minutes' drive, and on   5 a Saturday most of them seem to be trying to get into its car park.

Lakeside is a strange mixture of flashiness and plain grot. A "vertical feature" tells you the time and temperature as you drive along the M25. Then you turn off past the Essex Arena (for car racing) and the War Zone (for paintball games). A 20 acre lake offers windsurfing and an imitation Mississippi riverboat.

Opened only six years ago, by Princess Alexandra, its magnetism already terrifies Oxford Street, where traders   10 muse about the attraction of roofing their street over, and perhaps having their own security guards. Malls are mocked as a parody of a traditional city. But Jane Jacobs, heroine of the urban conservation movement, wrote that "the bedrock attribute of a successful city district is that a person must feel personally secure among all these strangers." Enclosed and video-scrutinised, they make people, especially women, feel safe. No panhandlers here. No need to carry bags slung across your chest.   15

The new centres are different from the basic air-conditioned shopping mall. The first in Britain opened at Brent Cross, North London, 20 years ago. But today's luxuriant, baroque centres are like mini-cities. Drive past the Meadowhall Centre outside Sheffield, and look down on its green dome in the old wasteland of the lower Don Valley. Apart from the shops, there are two office parks. Warner has opened an 11-screen multiplex cinema. Sheffield's first supertram line runs from the old city centre to Meadowhall. Locally, high hopes for regeneration   20 are placed on the "rippling-out" effect of Meadowhall.

Nobody planned that this should happen. When T Dan Smith, regional planning's flawed hero, started to weave motorways around and through Newcastle, the Gateshead MetroCentre was no part of his vision. Britain's first out-of-town shopping centre exploited a tax break intended to woo industry, not a retail heaven. It sometimes seems that the only people who like the centres are the millions of people who use them. Many of the complaints   25 have the giveaway taint of snobbery – in direct line of descent from 1930s moans about vulgar supercinemas or 1950s moans about unsightly television aerials.

I love these centres. The first time I went into the MetroCentre, I had been travelling the grey streets of the north-east. If the alternative was Sunderland High Street or Peterlee, then the MetroCentre is where I would shop. In design the centres have as much in common with theme parks as with department stores: perhaps more. At the Metro you can leave your children while you shop, in a pick 'n' mix amusement zone like the late-lamented Fun House at Blackpool Pleasure Beach. Shoppers go about with cheerful, sprightly step. They have dressed up to come here.

On the upper floor there is a classical corner with Corinthian columns and statues in creamy fibreglass, and box trees made of plastic. A sign welcomes you to "Roman Shopping." In architects' drawings of their city schemes, you find little groups of tables with happy urbanites chatting under the sunshades. A bit like a tourist brochure. You seldom see this in Britain in real life. But you see it in the Roman Forum at the MetroCentre, where the electricity always shines.

Adapted from an article in *Prospect Magazine* by Paul Barker

Source B:

by Henry Mayhew, first published in 1851

Henry Mayhew was a social researcher in favour of social reform. In this extract, he describes a Sunday morning market in London in the mid-19th century.

The Sunday Morning Markets

Nearly every poor man's market does its Sunday trade. For a few hours on the Sabbath morning, the noise, bustle, and scramble of the Saturday night are repeated, and but for this opportunity many a poor family would pass a dinnerless Sunday. The system of paying the mechanic late on the Saturday night – and more particularly of paying a man his wages in a public-house – when he is tired with his day's work lures him to the tavern, and there the hours fly quickly enough beside the warm tap-room fire, so that by the time the wife comes for her husband's wages, she finds a large portion of them gone in drink, and the streets half cleared, so that the Sunday market is the only chance of getting the Sunday's dinner.

Of all these Sunday-morning markets, the Brill, perhaps, furnishes the busiest scene; so that it may be taken as a type of the whole.

The streets in the neighbourhood are quiet and empty. The shops are closed with their different-coloured shutters, and the people round about are dressed in the shiney cloth of the holiday suit. There are no "cabs," and but few omnibuses to disturb the rest, and men walk in the road as safely as on the footpath.

As you enter the Brill the market sounds are scarcely heard. But at each step the low hum grows gradually into the noisy shouting, until at last the different cries become distinct, and the hubbub, din, and confusion of a thousand voices bellowing at once again fill the air. The road and footpath are crowded, as on the over-night; the men are standing in groups, smoking and talking; whilst the women run to and fro, some with the white round turnips showing out of their filled aprons, others with cabbages under their arms, and a piece of red meat dangling from their hands. Only a few of the shops are closed, but the butcher's and the coal-shed are filled with customers, and from the door of the shut-up baker's, the women come streaming forth with bags of flour in their hands, while men sally from the halfpenny barber's smoothing their clean-shaved chins. Walnuts, blacking, apples, onions, braces, combs, turnips, herrings, pens, and corn-plaster, are all bellowed out at the same time. Labourers and mechanics, still unshorn and undressed, hang about with their hands in their pockets, some with their pet terriers under their arms. The pavement is green with the refuse leaves of vegetables, and round a cabbage-barrow the women stand turning over the bunches, as the man shouts, "Where you like, only a penny." Boys are running home with the breakfast herring held in a piece of paper, and the side-pocket of the apple-man's stuff coat hangs down with the weight of the halfpence stored within it.

Presently the tolling of the neighbouring church bells breaks forth. Then the bustle doubles itself, the cries grow louder, the confusion greater. Women run about and push their way through the throng, scolding the saunterers, for in half an hour the market will close. In a little time the butcher puts up his shutters, and leaves the door still open; the policemen in their clean gloves come round and drive the street-sellers before them, and as the clock strikes eleven the market finishes, and the Sunday's rest begins.

Have you fully understood the passages? If not, read the questions and then read the passages again.

Section A: Reading

Practice questions

Answer **all** questions in this section.
You are advised to spend about 45 minutes on this section.

Use the marks indicated by each question to help you decide how much time to spend on it.

0 1   Read **Source A** again, from lines 1 to 15.

Re-read these lines only.

Choose **four** statements below which are TRUE according to the passage.

• Write the letters of the four true statements
• Choose a maximum of four statements.

You need to read the statements and check whether they are true. Be careful – some of them are partly but not wholly true.

A   The M25 runs close by the Thurrock Lakeside shopping centre.   ○

B   The Lakeside shopping centre alone occupies about two million square feet.   ○

C   You can go windsurfing on a nearby lake.   ○

D   Princess Alexandra opened Lakeside in 1990.   ○

E   The time and temperature are displayed on the dome of Lakeside.   ○

F   Shopping malls are like a traditional city.   ○

G   The Lakeside shopping mall is like a war zone.   ○

H   Women in particular like the security offered by shopping malls.   ○

[4 marks]

This question is worth 4 marks.

0 2   **You need to refer to Source A and Source B for this question:**

You need to refer to both sources.

Use details from **both** sources. Summarise the different reasons why people went to shopping malls in the 20th century and why they went to the Sunday morning markets in the 19th century.

[8 marks]

This question is worth 8 marks.

0 3   Read again lines 13 to 31 in **Source B**.

How does Henry Mayhew use language to show the reader what the Brill market is like?

You could include the writer's choice of:

- words and phrases
- language features and techniques
- sentence forms.

[12 marks]

0 4   For this question, you need to refer to **Source A** and **Source B**.

Compare how the two writers convey their attitudes to the places they describe.

In your answer, you could:

- compare their attitudes
- compare the methods they use to convey their attitudes
- support your ideas with quotations from **both** sources.

[16 marks]

Take note of these – you will not get marks for material taken from outside the stated lines.

These are prompts to help you.

Think about how the writer uses words for effect.

This might include features such as repetition, figurative language and punctuation used for effect.

This question is worth 12 marks.

Focus on variations in sentence lengths and structures for effect.

You need to refer to both sources.

These are prompts to help you.

This question is worth 16 marks.

Section B: Writing

Practice questions

You are advised to spend about 45 minutes on this section.
You are reminded of the need to plan your answer.
You should write in full sentences.
You should leave enough time to check your work at the end.

0 5   'People waste away their weekends mindlessly in shopping malls when they could be doing so much more with their free time.'

Write an article for a broadsheet newspaper in which you explain your point of view on this statement.

(24 marks for content and organisation
16 marks for technical accuracy)
[40 marks]

Take note of these instructions. They are given to help you.

Planning helps you structure your writing.

You must also write in Standard English.

Check your answer for technical accuracy. You can also make other improvements at this stage.

You are expected to write a developed article appropriate for a 'good quality' newspaper. You should focus on the quality of your content and craft, not on presentational features.

Your audience is newspaper readers; your audience is also your examiner; you will be assessed on how well you craft your writing.

In Paper 1, you assessed a range of responses to help you recognise what you need to do. In this section, you will further develop your exam skills by learning how to make focused notes to help you produce high-level responses. This needs practice. Use the advice here to get you started on making focused notes. The more exam practice you do, the more efficient you will become in making focused notes. These skills are transferrable to Paper 1. You can start to make your notes in your reading time.

Section A: Reading

Question 1

---

01   Read **Source A** again, from lines 1 to 15.

Choose **four** statements below which are TRUE according to the passage.

- Write the letters of the four true statements
- Choose a maximum of four statements.

[4 marks]

This question is designed to assess the first bullet point of AO1: Identify and interpret explicit and implicit information and ideas.

It is a relatively straightforward question. It asking you to identify four true statements.

1 You are awarded 1 mark for each correct choice. Check your answers against the following four correct choices and decide how many you identified correctly:

A   The M25 runs close by the Thurrock Lakeside shopping centre.
C   You can go windsurfing on a nearby lake.
D   Princess Alexandra opened Lakeside in 1990.
H   Women in particular like the security offered by shopping malls.

Question 2

0 2   You need to refer to **Source A** and **Source B** for this question:

Use details from **both** sources. Summarise the different reasons why people went to shopping malls in the 20th century and why they went to the Sunday morning markets in the 19th century.

[8 marks]

This question assesses both bullet points of AO1:

- Identify and interpret explicit and implicit information and ideas.
- Select and synthesise evidence from different texts.

You should:

- show that you understand the reasons and the differences between them
- interpret the detail given in each source
- synthesise evidence taken from the two sources
- refer to detail and use quotations to support the points you make.

It is important to focus closely on the question. You are not being asked to compare the reasons why people went to these places; you are being asked to summarise them. It is a good idea to quickly list the reasons before writing your answer. For example:

<u>20th century</u>

Convenient transport – M25/supertram

Like a day out for family – cinema/wind surfing/

MetroCentre amusement zone

People feel safe – video-scrutinised

You can see things you can't see in real life, e.g.

Roman Forum

<u>19th century</u>

Transport not an issue – on foot

Men went to smoke and talk – social reasons –

barber's

Women went to buy food for Sunday dinner –

all other shops closed - necessity

Mainly food market – lots of different things:

walnuts, apples – boys went to buy herrings

You can then use your lists to help you write your answer. For example:

There are lots of reasons why people go to shopping malls in the 20th century. The writer tells us that there is usually convenient transport, such as the M25 for Lakeside or the supertram to Meadowhall. This would not have been a reason in the 19th century as most people would have travelled by foot. It's like a day out for people in the 20th century. There's lots of things to do as well as visit the shops, such as go to the cinema at Meadowhall or go windsurfing at a lake near Lakeside. Some people went to the Sunday markets for social reasons; the men went to smoke and chat and the labourers and mechanics just 'hang about'. There wasn't a lot to do but the men sometimes went to go to the barber's. However, the women had a purpose – they were there to buy the Sunday dinner as they had not got any money from their husbands until late the night before. It was mostly food that was on sale, such as walnuts and apples.

Children go to both markets but for different reasons. In the 20th century their parents can put them in the amusement zone at the MetroCentre but in the 19th the boys went to buy herrings for breakfast. In the 20th century, women like to go because they feel safe there as they are video-scrutinised, but in the 19th century, women had no alternative. All the other shops were closed and they only had until eleven. Mainly people go to 20th-century shopping malls for leisure reasons, but women went to the 19th-century Sunday market for necessity.

2 Compare your answer with the sample given. Did you miss some points you could have included? Make a note of them. Did you include some other points? Check that all the points you made are relevant to the question.

Question 3

0 3	Read again lines 13 to 31 in **Source B**.

How does Henry Mayhew use language to show the reader what the Brill market is like?

You could include the writer's choice of:

- words and phrases
- language features and techniques
- sentence forms.

[12 marks]

This question tests your skills in AO2 and focuses on the writer's use of language – words, phrases, language features, language techniques and sentence forms.

You should:

- show that you understand the writer's use of language
- examine and analyse the effects of the writer's language choices
- select and use relevant quotations
- use appropriate subject terminology to discuss language use.

3 Develop your skills in making useful notes by:

- identifying things to write about
- selecting examples
- reminding yourself to write about effects.

Remember – you can start to make notes in your reading time. In the real exam, you can annotate the passage rather than making separate notes.

For this question, start by identifying three features in lines 13 to 31 that seem important. For example:

Sounds: simple sentence – 'sounds are scarcely heard'; long sentence – 'low hum' to 'noisy shouting' to 'the different cries become distinct' to 'the hubbub, din, and confusion of a thousand voices bellowing at once'. These sounds 'fill the air'. Discuss effects – verbs, nouns and adjectives.

Movement: starts 'as you walk through the market'; then 'at each step' – like walking with him; changes to 3rd person – 'road and footpath are crowded'; men are 'standing'; women 'run to and fro' – contrast – men 'sally' or 'hang about' while women 'streaming forth' and boys 'running'. Discuss effects – 'you' + contrast.

Use of lists: captures detail: 'the hubbub, din and confusion' (nouns); 'the men are standing in groups, smoking and talking' (verbs); 'Walnuts … corn-plaster (nouns)'. Discuss effects – build up.

Notes like these will help you write three good paragraphs. Here is one paragraph based on the notes for 'Sound':

Henry Mayhew uses language to show the reader different aspects of the market. He shows us the sounds of the market. He starts with a short simple sentence, which clearly states that at the entrance to the market the sounds can be 'scarcely heard'. He follows this with a contrasting long complex sentence, which he uses to show the gradual build-up of sounds. At the start there is a 'low hum' and this grows to noises that 'fill the air'. The range of nouns, all synonyms for sounds, effectively shows this growth moving from 'hum' to shouting, 'cries', hubbub' and 'din'. The noun phrase 'confusion of a thousand voices bellowing at once' is particularly effective, with its use of a specific number and the verb 'bellowing', which suggests a very loud and echoing sound, almost like a herd of cattle.

- awareness of variety of sentence structures
- correct use of terms
- quotes are appropriate
- effects are looked at in detail

4 Use the notes for 'Movement' and 'Use of lists' to help you add to your answer to this question. Remember to show that you can examine and analyse the effects of the writer's language choices.

> **0 4**   For this question, you need to refer to **Source A** and **Source B**.
>
> Compare how the two writers convey their attitudes to the places they describe.
>
> In your answer, you could:
>
> - compare their attitudes
> - compare the methods they use to convey their attitudes
> - support your ideas with quotations from **both** sources.
>
> **[16 marks]**

This question tests AO3: Compare writers' ideas and perspectives, as well as how these are conveyed, across two or more texts.

You should:

- show that you understand the ideas and perspectives
- compare the ideas and perspectives clearly and perceptively
- explain, analyse and compare the methods used to convey the ideas and perspectives
- use relevant quotations from both texts to support your comparison.

This question asks you to do several things. An analysis of the question shows what you need to do:

| Point out similarities and differences | | Viewpoint and perspective – what does tone show? |

Compare how the two writers convey their attitudes to the places they describe.

| Methods: language? structure? use of evidence? tone? |

Obviously you will not be able to point out the similarities and differences until you have worked out the perspectives, viewpoints and methods.

This table will help you identify similarities and differences in the two sources.

	Source A	Source B
Perspective / purpose / audience	20th-century journalist – Barker – mag. Article – adults Describes and argues and gives personal opinion – tries to persuade – has visited malls	19th-century social reformer – Mayhew Social record? Educated readers – future? Describes – has visited – doesn't persuade – shows positives
Viewpoint	In favour: I love these centres. Biased? – sees them as 'fantasy' places – not real life	Distant observer – doesn't interact with place or people – seems to like it - real place – shopping for Sunday dinner
Tone	Sometimes sarcastic, mocking, humorous	Impartial – informing – educating – addresses reader directly once
Language	Conveys tone: 'dumpy dome'; 'a strange mixture of flashiness and plain grot'; adjectives/verbs persuade: 'Shoppers go about with cheerful, sprightly step'; 'the electricity always shines'	Sounds/movements/lists (see Q3)
Structure	Third person at first – moves from one mall to another – explains attractions – personal viewpoint at end	Third person throughout – explains and then describes – ends with close of market
Use of evidence	Only positive details given – avoids negative – quotes expert to support argument	Details about place, e.g. sounds, movements – own experience only

Read this answer based on the table:

The writers of the sources have different purposes and audiences. Barker is a journalist writing for a magazine and a 20th-century audience that will probably already know about shopping malls. Mayhew is a social reformer. He is probably writing for educated people who would not have visited the Sunday market. Barker clearly has a strong personal opinion in favour of shopping malls: he says 'I love these centres'. Whilst Mayhew seems to quite like the Sunday market – he doesn't include any negative details about it – he certainly doesn't 'love' it and doesn't seem to be trying to persuade his readers to love it either in the way that Barker does. His purpose seems to be mainly to inform and describe, and maybe to record for the future.

Although both writers have visited the places they write about, they have different attitudes towards them. Barker seems to view shopping malls as 'fantasy' places that have little connection with real life. They are the kinds of places where you can do lots of different things and see things 'you seldom see in Britain in real life'. Mayhew, on the contrary, presents the Sunday market as a very real place where 'real' people go. These people are not 'dressed up'. They are doing things everyone does – hanging around, talking and buying food. Mayhew's account is about 'real' life, not fantasy.

At times Barker sounds sarcastic: 'Lakeside is a strange mixture of flashiness and plain grot'. But there is also affection in the way he refers to Lakeside's 'dumpy dome'. He also seems to have some respect for these 'mini cities'. In the phrase 'its magnetism already terrifies Oxford Street' he uses the words 'magnetism' and 'terrifies' to show both the attraction and power of these places. He stays positive throughout. He hints at potential for 'regeneration' showing the good such places can bring about through their 'rippling-out' effect. He also quotes an expert, Jane Jacobs, to support his views.

Barker is describing three different places in his article but Mayhew describes only one. However the place he describes – Brill – is chosen because it is typical of Sunday markets. He has a more detached and impartial tone than Barker. Whereas Barker uses language to argue and persuade as with the use of adjectives used positively in 'Shoppers go about with cheerful, sprightly step', Mayhew uses language to create a detailed picture of the Sunday market focusing on the sounds you can hear and the movements of the people and the contrast between the men and women.

Mayhew writes in the third person, though he does once address his reader directly, whereas Barker starts in the third person but in the penultimate paragraph he uses the first person to give emphasis to his personal viewpoint. They both end effectively. Mayhew uses the peaceful phrase 'and the Sunday's rest begins' to contrast with what has gone before and Barker ends with the very positive phrase 'where the electricity always shines' to emphasise the attractions of the malls.

5 Compare this answer with your own. Add points you could have made to your answer.

6 Make a note of the key words used in the first column of the chart. Aim to use these to help you plan for this question in the future.

Section B: Writing

Question 5

| 0 5 | 'People waste away their weekends mindlessly in shopping malls when they could be doing so much more with their free time.'

Write an article for a broadsheet newspaper in which you explain your point of view on this statement.

(24 marks for content and organisation
16 marks for technical accuracy)
[40 marks]

You should:

- communicate clearly, effectively and imaginatively
- choose and adapt your tone, style and register for purpose and audience
- develop, organise and structure your information and ideas
- make fluent links within and between paragraphs
- make effective use of structural features
- use a range of vocabulary for clarity, purpose and effect
- use a range of sentence structures for clarity, purpose and effect
- spell accurately and punctuate effectively.

> Notice that these are the same skills you needed in Section B of Paper 1.

7 Work with another student. Use the bullet points to help you assess the work of Students A and B.

8 Whilst Student A does some things well, Student B's article is clearly better. Can you work out why? List the reasons, using examples from the students' work to support them.

 Find annotated examples of these responses on Cambridge Elevate.

Student A

Did you know that there has been a 60% increase in the number of people visiting shopping malls in the last ten years? Maybe it's time that we stopped and thought about why this is happening.

I was at school yesterday and everyone was talking about what they were going to do at the weekend. At least half of my friends said that they were going to our local shopping mall, which is called the Bullring. I was simply shocked by this. It was a Saturday and they had nothing better to do than go and walk around a place like that. Let me tell you, it is not a very nice place to be. There are usually loads of people there and all they do is walk around all the time. There are a few nice shops there and some good places to eat but there's nothing much else to do. Would you like to spend a whole day there? I know I wouldn't and yet lots of people do.

And it doesn't stop there! Some people go there more than once a week and some of my friends were planning to go on Saturday and Sunday! I mean to say! One day is surely enough! Why don't they find better things to do with their time?

There are lots of things that people can do at the weekend depending on where they live and what they like. If they live in Birmingham they could go paintballing at Deltaforce or they could spend the day in a park. Birmingham has more parks than any other city in Europe – and that includes London! The best park is Cannon Hill Park and you can do all different things there like boating and tennis and you can go and have a picnic there. Birmingham also has lots of canals which you can walk along. There's so many things you can do why would you want to spend all day in the Bullring?

If you go to the Bullring you will find lots of families there. The kids are often whinging and not happy because they don't want to be there. You can see them crying and pulling at their Mum and Dad's hands because they want to go home. It's not good enough! They should be outside running about and enjoying the fresh air and getting fit and healthy. It's no wonder that so many children don't run any more when they spend all their weekends stuck inside a shopping mall.

Their parents should find better things for them to do. When I was little my Dad took me to watch the football every weekend. He would never have taken me to a shopping mall. We spent some really good times together and it was really good fun. He still asks me if I want to go with him and sometimes I do.

That's the kind of thing parents should be doing with their children. They should be having fun with them at weekends and not dragging them round somewhere they don't want to be.

Quite frankly, I think it has to stop. So many people going there week after week is just appalling. We should make sure that there are better things for everyone to do with their time at weekends. I don't know about you but I always find that if people know there are better things to do, they will do them. So let's work together and make sure that everyone does something different at the weekend.

Student B

The shopping mall has been an inherent part of my life for as long as I can remember. I was born in Kent and Bluewater was a place of awe and wonder for a three-year-old. Hands firmly clasped on both sides by loving, watchful parents, I would raise my eyes up and up again before I could see the top of the towering escalator and, like an intrepid explorer, I would firmly place my foot on the bottom step. Imagine my delight when on reaching the top I felt like a mountaineer who had conquered Everest!

And the delight didn't stop at three. At five years old, I was host to my first ever 'proper' birthday party. Friends and relatives gathered at Pizza Hut, bringing presents and hugs and a memory filled with laughter. A menu of Margherita and ice cream topped with a colourful array of hundreds and thousands may not sound so appealing to you but for me, in my shiny pink princess dress, it was a gourmet's delight. And the fun didn't stop there. After our meal we all went to the Pirate Cove Adventure Park for a relaxing ride on the pedalos. Birthdays at five don't come much better than this.

Now that I'm older I still go to Bluewater most weekends. The shiny pink princess dress has gone and my parents, though still loving and watchful, no longer hold my hands. In fact, Bluewater seems to have lost its appeal for them, the attractions of the garden and a comfy seat in front of the television apparently more suited to their middle-age needs. But Bluewater still draws me in, like a magnet does a metal filing. The shops glow seductively, their sensuous garments promising a better time – a better me. I've moved on though from Pizza Hut. McDonalds is now my restaurant of choice, where the scent of chips frying and the murmur of laughter and chatter never ceases.

I know what you're thinking – that I should be doing better things with my free time; I should be studying or working or improving myself. But you're wrong. I work hard all week at school. I keep fit by walking almost everywhere. I try to do an hour's practice on my violin at least three times a week and I babysit my younger brother every Tuesday night, a feat of great heroism and an emotional challenge! I deserve a break.

For the space of one single afternoon I can stroll at leisure through a brightly lit, warm and comforting place with no threat of danger, no need to listen for ominous footsteps in my wake. I don't need to hurry – the day stretches ahead of me. Of course, I'm not on my own. Bluewater is a social centre for the young. These days, when Youth Clubs have been chopped and libraries axed, where else are we meant to go? Where else offers such a retreat without an entrance charge?

We don't 'do' anything there, but life doesn't always have to be about 'doing'. Sometimes just 'being' is fine.

Explorations in creative reading and writing

Section A: Reading

- You are advised to spend some time reading Source A and thinking about the questions you have to answer.
- You should make sure you leave sufficient time to check your answers.

Source A

This is the opening of a short story, in which a boy ventures out into the early morning with only his dogs and his gun.

A Sunrise on the Veldt

Every night that winter he said aloud into the dark of the pillow: Half-past four! Half-past four! till he felt his brain had gripped the words and held them fast. Then he fell asleep at once, as if a shutter had fallen; and lay with his face turned to the clock so that he could see it first thing when he woke.

5 It was half-past four to the minute, every morning. Triumphantly pressing down the alarm-knob of the clock, which the dark half of his mind had outwitted, remaining vigilant all night and counting the hours as he lay relaxed in sleep, he huddled down for a last warm moment under the clothes, playing with the idea of lying abed for this once only. But he played with it for the fun of knowing that it was a weakness that he could defeat without effort; just as he set the alarm each night for

10 the delight of the moment when he awoke and stretched his limbs, feeling the muscles tighten, and thought: Even my brain – even that! I can control every part of myself.

Luxury of warm rested body, with the arms and legs and fingers waiting like soldiers for a word of command! Joy of knowing that the precious hours were given to sleep voluntarily! – for he had once stayed awake three nights running, to prove that he could, and then worked all day, refusing

15 even to admit that he was tired; and now sleep seemed to him a servant to be commanded and refused.

The boy stretched his frame full-length, touching the wall at his head with his hands, and the bedfoot with his toes; then he sprung out, like a fish leaping from water. And it was cold, cold.

He always dressed rapidly, so as to try and conserve his night-warmth till the sun rose two hours

20 later; but by the time he had on his clothes his hands were numbed and he could scarcely hold his shoes. These he could not put on for fear of waking his parents, who never came to know how early he rose.

As soon as he stepped over the lintel, the flesh of his soles contracted on the chill earth, and his legs began to ache with cold. It was night: the stars were glistering, the trees standing black

25 and still. He looked for signs of day, for the greying of the edge of a stone, or a lightening in the sky where the sun would rise, but there was nothing yet. Alert as an animal he crept past the dangerous window, standing poised with his hand on the sill for one proudly fastidious moment, looking in at the stuffy blackness of the room where his parents lay.

Feeling for the grass edge of the path with his toes, he reached inside another window further

30 along the wall, where his gun had been set in readiness the night before. The steel was icy, and numbed fingers slipped along it, so that he had to hold it in the crook of his arm for safety.

35 Then he tiptoed to the room where the dogs slept, and was fearful that they might have been tempted to go before him; but they were waiting, their haunches crouched in reluctance at the cold, but ears and swinging tails greeting the gun ecstatically. His warning undertone kept them secret and silent till the house was a hundred yards back: then they bolted off into the bush, yelping excitedly. The boy imagined his parents turning in their beds and muttering: Those dogs again! before they were dragged back in sleep; and he smiled scornfully. He always looked back over his shoulder at the house before he passed a wall of trees that shut it from sight. It looked so low and small, crouching there under a tall and brilliant sky. Then he turned his back on it, and on
40 the frowsting sleepers, and forgot them.

He would have to hurry. Before the light grew strong he must be four miles away; and already a tint of green stood in the hollow of a leaf, and the air smelled of morning and the stars were dimming.

From 'A Sunrise on the Veldt' by Doris Lessing, in *This Was the Old Chief's Country*

Section A: Reading

Practice questions

Answer **all** questions in this section.
You are advised to spend about 45 minutes on this section.

| 0 1 | Read again the first part of the source, lines 1 to 16. |

List **four** things that the boy does between going to bed at night and getting out of bed in the morning. **[4 marks]**

| 0 2 | Look in detail at this extract from the source: |

> As soon as he stepped over the lintel, the flesh of his soles contracted on the chill earth, and his legs began to ache with cold. It was night: the stars were glistering, the trees standing black and still. He looked for signs of day, for the greying of the edge of a stone, or a lightening in the sky where the sun would rise, but there was nothing yet. Alert as an animal he crept past the dangerous window, standing poised with his hand on the sill for one proudly fastidious moment, looking in at the stuffy blackness of the room where his parents lay.

How does the writer use language here to describe the scene?

You could include the writer's choice of:

- words and phrases
- language features and techniques
- sentence forms.

[8 marks]

| 0 3 | You now need to think about the **whole** of the source. |

How has the writer structured the text to interest you as a reader?

You could write about:

- how the writer shifts the focus
- how the writer develops her ideas
- any other structural features that interest you.

[8 marks]

| 0 4 | Focus this part of your answer on **lines 29 to the end**. |

'In these lines, the writer successfully captures the secrecy of the boy's actions and makes me worried about what might happen to him.' To what extent do you agree with this statement?

In your response, you could:

- explain what you learn from the boy's actions
- evaluate the extent to which the writer captures the secrecy of the boy's actions and makes the reader worried about what might happen to the boy
- support your opinions with quotations from the text.

[20 marks]

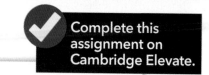
Complete this assignment on Cambridge Elevate.

Section B: Writing

Practice questions

You are advised to spend about 45 minutes on this section.
Write in full sentences.
You are reminded of the need to plan your answer.
You should leave enough time to check your work at the end.

0 5   You are going to enter a creative writing competition.

Your entry will be judged by a panel of published writers.

Either:

Write a story suggested to you by this photograph.

Or:

Write a story in which a secret plays an important part.

(24 marks for content and organisation
16 marks for technical accuracy)
[40 marks]

Set 2 practice Paper 2

Writers' viewpoints and perspectives

Section A: Reading

Insert

You are advised to spend some time reading through the source and all five questions you have to answer.

You should make sure you leave sufficient time to check your answers.

- **Source A:** An account about the hardships of factory life in the 19th century from *A Narrative of the Experience and Suffering of William Dodd*

- **Source B:** A newspaper article from *The Guardian, 2013*

Source A:

Dear Reader, – I wish it to be distinctly and clearly understood that I am not actuated by any motive of ill-feeling to any party with whom I have formerly been connected; on the contrary, I have a personal respect for some of my former masters; but having witnessed the efforts of some writers (who can know nothing of the factories by experience) to mislead the minds of the public upon a subject of so much importance, I feel it to be my duty to give the world a fair and impartial account of the working of the factory system, as I have found it in twenty-five years' experience. 5

Of four children in our family, I was the only boy; and we were all at different periods, as we could meet with employers, sent to work in the factories. My eldest sister was ten years of age before she went; consequently, she was, in a manner, out of harm's way, her bones having become firmer and stronger than ours, and capable of withstanding the hardships to which she was exposed much better than we could. My second sister went at the age of seven years, and, like myself, has been made a cripple for life, and doomed to end her days in the factories or workhouse. My youngest sister also went early, but was obliged to be taken away, like many more, the work being too hard for her. 10

I was born on the 18th of June, 1804; and in the latter part of 1809, being then turned of five years of age, I was put to work at card-making, and about a year after I was sent, with my sisters, to the factories. I was then a fine, strong, healthy, hardy boy, straight in every limb, and remarkably stout and active. It was predicted by many of our acquaintance, that I should be the very model of my father, who was the picture of robust health and strength. 15

From six to fourteen years of age, I went through a series of uninterrupted, unmitigated suffering, such as very rarely falls to the lot of mortals so early in life, and such as I could not have withstood, had I not been strong and of a good constitution. 20

My first place in the factories was that of piecer, or the lowest situation. The piecers are the servants of the spinners, and both are under an overlooker; and liable to be dismissed at a week's notice. In order to induce the piecer to do his work quick and well, the spinner has recourse to many expedients, such as offering rewards of a penny for a good week's work; as a last resource, when nothing else will do, he takes the strap, or the billy-roller, which are laid on most unmercifully, accompanied by a round volley of oaths. 25

On one occasion, I remember being thrashed with the billy-roller till my back, arms and legs were covered with ridges as thick as my finger. This was more than I could bear and I stole off home, along some by-ways, so as not to be seen. Mother stripped me, and was shocked at my appearance. The spinner had to beg that mother would let me go again, and promised not to strike me with the billy-roller any more. He kept his promise, but instead of using the roller, he used his fist. 30

A Narrative of the Experience and Suffering of William Dodd

Source B:

Admit it. You love cheap clothes. And you don't care about child slave labour

Until three years ago I did not believe in magic. But that was before I began investigating how western brands perform a conjuring routine that has cast a spell over the world's consumers.

This is how it works. Well Known Company (WKC) makes shiny, pretty things in India or China. *The Observer* reports that the people making the shiny, pretty things are being paid buttons and, what's more, have been using children's nimble little fingers to put them together. There is much outrage, WKC professes its horror that it has   5
been let down by its supply chain and promises to make everything better. And then nothing happens. WKC keeps making shiny, pretty things and people keep buying them. Because they love them. Because they are cheap. And because they have let themselves be bewitched.

In the last few years, companies have got smarter. It is rare now to find children in the top level of the supply chain, because the brands know this is PR suicide. But the wages still stink, the hours are still brutal, and the   10
children are still there, stitching away in the backstreets of the slums.

Drive east out of Delhi for an hour or so and take a stroll down some of the back lanes. Take a look through some of the doorways. See the children stitching the fine embroidery and beading? Now take a stroll through your favourite mall and have a look at the shelves. Recognise some of that handiwork? You should.

Suppliers now subcontract work out from the main factory. The work is done out of sight, the pieces sent back   15
to the main factory to be finished and labelled. And when the auditors come round the factory, they can say that there were no children and all was well.

A young boy working in a textile factory in Delhi, India

Need fire extinguishers to tick the safety box? Hire them in for the day. The lift is a deathtrap? Stick a sign on it to say it is out of use and the inspector will pass it by. We, the consumers, let them do this because we want the shiny, pretty thing. 20

But times are tough, consumers say. Here's some maths from an *Observer* investigation last year in Bangalore. We can calculate that women on the absolute legal minimum wage, making jeans for a WKC, get 11p per item. Now wave your own wand and grant them the living monthly wage – the £136 needed to support a family in India today. It is going to cost a fortune, right? No. It will cost 15p more on the labour cost of each pair of jeans.

The very fact that wages are so low makes the cost of fixing the problem low, too. Someone has to absorb the hit, 25 be it the brand, supplier, middleman, retailer or consumer. But why make this a bad thing? Why be scared of it?

Here is the shopper, agonising over ethical or cheap. What if they can do both? What if they can pluck two pairs of jeans off the rail and hold them up. One costs £20. One costs £20.15. It has a big label on it, which says "I'm proud to pay 15p more for these jeans. My jeans were made by a happy worker who was paid the fair rate for the job." 30

Go further. Stitch it on to the jeans themselves. I want those jeans. I want to know I'm not wearing something stitched by kids kept locked in backstreet godowns, never seeing the light of day, never getting a penny. I want to feel clean. And I want the big brands and the supermarkets to help me feel clean.

I want people to say to them: "You deceived us. You told us you were ethical. We want you to change. We want you to police your supply chain as if you care. We want to trust you again, we really do, because we love your 35 products. Know what? We don't mind paying a few pennies more if you promise to chip in too."

And here's the best part: I think they would sell more. I think consumers would be happier and workers would be happier. And if I can spend less time trawling through fetid backstreets looking for the truth, I'll be happier.

Adapted from an article in *The Guardian* by Gethin Chamberlain

---

Section A: Reading

Practice questions

Answer **all** questions in this section.
You are advised to spend about 45 minutes on this section.

---

0 1   Read **Source A** again, from lines 1 to 13.

Choose **four** statements below which are TRUE according to the passage.

- Write the letters of the four true statements
- Choose a maximum of four statements.

A   The writer has no ill feeling towards his former masters.   ⬭

B   Some writers have tried to mislead the public about factory life.   ⬭

C   There are many other reliable accounts of children's lives in the factory system.   ⬭

D   The writer had four sisters.   ⬭

E   The four children all started factory work at the same age.   ⬭

F   One of his sisters was strong enough to withstand the hardships of factory work.   ⬭

G   His second sister ended up in a workhouse.   ⬭

H   Factory work was too hard for the writer's youngest sister.   ⬭

[4 marks]

0 2   You need to refer to **Source A** and **Source B** for this question:

Use details from **both** sources. Write a summary of the different hardships faced by children in the 19th and 21st centuries.

[8 marks]

0 3   Read again **lines 1 to 14** in **Source B**.

How does the writer use language to influence the reader's opinion?

You could include the writer's choice of:

- words and phrases
- language features and techniques
- sentence forms.

[12 marks]

0 4   For this question, you need to refer to **Source A** and **Source B**.

Compare how the two writers convey their attitudes to child labour.

In your answer, you could:

• compare their attitudes
• compare the methods they use to convey their attitudes
• support your ideas with quotations from **both** sources.

[16 marks]

Section B: Writing

Practice questions

You are advised to spend about 45 minutes on this section.
You are reminded of the need to plan your answer.
You should write in full sentences.
You should leave enough time to check your work at the end.

0 5   'Unless ordinary people speak out about things they believe to be wrong, nothing will ever change.'

Write a letter to your local Member of Parliament about something that you believe to be wrong. Explain your views and persuade him or her to take action.

(24 marks for content and organisation
16 marks for technical accuracy)
[40 marks]

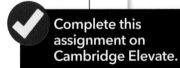
Complete this assignment on Cambridge Elevate.

Glossary

active voice a verb used to indicate that the subject of a sentence is being performed (e.g. 'She hit the ball.')

adjective a word used to enhance the meaning of a noun

adverb a word that adds to the meaning of a verb, adjective or another adverb (e.g. 'very', 'easily')

alliteration repetition of the initial letter in adjacent words (e.g. 'dark, dank dungeon')

anecdote a personal story

audience the intended readers of a piece of writing

bias using language to influence a reader

clause a group of words that contain a finite verb

closed question a question that typically only requires a 'yes' or 'no' response

complex sentence a sentence consisting of a main clause and at least one subordinate clause

compound sentence a sentence formed from two simple sentences using 'and', 'but', 'so' or 'or' (e.g. 'he ate supper and went to bed')

connotation an additional associated meaning of a word

coordinating conjunction a conjunction such as 'and', 'but' or 'or'

denotation the main meaning of a word

dialogue a conversation, or part of a conversation, in a piece of writing

emotive language using words to influence how a person feels

figurative language non-literal use of language

finite verb a verb that has a subject

first person the form of a verb or pronoun used when you are speaking or writing about yourself

homograph a word that shares the same spelling as another word, but is pronounced differently and has a different meaning

homonym a word that shares the same spelling and punctuation with another word, but has a different meaning

homophone a word that shares the same pronunciation as another word, but has different meanings and spellings

imagery the use of words to create a picture or scene

infinitive the base form of a verb

intonation the rise and fall of the pitch of the voice when speaking

metaphor a word or phrase that describes one thing as something else

motif a recurring element or theme in a piece of writing with symbolic significance

noun a word that refers to a person, place or thing

noun phrase a group or words that act like a noun

objective a piece of writing presented without emotion or bias

open question a question that requires a full, descriptive response

pace the perceived speed of a piece of writing or speech

passive voice where the subject of the sentence receives the action of the verb (e.g. 'He was hit by the ball.')

personification giving human attributes to non-human things

pronoun a word that replaces, or is used in place of a noun phrase

purpose the reason a piece of writing has been written

register the level of formality used in a piece of writing

rhetorical question a question that is asked for effect rather than to obtain information

second person the form of the verb or pronoun used for a person you are speaking or writing to

simile a comparison using 'as' or 'like' (e.g. she was like a fish out of water)

simple sentence a sentence consisting of a single main clause

Standard English the form of English most commonly used in formal situations

subjective a piece of writing based on personal opinion, thoughts and feelings

subordinate clause a clause that functions in the same way as a noun, adjective or adverb, but cannot stand as a sentence on its own

subordinating conjunction a conjunction that precedes a subordinate clause, such as 'although', 'if', 'because'

synonym a word or a phrase with a similar meaning to another word

third person the form of the verb or pronoun used when you are speaking or writing about another person

tone the mood or attitude the writer conveys in a piece of writing

verb a word that conveys an action in a sentence

Acknowledgements

The authors and publishers acknowledge the following sources of copyright material and are grateful for the permissions granted. While every effort has been made, it has not always been possible to identify the sources of all the material used, or to trace all copyright holders. If any omissions are brought to our notice, we will be happy to include the appropriate acknowledgements on reprinting.

p. 9 Guinness World Records © 2013; p. 10 Contains public sector information licensed under the Open Government Licence v2.0, The National Archives; p. 13 William Alevizon with permission; p. 14 Reprinted by permission of HarperCollins Publishers Ltd © 2001 John Gillham and Ronald Turnbull; p. 15 Bloomsbury, Curtis Brown, Random House Canada and Random House Inc; p. 16 NAME ALL THE ANIMALS by Alison Smith with permission from Simon & Schuster UK and Simon & Schuster Inc; p. 17 Orion Publishing Group Ltd and Capel & Land Ltd; p. 20 (l) The Random House Group; p. 20 (r) sse.com with permission; p. 21 Headline Publishing Group; p. 23 United Agents; p. 25 (t) Nick Middleton, 2004, Pan Books; p. 25 (b) W. W. Norton & Company and The Random House Group; p. 26 The Random House Group and Harper Collins Inc; p. 27 (t) Mirrorpix; p. 27 (b) The Random House Group; p. 28 Penguin Books Limited and Rogers, Coleridge and White; p. 30 Houghton Mifflin; p. 33 (l) Penguin Books Ltd; p. 33 (r) Hodder & Stoughton Ltd; p. 34 Copyright Guardian News & Media 2013; p. 35 Excerpt from 'A Hanging' from A COLLECTION OF ESSAYS by George Orwell. Copyright 1950 by Sonia Brownell Orwell. Copyright © renewed 1978 by Sonia Pitt-Rivers. Reprinted by permission of Houghton Harcourt Publishing Company. All rights reserved. / A Hanging by George Orwell (Copyright © George Orwell, 1931) / Penguin Books Ltd; p. 36 Daily Mail; p. 37 The Random House Group; p. 38 Longman; p. 39 The Random House Group; p. 43 New Scientist; p. 46 Daily Mail; p. 48 The Times 2012; pp. 49-50, 54 The Random House Group; p. 62 Daily Mail; p. 68 Copyright Guardian News & Media 2014; p. 70 Copyright Guardian News & Media 2014; p. 72 Jeremy Dean; p. 73 The Telegraph 2014; pp. 76-80 Andre Deutsch Ltd; p. 84 Headline Publishing Group and Brandt & Hochman Literary Agents, Inc.; p. 85 The Independent; p. 87 The Independent; p. 88 And Did Those Feet: Walking Through 2000 Years of British and Irish History by Charlie Connelly, Published by Abacus; p. 89 Global Post; p. 90 The Sunday Times; p. 92 HarperCollins Inc, The Random House Group, Random House Canada; p. 95 Curtis Brown; p. 97 Penguin Books Ltd and Aitken Alexander Associates Ltd; p. 100 Faber & Faber and United Agents; p. 102 I Spy by Graham Greene published by Penguin; pp. 103–104 David Attenborough Productions Ltd; p. 105 Macmillan Inc; p. 107 Bloomsbury and ICM; p. 108 (t) The Random House Group; p. 109 (t) From THE KITE RUNNER by Khaled Hosseini, copyright © 2003 by Khaled Hosseini. Used by permission of Riverhead Books, an imprint of Penguin Group (USA) LLC, Bloomsbury and Random House Canada; p. 109 (b) Nineteen Eighty-Four by George Orwell (Copyright © George Orwell, 1948) Reprinted by permission of Bill Hamilton as the Literary Executor of the Estate of the Late Sonia Brownell Orwell / Penguin Books Ltd / Harcourt Brace & Co; pp. 114–115 Down and Out in Paris & London by George Orwell (Copyright © George Orwell, 1933) Reprinted by permission of Bill Hamilton as the Literary Executor of the Estate of the Late Sonia Brownell Orwell / Penguin Books Ltd / Harcourt Brace & Co; p. 117 Copyright Guardian News & Media 2014; p. 123 The Telegraph; p. 135 Simon & Schuster Ltd; pp. 138, 142 Penguin Books Limited; p. 140 Arcadia Books Limited; p. 157 Professor David Crystal with permission; p. 160 Excerpt from THE ROAD TO WIGAN PIER by George Orwell. Copyright © 1958 and renewed 1986 by the Estate of Sonia B. Orwell. Used by permission of Houghton Mifflin Harcourt Publishing Company.

Picture credits

p. 8 Mimadeo/Shutterstock; p. 9 (background) Anton Balazh/Shutterstock; p. 9 FocusDigital/Alamy; p. 11 Peter Fuchs/Shutterstock; p. 12 Elena Elisseeva/Shutterstock; p. 13 Rich Carey/Shutterstock; p. 14 (background) hobbit/Shutterstock; p. 14 Phil MacD Photography/Shutterstock; p. 16 Dudarev Mikhail/Shutterstock; p. 17 Gerritt de Vries/Shutterstock; p. 18 Hill Street Studios/Thinkstock; p. 19 (t) Bloomua/Shutterstock; p. 19 (b) Elena Rostunova/Shutterstock; p. 21 bojangles/Shutterstock; p. 22 Heartland Arts/Shutterstock; p. 23 Barry Lewis/Alamy; p. 25 HPH Image Library/Shutterstock; p. 26 Tony Campbell/Shutterstock; p. 28 Mihai Simonia/Shutterstock; p. 29 (t) Vladitto/Shutterstock; p. 29 (b) Stockbyte/Thinkstock; p. 30 Suzanne Tucker/Shutterstock; p. 31 Classic Image/Alamy; p. 32 Print Collector/Getty Images; p. 33 La_Corivo/Thinkstock; p. 34 La_Corivo/Shutterstock; p. 35 Fototaras/Shutterstock; p. 36 United Archives/Topfoto; p. 38 javarman/Shutterstock; p. 39 Tom Grundy/Shutterstock; p. 41 © The National Army Museum/Mary Evans Picture Library; p. 42 Topical Press Agency/Getty Images; p. 44 (t) Purestock/Thinkstock; p. 44 (b) CoolR/Shutterstock; p. 46 Michaelpuche/Shutterstock; p. 49 weerapatkiatdumrong/Thinkstock; p. 51 (t) Sergey Nivens/Shutterstock; p. 51 (m) Tim Whitby/Alamy; p. 51 (b) Jon Arnold Images/Alamy; p. 52 John Charles Dollman/Getty Images; p. 60 Universal History Archive/Getty Images; p. 61 (t) Vladek/Thinkstock; p. 61 (b) Bloomua/Shutterstock; p. 62 simonkr/Thinkstock; p. 68 Wavebreakmedia Ltd/Thinkstock; p. 69 Oleksiy Mark/Thinkstock; p. 71 Markus Mainka/Shutterstock; p. 72 Warren Goldswain/Thinkstock; p. 73 Roger Bamber/Alamy; p. 74 (tl) i4images_music/Alamy; p. 74 (tr) dwphotos/Thinkstock; p. 74 (bl) muzsy/Shutterstock; p. 74 (br) Shirlaine Forrest/Getty Images; p. 76 (t) f9photos/Shutterstock; p. 76 (b) panphai/Shutterstock; p. 79 mazzzur/Thinkstock;

p. 82 wonry/Shutterstock; p. 83 orbandomonkos/Thinkstock; p. 84 behindlens/Thinkstock; p. 86 Daniel Prudek/Shutterstock; p. 87 Morley Read/Thinkstock; p. 88 Chris Parypa/Thinkstock; p. 89 meunierd/Shutterstock; p. 92 Jjustas/Shutterstock; p. 93 (t) Shutter_M/Shutterstock; p. 93 (b) Annette Shaff/Shutterstock; p. 95 dragosgrijincu/Shutterstock; p. 97 NeonLight/Shutterstock; p. 100 mark yuill/Thinkstock; p. 103 Ollyy/Shutterstock; p. 106 thomas-bethge/Thinkstock; p. 107 olavs/Shutterstock; p. 109 Stephen Morris/Thinkstock; p. 112 Suzanne Tucker/Shutterstock; p. 113 Culture Club/Getty Images; p. 115 Sasha/Getty Images; p. 117 Daniel Atkin/Alamy; p. 119 sam chamberlain/Thinkstock; p. 122 (t) Simone van den Berg/Shutterstock; p. 122 (b) Stocktrek Images/Getty Images; p. 123 UPP/Topfoto; p. 125 Thomas Pickard/Thinkstock; p. 127 (t) Ana Blazic Pavlovic/Shutterstock; p. 127 (mt) savageultralight/Thinkstock; p. 127 (mb) nyul/Thinkstock; p. 127 (b) IPGGutenbergUKLtd/Thinkstock; p. 130 (t) Diego Cervo/Shutterstock; p. 130 (b) GatorDawg/Thinkstock; p. 132 ArtisticPhoto/Shutterstock; p. 137 ra2studio/Shutterstock; p. 138 mark wragg/Thinkstock; p. 139 CBCK-Christine/Thinkstock; p. 140 Phil Wills/Alamy; p. 141 Jaroslaw Kubak/Shutterstock; p. 144 Marie C Fields/Shutterstock; P. 145 (TL) Mike Watson Images/Thinkstock; p. 145 (tr) kadmy/Thinkstock; p. 145 (bl) Ammit/Thinkstock; p. 145 (br) Horsche/Thinkstock; p. 146 Joe Daniel Price/Getty Images; p. 150 (t) Air Images/Shutterstock; p. 150 (b) Brian Jackson/Thinkstock; p. 151 poplasen/Thinkstock; p. 154 Marcos Mesa Sam Wordley/Shutterstock; p. 155 CandyBox Images/Shutterstock; p. 157 (t) shironosov/Thinkstock; p. 157 (b) dslaven/Shutterstock; p. 158 alphaspirit/Thinkstock; p. 160 Geogphotos/Alamy; p. 162 Ammit Jack/Shutterstock; p. 163 Dennis W. Donohue/Shutterstock; p. 165 Ingram Publishing/Thinkstock; p. 166 Daniel Fung/Shutterstock; p. 167 (t) Andrew Zarivny/Shutterstock; p. 167 (b) Stephane Bidouze/Shutterstock; p. 168 Leksele/Shutterstock; p. 171 IdealPhoto30/Thinkstock; p. 172 Tupungato/Shutterstock; p. 173 EpicStockMedia/Shutterstock; p. 175 evantravels/Shutterstock; p. 176 Linda Bucklin/Thinkstock; p. 177 (t) iraua/Shutterstock; p. 177 (b) Nathan Allred/Thinkstock; p. 178 Antonis Liokouras/Thinkstock; p. 181 Topfoto.co.uk; p. 183 Dylan Ellis/Thinkstock; p. 186 Zacarias Pereira da Mata/Thinkstock; p. 187 Chones/Shutterstock; p. 188 (l) Monkey Business Images/Shutterstock; p. 188 (r) Monkey Business Images/Thinkstock; p. 189 Alexandra Gl/Shutterstock; p. 190 Chris Elwell/Thinkstock; p. 193 Kane Skennar/Thinkstock; p. 194 Thinkstock Images/Thinkstock; p. 197 (t) Minerva Studio/Thinkstock; p. 197 (b) Aleshyn_Andrei/Shutterstock; p. 199 GordonBellPhotography/Thinkstock; p. 201 Paul J Martin/Shutterstock; p. 203 stanciuc/Shutterstock; p. 205 Chantal de Bruijne/Shutterstock; p. 212 catalin_grigoriu/Thinkstock; p. 213 Matthew Mawson/Alamy; p. 214 msgrafixxy/Shutterstock; p. 218 Keystone/Getty Images; p. 230 Robert Estall photo agency/Alamy; p. 248 pgaborphotos/Thinkstock.

Produced for Cambridge University Press by

White-Thomson Publishing
+44 (0)843 208 7460
www.wtpub.co.uk

Managing editor: Sonya Newland
Designer: Clare Nicholas